Political
Economics

WITHDRAWN
NDSU

CALIFORNIA SERIES ON
SOCIAL CHOICE AND POLITICAL ECONOMY

edited by Brian Barry and Samuel L. Popkin

Political Economics

James E. Alt
K. Alec Chrystal

UNIVERSITY OF CALIFORNIA PRESS
Berkeley • *Los Angeles* • *London*

University of California Press
Berkeley and Los Angeles, California
© 1983 by
The Regents of the University of California
Printed in the United States of America

1 2 3 4 5 6 7 8 9

Abridged excerpts from *Free to Choose* by Milton
and Rose Friedman are reprinted by permission of
Harcourt Brace Jovanovich, Inc., © 1980 by
Milton Friedman and Rose D. Friedman.

Library of Congress Cataloging in Publication Data

Alt, James E.
  Political economics.

  (California series on social choice and political economy)
  Bibliography: p.
  Includes index.
  1. Economics. 2. Political science. 3. Economic
policy. I. Chrystal, K. Alec, 1946–   . II. Title.
III. Series.
HB73.A42   1983   330   82–23721
ISBN 0–520–04934–9
ISBN 0–520–04983–7 (pbk.)

HB
73
A42
1983

To our parents

Contents

Tables

Figures

Preface

Our aim is to give those acquainted with economics and politics a framework for analyzing the making of economic policy. For those familiar with only one of these disciplines, we hope that this book will demonstrate the relevance of the other. Our focus is on concepts and theories, which are evaluated for logical consistency and empirical support. We offer a synthesis of important points rather than a detailed critique of all existing work.

The book evolved through several years of offering undergraduate and graduate seminars on the connection between politics and economics. An earlier version of parts of Chapters 9 and 10 appeared in the *Journal of Public Policy*, volume 1. John Woolley co-authored with Alt a version of part of Chapter 6, which appeared in volume 26 of the *American Journal of Political Science*. We also express our gratitude to him for comments on other chapters. For helpful comments on the manuscript, we wish to thank Tony Atkinson, Neal Beck, Randy Calvert, Mono Chatterji, Hugh Heclo, Roberta Herzberg, Ray Jean, Bill Keech, Mike Krassa, Margaret Levi, Miguel Martinez, Ned McClennen, and, of course, the series editors, Brian Barry and Sam Popkin. Much of the manuscript was carefully typed and retyped by Tina Maines. We also wish to acknowledge the financial support of the National Science Foundation under grant SES80–06488.

PART ONE

Background

Background

Introduction

The fundamental questions of political economics are "What part does the government play in the economy? What part should it play? How well does it do what it does?" Questions this big do not have simple and straightforward answers. The purpose of this book is to bring together diverse ideas necessary to a comprehensive study of these issues.

The study of economic policy cuts across the domains of economics and political science. There is a real distinction between "economic" questions and "political" questions in this area, and we shall say something about the differences. But treating our opening questions as belonging exclusively to one approach or the other restricts us to giving at best partial answers. We have two principal purposes in writing this book. First, we hope to help those familiar with some politics and economics to find a structure in which to answer questions like the ones above. Second, we hope to help those whose familiarity is with only one of these fields to see the relevance of the other.

In the past decade, theoretical and empirical work has increasingly spanned the boundaries between economics and politics. We believe that this is desirable for both fields. We will see how far this growing literature has succeeded in explaining or calling attention to important phenomena. Although the research appears in diverse places, we shall show that it is theoretically coherent. There is much to be gained from an attempt to integrate the concerns of economics and politics. Indeed, a little common sense will suggest that such integration is not just desirable but also unavoidable.

ECONOMICS WITHOUT POLITICS AND POLITICS WITHOUT ECONOMICS

The concerns of political economics have grown more important during the last decade, a time of economic difficulty for most Western industrial countries. Increasing inflation together with prolonged economic recession have led to doubts about much of the economic orthodoxy of the earlier postwar period. Confidence declined that appropriate fine-tuning could avoid major economic problems. Professional economists began to disagree over the policy advice they gave for dealing with the macroeconomy. Increasingly, scholars began to doubt that the field of economics alone held the answers to economic problems. Policy documents written by economists and purporting to offer economic remedies to economic problems actually offer up instead a variety of political, social, and psychological diagnoses of international recession and inflation (Keohane, 1978). The proposed remedies express the political values of the authors and are also expressly political in the sense that they call for action on the part of governments.[1]

Political arguments thus underlie economic arguments. But the direction is not only one way. Politics and economics must be dealt with simultaneously. Readers will see this by trying to recommend policy to reduce inflation in some country's economy. They will quickly find that no exclusively economic or political recommendation is possible. Suppose we try for an exclusively economic remedy. We might call for a reduction in public spending or tighter controls on the supply of money or both. These are typical of the remedies which economists

---

1. Keohane reviewed the McCracken report (McCracken et al., 1977) which was commissioned by the Organization for Economic Cooperation and Development as a study of major policy issues in the pursuit by member countries of noninflationary economic growth.

prescribe. Underlying them is some macroeconomic theory in which, say, the rate of inflation has been linked deductively to public spending and the rate of growth of the money supply. There is no need to elaborate the theory here. Rather, let us see how far such policy recommendations are really "economic." It is not part of economic theory to say whether the government of the day has the ability to implement the recommended policy. Public spending cuts affect many recipients, who may resist. Do outcomes differ where spending is decided in a decentralized legislature (like the U. S. Congress and its system of committees and subcommittees) rather than in a parliamentary system with close ministerial control over spending? Within parliamentary systems, it makes a difference if the government is formed by a single party or represents a diverse coalition whose members bargain among themselves before agreeing on an initiative. A certain package may be feasible in one case but not the other.

Moreover, the economist's policy recommendation may not agree with the expressed goals of the government in power. Indeed, economic theory has no claims to set goals for societies or governments. Economists may assert that the appropriate goals should reflect the public's preferences or desires. Nevertheless, the assertion that something should be done because people prefer it is itself political rather than economic. Moreover, there are many ways in which preferences can be aggregated, and the choice among them does not come from economic theory. For all these reasons the economic remedy appears to be also unavoidably political.

Now let us try it the other way. In an effort to offer an exclusively political solution to inflation, we might think first of controlling prices administratively. If we want prices to rise by a fixed amount each year, we simply set them to do so. Whether such a policy would work depends on whether it is administratively feasible to control prices. As before, it matters whether such a policy is compatible with the beliefs and other objectives of the government that implements it. Moreover, we must ask if it can emerge from the relevant institutions. But these are still political questions, and so the solution is still political. Why might we have to think about economics as well?

First, other things might begin to happen in the economy which could be related to the price controls. The domestic production of some goods might increase while that of others decreased, with the result that some workers lost their jobs. Pursuing the logic of the previous remedy, we might attempt to control quantities of production and employment as well. Now shortages or production bottlenecks might appear in different industrial sectors. We could try to fix that with controls too. There is no need to pursue the possible chain of fixes, each of which will have some further consequences. The point is that at some stage we will have begun to think about a variety of economic outcomes as linked to each other by a set of regularities so that varying one causes the other to vary in a certain way. At this point we have begun to do economics, and it will pay to have some idea of the work in these areas that economists have already done.

Economics functions here both as a mode of reasoning and as the accumulation of such reasoning about a particular class of phenomena having to do with the production and distribution of goods and services. As a mode of reasoning, economics proceeds by building deliberately simplified models of relationships among economic variables. The power of economic reasoning lies in producing determinate hypotheses which can be tested against data. Contrasting approaches enumerating all possible structures and outcomes are most useful when they underlie subsequent attempts to provide explanations. We will evaluate how far politicoeconomic research produces testable hypotheses.

THE STUDY OF ECONOMICS AND THE STUDY OF POLITICS

Most economic theory involves a conception of human activity as *exchanges among optimizing individuals*. Individuals interact within a framework provided by a "market." The existence of a market does not necessarily entail its being "free" or "perfectly competitive." However, the idea of the competitive market does function as a reference point to which other economic structures may be compared. This economic conception of human action does not generally underlie political science research. Because we want to integrate politics and economics, we should consider how the concerns of political scientists and economists differ. Political science has no core concepts shared by all its practitioners. Nevertheless, political scientists regularly show a concern with *power* and with *groups and institutions*.

ECONOMICS

At least since Adam Smith, economists have treated exchange as the basic concept of human activity. In an exchange, one person gives up something of value in order to receive something else of value, the subjective value received being greater than that given up. Note that the "subjective" value of a good depends on the good's marginal benefit to the party to the exchange. It is not necessarily the same as "market value," which depends on many exchanges, "factor cost," its value in terms of production inputs like labor, or indeed any "real" value placed on the good from the standpoint of some external theory.[2] The concept of exchange involves choice and voluntarism. Not all economic models conform to the assumption of perfect or free competition. However, even monopoly models assume that other actors are free to choose whether or not to trade with the monopolist.

Economists assume that actors make exchanges in a rational way. This means that given a certain set of alternatives, individuals choose the one giving the greatest subjective benefit net of cost (including the "opportunity" cost of not doing something else). Some theories appear to avoid the assumption of maximizing. A well-known example is the model of "satisficing" behavior, in which actors are assumed to be satisfied with certain threshold levels of benefit. However, no such theory asserts that an individual faced with a costless choice between greater and lesser net benefits would deliberately choose the lesser. What satisficing theories show is that limited goals are optimal in the face of adjustment costs or limited information.

Equally basic to economics is the conception of the unitary actor. In large part, this is because optimizing behavior requires that actors

2. Economics consigns the origins of subjective value to "tastes," and the origins of tastes to the field of psychology.

have well-defined preferences. Of course, not all transactions involve individuals. Thus, economists frequently treat the preferences of individuals within groups as homogeneous or speak of the preferences of a "typical" member of the group. If there is no typical member and decisions are collectively made, economists seek a decision rule with well-defined properties to characterize preferences. Economic models rarely assume that a single collective expression of individual preferences does not exist.

POLITICS

Power and institutions are commonly the focus of political science. Having power is the possession of resources which are of value in getting one's way. These resources are partly material, but nonmaterial resources such as information, skills, and access to other individuals and important positions also count. Power is exercised by offering inducements and making threats. Political science usually assumes that decisions result from the exercise of power rather than from voluntary choices. It is possible to conceive of all activity as voluntary exchange since choices where actions induce sanctions can be viewed in the same framework. However, there is an important difference between cases where abstention leaves the actor no worse off and those into which he is coerced by threat of some punishment. Lindblom (1977) makes this the central contrast between politics and economics, though he calls authority what we call power.

Political scientists characteristically assume that decisions are made through the interaction of groups in the context of institutions.[3] Institutions are complex organizations that embody a multitude of conflicting goals and constraints on individual action. Institutions affect how agendas are set, who participates in decisions, and what

3. Groups are commonly hierarchical organizations. When economists recognize the existence of hierarchical relationships (and other human factors) which impinge on the ability of some group members to form preferences autonomously, these are characterized as "organizational failures" (O. Williamson, 1975). Political scientists, on the other hand, treat the existence of hierarchy in organizations as natural and omnipresent rather than as a sort of "failure."

means are available for solving particular policy problems. Political science assumes the importance of institutions and describes their workings in various settings.

In economics, an actor's choices are usually assumed to be separable from those of others and thus made on the basis of direct costs and benefits alone. Some choices have effects on others not participating in the decision. Economists treat these as externalities.[4] In political science the distinction between internal and external costs and benefits is less common. The unitary transaction gives way to the assumption of multiple participants reflecting the multiple aspects of any policy problem (Lindberg and Maier, 1983). Moreover, individuals within an institution have to consider simultaneously the survival of the institution, their own position and interests within the institution, and the "internal" merits of the problem for which a decision must be taken.

The assumption of optimizing appears to separate economics and politics insuperably. A common criticism of optimizing is that an unequal distribution of resources or power so constrains choice as to make alternative benefit streams irrelevant. Within a framework of choice, the information requirements of maximizing behavior seem formidable. Learning about how modern economic systems work is a time-consuming and costly business, though such costs can be included in the optimization problem (Feige and Pearce, 1976). There are economic theories of the consequences for markets of limited and asymmetrically distributed information (Akerlof, 1970; Bates, 1981). The working of actual markets depends on not only the distribution of information within them but also legal procedures governing ownership and exchange. This is an important extension of the standard economic approach, though it is rarely found in the macroeconomic formulations underlying economists' policy advice. Political scientists see habit, ideology, and the ideas of group leaders or the media as more

4. Externalities are discussed in Chapter 8. Political science does not reject the existence of externalities, but it also does not focus on individual transactions so that many costs which economists might treat as external remain part of the decision being analyzed.

likely sources of popular preferences. The determination of preferences by habit or the copying of ideas of trusted others can be reconciled within an economic framework. These are devices which reduce the cost of obtaining sufficient information to make a decision, though not much is gained by this translation into rational choice terms.

POLITICAL ECONOMICS

Political economics starts from a particular conception of optimizing behavior, which is that optimization is context-bound. The application of optimizing depends on an appropriate specification of the areas in which decision-makers have discretion. This in turn requires a specification of the constraints under which they operate. Constraints include behavioral regularities, the limits of available abilities and ideas, and organizational structures. The fact that constraints are often provided by assumption gives the character of economic analysis to much of our discussion. Nevertheless, including these assumptions avoids the error of falsely assuming that all policy outcomes reflect discretionary actions or choice, whether the discretion is assumed to lie with elected leaders, bureaucrats, interest groups, or individual citizens.

PLAN OF THE BOOK

The fundamental questions of political economics involve the responsibility of governments for economic policy. Most of this book focuses on the role of elected governments in the mixed economies of Western industrial democracies. The first four chapters provide background information. Chapter 1 of Part I lays out the basic issues involved in analyzing state activity in the market economy from the point of view of both economic and political theory. Chapters 2, 3, and 4 comprise Part II. (Each part has a short introduction to place its contents in context.) Part II outlines the constraints on policy imposed by political institutions, economic ideas, and the international environment. Chapter 2 reviews political aspects of economic policy, suggesting the principal ways in which social and political institutions affect economic outcomes. Chapter 3 develops the history of thought about the role of macroeconomic policy. The important constraints on policy arising from the international economy and international institutions are set out in Chapter 4.

Part III consists of a discussion of the central ideas and methods of analysis of the existing "politicoeconomic" literature. Chapter 5 contains a critique of analyses of political business cycles. The view of policy as an optimization problem is developed in Chapter 6, with a discussion of the use of reaction functions for policy analysis. Chapter 7 surveys the influence of the state of the economy on voting behavior and the analysis of voting behavior from a choice theoretic point of view.

The behavior of governments is the subject of Part IV. Chapter 8 outlines first the economic analyses of the functions of the public sector and then discusses several arguments about the growth of government. Some evidence about the actual growth of government is presented in Chapters 9 and 10. Chapter 9 contains broad comparative analysis. Chapter 10 tests specific hypotheses about expenditures for the cases of Britain and the United States. The main arguments of the book and some important themes and implications are drawn out in the Conclusion.

CHAPTER ONE

Politics and Economics

A central issue of political economy is now, and always has been, the role of uncontrolled "market" forces versus "political" or government intervention. Most recorded history contains debates related to this fundamental problem. To what extent should individuals be allowed to pursue their own self-interest? To what extent should the political authorities of the state direct areas of economic behavior? The origins of this debate are often ascribed to Adam Smith's famous book, *An Inquiry into the Nature and Causes of the Wealth of Nations,* written in 1776. However, some tensions of this kind have existed for as long as market economies have existed. For example, the biblical admonition that "the love of money is the root of all evil" and stories like that of Jesus overturning the tables of the money lenders have more than religious significance. They speak to moral dilemmas accompanying the pursuit of economic self-interest.

There is a set of assumptions under which markets will be perfectly competitive, and the workings of such a market economy will make us as well off as we can possibly be. Arguments for political intervention claim either that real markets are not perfectly competitive or that individual resources are distributed so inequitably that market outcomes are not fair.

We proceed with a highly selective survey of the key issues relating to the behavior of the central government sector in modern Western economies. At times the debate has appeared to turn on more fundamental issues. Sometimes characterized as between capitalism and socialism or the market and planning, the problem has more recently been argued to be the incompatibility of capitalism and democracy. The debate is presented in four stages. Adam Smith's work introduces the ideas of markets and perfect competition. The writings of Karl Marx argue that nothing justifies the distribution of existing endowments or property rights underlying market outcomes. Oskar Lange, Ludwig von Mises, and F. A. Hayek among others proposed and attacked "socialist" solutions to this problem in the 1920s and 1930s. Finally, welfare economics and the attack on market failure appeared to offer a nonsocialist way out, though criticisms of this approach appear in the writings of the new marketeers.

There is no reason to expect that the many phases of this debate will ever reach a conclusion. This is partly because arguments exclude possible improvements by assumptions about the nature of government as much as by observation of real interventions in markets. It is important to realize, however, that many of the protagonists of the contemporary debates about more or less government see themselves as continuing the old arguments. Some, indeed, like Hayek have been involved for half a century. While many arguments today are concerned with whether the government should do a bit more or a bit less, it is impossible to escape entirely from arguments about the basic choice of an economic system.

ADAM SMITH

It is convenient to start with the contribution of Adam Smith. Smith provided the intellectual basis for the policy of laissez faire by defining what he regarded as the proper role of governments. The British policy of free trade in the nineteenth century owed a great deal to the influence of Smith's ideas, as did the general belief in the benefits of uncontrolled economic growth which survived even longer.

The central idea that Smith proposed was that an economy made up of individuals each pursuing his own self-interest may work for the good of all. Within a framework of the rule of law, economic transactions will be *voluntary* for both the buyer and seller of any good or service. Voluntarism means that no exchange can take place which does not benefit both parties. Since transactions are *presumed* to affect only those directly participating, a trade which is good for the parties involved and harms no one else can only be socially beneficial. The more such trades there can be, the better off more people must become. Central direction is unnecessary since distribution of available resources is achieved by a vast number of decentralized exchanges between mutually benefiting individuals. As a result, Smith wrote, an individual who

intends only his own gain is led as if by an invisible hand to provide an end which was no part of his intention. Nor is it always the worse for the society that it was not part of it. By pursuing his own interests, he frequently promotes that of the society more effectually than when he really intends to promote it. I have never known much good done by those who affected to trade for the public good. (Bk. IV, Ch. 2, p. 199)

The idea was later formalized into the perfect competition model of economics. In this model, under certain preconditions, the free market economy leads to an "optimal" or "efficient" allocation of resources. The status of this result and the interpretation of "optimal" in this context are, of course, at the heart of the controversy. For now, note that according to Smith, there was no direct role for the government in private economic relations:

The sovereign is completely discharged from a duty, in the attempting to perform which he must always be exposed to innumerable delusions, and for the proper performance of which no human wisdom or knowledge could ever be sufficient; the duty of superintending the industry of private people, and of directing it towards the employments most suitable to the interest of society. (Bk. IV, Ch. 9, p. 311)

This did not mean that there was no need for central government, however.

The sovereign has only three duties to attend to; three duties of great importance, indeed, but plain and intelligible to common understandings: first, the duty of protecting the society from the violence and invasion of independent societies; secondly, the duty of protecting, as far as possible, every member of the society from the injustice or oppression of every other member of it, or the duty of establishing an exact administration of justice; and, thirdly, the duty of erecting and maintaining certain public works and certain public institutions, which it can never be for the interest of any individual, or small number of individuals, to erect and maintain, because the profit could never repay the expense to any individual or small number of individuals, though it may frequently do much more than repay it to a great society. (Bk. IV, Ch. 9, p. 311)

The first two functions, defense and law and order, are straightforward and uncontroversial. The administration of law includes the creation and enforcement of property rights. Many interpretations of the third function are possible, however. Since it calls for public works and public institutions, a political judgment is needed to decide if some expenditure "will more than repay it to a great society." So Smith's restrictive definition of the job of governments still left considerable scope for justifiable expansion. This issue is exactly the concern of most of the recent arguments: "what is the appropriate level of public works?" and "what is the proper role of public institutions?"

KARL MARX

Most of the "classical" economists who followed Smith developed more detailed analyses of how the market economy worked. An important trend owing more to Ricardo and Malthus than Smith was the development of interest in the distribution in addition to the total level of incomes and wealth. Nineteenth-century politics contained a growing minority who rejected Smith's argument that the free market economy served the best interest of all. At first dissatisfaction focused on the poor conditions in which the mass of the population lived or worked. Marx's writings raised particularly serious intellectual issues.

A major contribution was Marx's insistence on the importance of the "dominant mode of production" in determining broader social, political, and economic relations. His elaboration of the impoverishment and exploitation of the working class by profit-maximizing entrepreneurs in the face of the diminishing profitability of enterprise is still central to contemporary neo-Marxist political economy. This stresses the role of modern government in increasing effective demand for production to ensure private accumulation of profits (see, for example, Baran and Sweezy, 1966) or in directly providing social capital to ensure profitability of the capitalist sector (O'Connor, 1973).

The important point for present purposes is that not everyone benefits in the free market system. Marx pointed out that even if trade is voluntary for both parties, economic outcomes are not "fair" because people do not start with equal endowments. He adopted the approach of the classical economists who divided society into two classes, "capitalists" and "labor." For Marx the nature of the capitalist system was such that labor would inevitably be "exploited" by the capitalist class. The latter, for the most part, were seen to achieve their status not by any intrinsic merit but rather by the good fortune to have been born "rich."

Political economy conceals the estrangement inherent in the nature of labor by not considering the direct relationship between the worker (labor) and production. It is true that labor produces wonderful things for the rich—but for the worker it produces privation. It produces palaces—but for the worker, hovels. It produces beauty—but for the worker, deformity. It replaces labor by machines, but it throws one section of the workers back to a barbarous type of labor and it turns the other section into a machine. It produces intelligence—but for the worker, stupidity, cretinism. (Marx, 1970, pp. 109–10)

His insight was that free market outcomes are determined by the initial distribution of endowments, which reflect the distribution of property rights among members of society. The analyses of Marx and his followers, together with the conditions of the time, led many intellectuals to seek a "better" system of social and economic organization. A dominant idea was that labor should, by force if necessary, take over the means of production and run them in the interests of labor. Capital would thus become the property of society at large and all could share in the profits.

Those who proposed communal ownership of the means of production and the abandonment of the principles of the free market economy faced important questions. What would determine which goods to produce and at what price they would sell? How was an economy to be organized in the absence of Adam Smith's invisible hand of market forces? How could it be decided where people should work and what should be available in which shops in which towns? If a group of planners were going to direct the economy centrally, what principles should they use to allocate resources to various areas of activity?

This problem of organizing the new system inevitably had to be faced in the Soviet Union after 1917. It was also of considerable interest in the West, particularly in Western Europe. This interest became stronger in the 1930s when many believed that the Great Depression was proving the inadequacies of the market system. There was a possibility that more countries might choose a socialist system. There followed a lengthy academic debate, labeled as "Capitalism versus Socialism" or "the Market versus Planning," or even "Right versus Left." Its essence was whether the gains from government intervention outweighed possible losses of efficiency in departures from market outcomes. It is a debate which still continues in many forms, though the argument now tends to be about a bit more or less government intervention rather than about a fundamental change of system.

THE GREAT DEBATE: VON MISES, LANGE, AND HAYEK

Von Mises, in "Economic Calculation in the Socialist Commonwealth" (1920), argued that a rational socialist system was a logical impossibility, for "where there is no free market, there is no pricing mechanism, there is no economic calculation." The basic problem of economics is the allocation of scarce resources to competing uses. Von Mises conceded that goods produced could be directed to uses decided by a socialist planner, but not that the planner could organize production itself in the absence of profit motives and a capital market.

The administration may know exactly what goods are most urgently needed. But in so doing, it has only found what is, in fact, but one of the two necessary prerequisites for economic calculation. In the nature of the case, it must, however, dispense with the other—the valuation of the means of production . . . exchange relations between production goods can only be established on the basis of private ownership of the means of production. (p. 107)

This did not mean that a socialist economy could not exist but that it must *necessarily* allocate resources worse than a market economy. A socialist economy could convert raw materials and effort into some output combination, but it would be "inferior" to the output achieved by a market economy with the same resources. Here, *inferior* refers to a typical consumer's evaluation of the volume or diversity of products.

In contrast, Lange (in Lange and Taylor, 1938) argued that the socialist solution was feasible, practical, and desirable.[1] If we could create a socialist system with no transitional problems, how would it work? Lange's hypothetical world contains four groups of actors. First, there are households. They can work largely as before in any occupations for which they are suitably qualified, provided they accept the going wage and do not choose to be unemployed. They may freely choose to spend their income on any consumer goods. However, they cannot have any income from property or investments since capital is now collectively owned. The second group are firms which are collectively owned but managed by socialist enterprise managers. Given the prices of inputs and outputs, their job is (1) to produce at lowest possible cost for any given volume of output and (2) to select that volume of output where price equals marginal cost. This ensures that firms are "profit-maximizing" as they would be under perfect competition. The third group are socialist industrial managers, who regulate the number of firms so that in each industry marginal cost is equal to price.

The final, and critical, group are the central planners. They have three major functions. They determine the rate, but not the direction, of investment. This ensures an "adequate" overall rate of economic

1. In fact, the logical possibility of a socialist solution was already demonstrated by Enrico Barone in "The Ministry of Production in a Collectivist State" (in Hayek, ed., 1935). He showed that all prices of inputs and outputs were part of a determinate solution to a system of equations, though he was unable to describe how these prices would be determined *in practice*.

growth. Second, they decide appropriate production levels for "public" goods such as defense, law and order, health services, and education, which the market provides poorly. Third, they determine the prices of all inputs and outputs. Prices can be adjusted by trial and error until demand equals supply in all markets.

An obvious danger is that this system might respond slowly and inflexibly to changes in circumstance. Lange himself argued that equilibrium prices will be reached *faster* under this socialist system than under capitalism because the planners can anticipate the effects of one price change on all others. Since all firms would equate marginal cost to price, the socialist system avoids the inefficiency caused by capitalist monopolies, which do not equate price to marginal cost. Three major benefits claimed for this system were that (1) any desired growth rate could be achieved whereas in capitalism the growth rate emerged by accident, (2) full employment would be achieved by adjustments of factor prices and government purchases, and (3) income distribution becomes significantly fairer. Since paid employment is the only personal source of income, wage differentials only reflect rewards for hard work, danger, or the acquisition of useful skills.

Critics attacked several features of Lange's scheme. For example, the planners might not act efficiently. How to measure their efficiency is unclear. Schumpeter (1966) argued that socially responsible planners would lack the ability to profit exploitatively from new inventions, stifling innovation. Others attacked Lange's system more generally. For instance, Hayek never accepted the possibility of the planners adjusting prices in anything like an optimal manner.

The difference between such a system of regimented prices and a system of prices determined by the market seems to be about the same as that between an attacking army where every unit and every man could only move by special command and by the exact distance ordered by headquarters and an army where every unit and every man can take advantage of every opportunity offered to them. (Hayek, 1940, p. 131)

Hayek argued that Lange's scheme would be slower than a market economy to adjust to the ever-changing equilibrium of a constantly changing world. It would be impractical to change all prices frequently, so they would only change after quite long intervals. The planners could neither make price differentials reflect all the quality differences which consumers recognize nor possibly collect and process enough information to avoid considerable inertia in the planning process. Information processing is time-consuming even in the computer age. Hayek's case must have seemed overwhelming in the interwar period.[2]

The political objections were even stronger than the economic ones. As even Lange was aware, his socialism requires a large bureaucracy, and nothing in the theory says how much this will cost. Although intended to be more equitable for the average person, the system could easily be worse for many by reducing political and economic opportunities. The problem was the excessive power of the central planner.

Some fear this will inevitably lead to a general restriction of personal freedom, as the government begins to use its enormous power to allocate resources for investment and collective consumption. At first, it will paternalistically try to change public opinion on these matters by propaganda, an organized campaign, very much like the advertising of private profit-making industry, to make people *like* future consumption and collective consumption rather than private consumption now. Eventually, however, there is bound to be, so the argument goes, authoritarian despotism. As propaganda fails to create the extensive agreement about society's goals that is desired by the government, it will impose those goals by force. (Kohler, 1968, pp. 80–81)

The argument that a socialist system restricts the freedoms of individuals is prominent in Hayek's *The Road to Serfdom* (1944):

Although the professed aim of planning would be that man should cease to be a mere means, in fact—since it would be impossible to take account in the plan of individual likes and dislikes—the individual would more than ever become a mere means, to be used by the authority in the service of such abstractions as the "social welfare" or the "good of the community." (p. 96)

Proponents of intervention stressed the ability of government to produce net social benefits in terms of an equitable distribution of incomes and elimination of inefficiencies in production.[3] Opponents

2. Hayek's argument is still relevant in communist countries; see, for example, Martin, 1977.
3. Lange was explicitly concerned with the ability of a socialist commonwealth to reproduce exactly that "optimal" outcome which perfect competition would have pro-

argued that the bureaucratic cost of intervention would outweigh any benefits provided. As widespread transitions to socialism in the West became less likely, interest in the choice of system faded. Nevertheless, even in the context of the so-called "mixed economy," there continue to be serious disagreements about the appropriate extent of national ownership of industry, government regulation of monopoly, protection from foreign competition, and public expenditure on social services and welfare.

THE CONTINUING DEBATE: WELFARE ECONOMICS AND THE NEW MARKETEERS

The problems of the capitalist system in the interwar period convinced many people that the market mechanism would not achieve optimal outcomes on its own. A middle-of-the-road remedy short of full socialism emerged. Its intellectual basis was the newly emergent welfare economics particularly associated with A. C. Pigou. This called for intervention to offset the effects of specific cases of "market failure."

The perfect competition model characterizes the economy as a number of firms which compete with one another. By itself, no firm can influence the price of what it produces or consumes, so each takes the market price as given. Such a perfectly competitive market produces an "efficient" outcome in which prices equal marginal costs. Competition ensures that there are no "excess" profits.[4] The assumptions required for perfect competition are very strict, requiring at a minimum[5] (1)

---

duced. Other critiques of market systems stress instead the need to produce a different outcome, one which is optimal in terms of goals other than those reached through perfect competition.

4. Welfare economics places heavy reliance on the concept of "Pareto optimality." Trades are Pareto efficient if at least one person gains and no other loses. The outcome is optimal when no more such trades are available, that is, when only trades with no losers are made and all such trades have been made. The problem with this is that there may be infinitely many Pareto-optimal outcomes consistent with each initial distribution of endowments. Once anyone must *lose* from an action, the outcome cannot be evaluated by reference to economic theory and becomes intrinsically a "political" problem (see Mishan, 1982).

5. A further assumption is often added that preferences of individuals are not

absence of economies of scale and therefore no monopolies, (2) no external effects, (3) no public goods, and (4) no significant information or transaction costs. The most important cases of market failure are associated with violations of these assumptions.

First, economies of scale mean that unit costs of production diminish as the output of an individual firm increases. A big firm would then produce at lower unit costs than a large number of smaller firms. Competition would thus lead a small number of large firms (oligopoly) or even one large firm (monopoly) to dominate the market. A monopoly maximizes profits by setting price above marginal cost and, in effect, restricting output.

Antimonopoly legislation as been common for many years. In some countries, "natural" monopolies are nationalized, that is, taken into public ownership. Natural monopolies are those for which economies of scale are so great that competing firms would be inefficient or impractical, including cases where high "start-up" costs deter entry of new firms into a market. Utilities like electricity, gas, and telephones as well as rail and road systems are almost universally nationalized in Western Europe. In the United States they are mostly privately owned but publicly regulated. In principle there are ways of neutralizing or at least ameliorating the effects of monopoly. In practice there has always been a tension between discouraging monopoly and encouraging efficiency.

The second sort of market failure arises from "external" costs and benefits. Individual firms consider only their own direct costs and benefits in making decisions. The costs and revenues of a firm may differ from the costs and benefits they impose on others and to society as a whole. Pollution exemplifies how one firm's activities can impose costs on others. A firm's consumption of exhaustible resources is another case in which the calculations of one firm exclude consideration of real costs to another. In general, firms which ignore the costs they impose on others overproduce relative to the social optimum. The

---

interdependent. Each individual or firm cannot affect the preferences of others but must take them as given. Independence of preferences is a precondition for individual optimization rather than a potential source of market failure.

remedy is government intervention to restrict the activities of the externality-producing firm by taxes or production quotas.

Third, the market will not produce some goods because competitive pricing could never cover total cost. These are known as "public goods." Common examples are national defense and street lighting. Public goods are defined by joint consumption and nonexcludability. Once the good exists, joint consumption means that one individual's benefit from it is unaffected by how many others also benefit. Non-excludability means that no one can be excluded from consuming it. Any individual can benefit as long as *someone* has bought it and he thus has no incentive to buy it for himself. It may be appropriate to provide without charge (financed out of general taxation) goods which it is difficult to exclude people from consuming. Do not confuse public goods with those which will not be produced simply because there is no demand for them.

The existence of significant information and transaction costs prevent many otherwise profitable exchanges from taking place. Public intervention to reduce these costs is common. The legal system reduces transaction costs by enforcing contracts. Aid for those involuntarily unemployed through the cost of moving or training for employment is a further example. Laws controlling false advertising reduce the cost to consumers of ascertaining product quality. All these interventions are intended to have net positive social effects. Public goods are produced which individuals would not rationally purchase and competing firms would not produce. Monopolists are prevented from restricting production to gain higher prices. Alternatively, the state acts as a monopolist, but the "surplus" profit is distributed to the public or accrues to government revenues.

Redistribution is different. Intervention to redistribute incomes does not cure market failures but achieves something that markets could not. Although in the market model trade must be beneficial to participants, the total product need not be shared equitably, and there may be people who cannot survive at all. The competition model assumes that actors are arbitrarily endowed with resources (through accident or inheritance). Those who start off with most will normally end up with most. Those who start with no resources have no guarantee of being able to sell their labor at a price sufficient to ensure survival.

All governments in Western industrial economies have intervened for all these reasons, and possibly others, which is why these economies are called "mixed." The extent of intervention varies from country to country. Since the end of World War II, intervention has led to a steady and substantial increase in state activity. There are many who believe that this has gone much too far. A prominent advocate of the renewed plea for the market is Milton Friedman. On the whole, he accepts the *theoretical* case that markets may fail, though he argues with some force that the cure of government intervention is typically worse than the disease. Government is inefficient and bureaucratic, so its interventions are ponderous and inflexible. The choice according to Friedman in *Capitalism and Freedom* (1962) is between an imperfect but flexible market and an imperfect and rigid government agency.

In a rapidly changing society . . . the conditions making for technical monopoly frequently change and I suspect that both public regulation and public monopoly are likely to be less responsive to such changes in conditions to be less readily capable of elimination, than private monopoly. (p. 28)

It is now widely argued that agencies initially set up to regulate monopoly come to be the principal obstacle to increased competition. As an example, Friedman himself argued:

If railroads had never been subjected to regulation in the U.S., it is certain that by now transportation, including railroads, would be a highly competitive industry with little or no remaining monopoly elements. (p. 29)

Friedman also argues that external costs (which he calls "neighborhood effects") have been improperly used to justify intervention.

Considerations like those I have treated under the heading of neighborhood effects have been used to rationalize almost every conceivable intervention. . . . this rationalization is special pleading rather than a legitimate application of the concept of neighborhood effects. Neighborhood effects cut both ways. They can be a reason for limiting the activities of government as well as for expanding them. Neighborhood effects impede voluntary exchange because it is difficult to identify the effects on third parties and to measure their

magnitude; but this difficulty is present in governmental activity as well.
. . . when government engages in activities to overcome neighborhood effects,
it will in part introduce an additional set of neighborhood effects by failing to
charge or to compensate individuals properly. Whether the original or the new
neighborhood effects are the more serious can only be judged by the facts of
the individual case. (p. 32)

The recent book *Free to Choose* (Friedman and Friedman, 1980)
reasserts the value of freedom under the market by investigating cases
of government inefficiency and points to the damaging cumulative
effect of apparently well-meant interventions.

As consumers we are not even free to choose how to spend the part of our
income that is left after taxes. We are not free to buy cyclamates or laetrile, and
soon, perhaps, saccharin. Our physician is not free to prescribe many drugs for
us that he may regard as the most effective for our ailments, even though the
drugs may be widely available abroad. We are not free to buy an automobile
without seat belts. . . .You are not free to offer your services as a lawyer, a
physician, a dentist, a plumber, a barber, a mortician . . . without first getting
a permit or license from a government official. You are not free to work
overtime at terms mutually agreeable to you and your employer, unless the
terms conform to rules and regulations laid down by a government official.
. . .You are not free to set up a bank, go into the taxicab business . . . without
first receiving permission from a government official. . . .You are not free to
raise funds on the capital markets unless you fill out numerous pages of forms
the SEC requires and unless you satisfy the SEC that the prospectus you
propose to issue presents such a bleak picture of your prospects that no
investor in his right mind would invest in your project if he took the prospectus
literally. And getting SEC approval may cost upwards of $100,000—which
certainly discourages the small firms our government professes to help. (p. 66)

Not only may interventions involve a substantial loss of freedom, but,
also, the very intervention agencies may work against each other.

In one massive building in Washington some government employees are
working full-time to devise and implement plans to spend our money to
discourage us from smoking cigarettes. In another massive building . . . other
employees are working full-time spending our money to subsidize farmers to
grow tobacco. . . .The situation would be ludicrous if it were not so serious.
While many of these effects cancel out, their costs do not. Each program takes
money from our pockets that we could use to buy goods and services to meet

our separate needs. Each of them uses able, skilled people who could be engaged in productive activities. Each one grinds out rules, regulations, red tape, forms to fill in that bedevil us all. (pp. 291–92)

This case against government activities is emotive. It is also somewhat persuasive. Friedman's earlier concern for evidence to be "judged by the facts of the individual case" would make it more persuasive. He points out effectively that while market failure can justify state intervention, it is no guarantee that every intervention in fact cures (or even tries to cure) a market failure. He fails to establish that because state intervention *may* cause or exacerbate a market failure, intervention inevitably does so. We shall look in Chapter 8 at some reasons why public sector activities can be inefficient. They need not be inefficient in principle unless one makes some special assumptions. Demonstrating their inefficiency requires careful comparisons of the costs of public sector activity with the costs of doing without it.

Giving compelling evidence in individual cases is not easy, but this does not mean that nothing can ever be said. Government intervention, say, to prevent transportation monopoly, by requiring equal statutory charges for all carriers, has costs. Some cheaper alternatives cease to be available. This is bad, but the loss of efficiency may be offset by saving some transport sector from extinction (Noll, 1971). The preservation of an endangered sector is not equally important at all times. Ensuring that intervention continues to serve its original purposes is a serious problem. Franchises or licenses which restrict competition also create inefficient outcomes since they are equivalent to state-sanctioned monopolies. But if taxicab rides are equally expensive in cities with and without medallion licensing, the real choice is between state-sanctioned and unofficial monopolies. Efficiency losses may be offset by some distributional gains, depending on the size of efficiency loss. Its estimation requires clarity about the alternatives, about how the particular market will function with the government removed, and especially whether it will resemble a perfectly competitive market in the absence of government intervention. Since the argument will involve offsetting costs and benefits of different types and uncertain magnitudes, there will be few simple economic answers.

THE STATE IN THE MIXED ECONOMY

The "great debate" continues because the "perfect competition" market (with no economies of scale, no interdependent preferences, no transaction or information costs, no public goods, and no externalities) is no more realistic or attainable in practice than an idealized state-oriented nonmarket alternative. The efficiency of market systems requires that all the perfect competition assumptions be met. When they are not, government intervention could improve the situation. But will it? The answer is often smuggled in by assumption about the nature of the state rather than by observation of intervention in practice.

The state is a human community. It is both an abstract entity and simultaneously the people who do whatever it is the state does. To a neoclassical economist, the state provides basic rules of the game. These are called "property rights," which in turn define the structure of competition and cooperation in the economy (North, 1981). Property rights define ownership of resources and as a result they define which exchanges are feasible. The usual political conception of the state is that it "claims the monopoly of the legitimate use of physical force within a given territory" (Weber, 1958). The monopoly of legitimate violence can be exploited to make people do what they otherwise might not. Those who see in the state's monopoly position an opportunity for personal gain will compete to control it.

There are three ways to describe the nature of the state, as sketched in Figure 1.1. These are protective, productive, and exploitative. The protective state is the minimal state of classical and neoclassical liberal theory like Smith's with the basic functions of defense and law and order. This state protects its citizens against both external threat and the depredations of fellow citizens. The productive state is one whose active intervention produces net social benefits. It produces more than minimal public goods. Like Lange's state, it reduces market inefficiency through improved information and communication. It is the public interest state of welfare economics, in which the preferences of those in the state apparatus lead to policies of maximum net benefit to the population at large.

Like the productive state the exploitative state is also active, but its interventions maximize the benefit to those in the state apparatus, their agents or captors. The exploitative state is Marx's bourgeois state which exploits the proletariat, but it also includes ideas of a Leviathan state. The exploitative state can be partly productive. Brennan and Buchanan's (1981) Leviathan state maximizes social output only to tax it maximally. Hobbes's citizens have Leviathan but benefit from the possibility of trade. The bourgeois state survives as long as the social surplus extracted exceeds the costs of averting revolution.

Intervention poses a problem. Creating a productive state from a minimal, protective state involves increasing state autonomy, if only for the flexibility and speed of response described by Lange. An increase in state autonomy increases opportunities for self-serving exploitation. Increasing state autonomy by reducing formal restraints on state activity or creating new powers can be seen as a move away from the protective state toward the bottom of Figure 1.1. But is the move to the bottom left or right? It depends on whether institutions exist to restrict opportunities to productive and not exploitative activities.

It is thus an issue of constitutional design. Rawls (1971) derives the desirability of a state which maximizes liberties and opportunities (subject to constraints of equality and/or protection of the weakest or worst off) from prudent individuals' calculations of personal advantage under strong uncertainty. Brennan and Buchanan (1981) deduce a rational preference of individuals for whatever economic or-

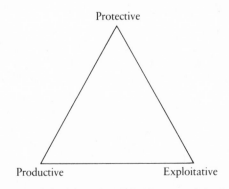

FIGURE 1.1. Three Possible Natures of the State

ganization will minimize the maximum tax share which can be extracted from the economy. Both theories have uncertain but rational individuals behind a "veil of ignorance." They are distinguished by their state's likely activities. Rawls's state is on the protection-production frontier, Brennan and Buchanan's in the exploitative corner.

The problem of intervention is to increase productive possibilites without increasing exploitative ones. The state is a social institution. The nature of the state is no better and no worse than those people who make up the state's institutions, given their incentives and constraints. The constraints are the subject of Part II. Models of the consequences of different incentives and opportunities, and their implications for the apparent nature of the state, form Part III. Part IV returns to the empirical problem of the scale of public activities.

PART TWO

The Political
and Economic Context

Chapter 1 outlined theoretical issues which underlie debates about the structure of economic systems and the role of government within them. At this point we move from the largely normative perspective of Chapter 1 to positive theories of politics and economic policy. We are concerned with the discretionary activities of policymakers. To follow Chapter 1, we begin with the role of the state in contemporary political economy. Each of the next three chapters looks closely at an important aspect of the formation of economic policy in the real world rather than in abstract economic systems. Chapter 2 explains why political institutions are important and how political influence can be brought to bear on the formation of economic policy. The development of theories of the appropriate conduct of macroeconomic policy is discussed in Chapter 3. Chapter 4 describes the importance of the international environment for policy problems of the domestic economy. Each of the three chapters thus discusses a major constraint on policymakers. The first constraint is the political institutions, the second is beliefs about how the economy works, and the third is the external environment within which policies must be made.

CHAPTER TWO

Politics and Economic Policy

Economic policy is political because it affects the distribution of wealth and incomes in society. Therefore, understanding policy requires understanding the distribution of power among major social interests. Economic policy is also political because it reflects decisions made by elected politicians in an institutional context. These policy decisions are based on social benefits and popular preferences, the interests of the politicians, and the incentives and constraints imposed by the institutions. This chapter treats systematic relationships between major social, economic, and political institutions in a context of economic development and constitutional and legal structure as the major political influences on the formulation of economic policy.

CONTEMPORARY POLITICAL ECONOMY

The first question is what role the state is to play in any account of policy. Contemporary political economists have replaced the concept of the state as passive arbiter among contending interests with the autonomous or discretionary activities of politicians. This has happened simultaneously in diverse schools of thought. Three examples, a "statist" view, a neo-Marxist one, and one from the public choice tradition, respectively, treat discretion as the implementation of a consistent set of preferences on behalf of society, adjustment between major interests in periods of overt conflict, and the active pursuit of reelection. Any description of political discretion requires simultaneous specification of the constraints on that discretion. Each of these three approaches does this differently.

It is possible to define political economy as the study of discretionary state activities. Krasner (1978) introduces his "statist" approach by arguing that the state is

an autonomous actor. The objectives sought by the state cannot be reduced to some summation of private desires. . . . For a statist approach explanation and description involve (a) demonstrating empirically that American decision-makers have sought a consistent set of goals . . . and (b) defining the conditions under which they have been able to attain their goals in the face of international and, more importantly, domestic constraints. (p. 6)

But while consistent goals were pursued by American central decision-makers in foreign raw materials investment policy, there were constraints.

This is not to say that the policies actually implemented by the United States have been coherent. Looking at what the American government actually did, as opposed to what central decision-makers preferred, presents a complicated picture. The fragmentation of power in the political system has allowed powerful private groups to block many state initiatives. (p. 331)

The broader empirical problem in this sort of political economy is to find circumstances under which state officials can pursue consistent goals in spite of sectional pressures.

Skocpol (1980) reviews neo-Marxist analyses of the New Deal. New Deal policy offers superficial support to those who see in it either a subservient state implementing the conscious strategy of capitalists or an active state producing policies which support capitalism. But Skocpol argues that such accounts overlook the failure of the New Deal to gain the confidence of business entrepreneurs, the hostility of much of business to many New Deal policies, and the absence of developed administrative cohesion in implementing policy. Some see the New Deal as the result of "pressure from below," eventually made consistent with continued capitalism by compromise on the part of those who initially resisted it. In contrast, Skocpol points out that "independent initiatives by liberal politicians within the Democratic party were decisive. . . ." The broad common interests of the New Deal coalition of urban liberals, workers, the unemployed, those on welfare, and the new federal administrators, together with the enhanced executive power of New Deal agencies, produced the opportunity for a social-democratic breakthrough. However, "patterns of institutional power" (notably individuals and committees in Congress) and the structural weakness of the Democratic party limited the extent to which liberal gains within the party could be translated into policy.

Wright (1974) argues that the New Deal "can be understood as a rational effort to maximize the prospect of electoral success" by the Democratic administration. This involved manipulating the distribution of New Deal expenditures. His point is that a programmatic innovation in the structure of the political and economic system also offered incentives for actions far from the original purposes of the innovation. The president dominated the political environment. Most relief agencies were closely identified with the New Deal. Spending more where it might make a difference to the Democrats' electoral chances should have paid dividends. This could not be the whole story. Wright's evidence does not suggest that the New Deal was only a vote-buying gimmick. Most assistance would go where relief was needed. "The distribution of jobs, even at election time, was strongly related to relief and unemployment levels. . . ." But political strategy had a role in the state-by-state distribution of relief expenditures.

From all these points of view, the central problems of the study of economic policy are to disentangle *discretion* from *constraint* in an institutional context and to reconcile political and economic approaches. Institutions provide both incentives for discretionary action and constraints on it. The major institutions in economic policy are labor, business, and finance in the context of a given level of economic development and political structure. Some way must also be found to say which economic outcomes arose from the economic system independent of the desires and actions of policymakers and those who sought to influence them, and which outcomes resulted from deliberate interventions. Some interventions do not have their intended consequences. Many consequences of interventions turn out not to have been intended at all. However, the problem is not intractable.

ECONOMIC AND POLITICAL EXPLANATIONS

Economic and political accounts of differing episodes are not incompatible. Gourevitch's (1977) account of trade crises[1] and tariff policy includes a simple and powerful "economic" explanation of whether or not tariffs were adopted between 1873 and 1896. It rests on "a large bloc of economic interest groups gaining significant economic advantages from the policy decision adopted concerning tariffs" (p. 306). But there is room for a "political" explanation as well. "The translation of economic advantage into policy does require action, organization, and politics . . ." (p. 308). The ability of an economic interest group to organize depends on the urgency and specificity of the benefits sought and the compactness and structural position of the group.

A satisfactory demonstration of the effects of discretionary interventions on economic outcomes requires what economists describe as a model of *demand* and political scientists describe as a model of *power*. (Political scientists also speak of demands but mean something different.) The economists' model of demand is of a force on one side of a market. It reflects preferences (rankings of outcomes) and a resource constraint which limits what can be achieved.

A preference for an outcome is not the same as the demand for an outcome.[2] Preferences become demand when people are prepared to

1. The advantages of studying crises are that they are periods when, literally, the chips are down. The disadvantage is that attention is focused on political activity in a crisis. The pattern of outcomes in the crisis period need not be reflected during calmer times. This point is particularly important in economic policy where any intervention alters the structure of some market in which transactions take place, causing adjustments to the new market structure. These take place over a prolonged period and involve political activity as well as economic adaptation.

2. We shall see in Chapter 7 that not all economic policies have neatly delineable outcomes allowing the analyst to impute preferences to readily identifiable social groups.

bear the cost of political activity. Olson (1965) argues that those with common interests will not organize unless the costs of organization are offset by its expected rewards. These costs can never be offset where the good sought is "public" since none could subsequently be excluded from its enjoyment whether or not they participated in securing it. Where possible, groups will organize to provide selective benefits from which those not bearing a share of the cost of organizing can be excluded.

The language of politics replaces the economic concept of demand with preferences and the power to achieve them.[3] Power resides partly in resources like money, time, and organization. Access to information not freely available to all is also a source of power. This includes specific information about values of some economic variables and about how the economy works. The private sector's monopoly of skilled personnel is a source of power when policymakers depend on recruitment from the private sector for people with the ability to formulate and implement policy. This is a feature of the relationship between private banks and the central bank in the execution of monetary policy. The focus on power stresses the restricted process by which preferred outcomes are obtained politically. In contrast, demand assumes a market in which transactions take place. We will discuss power in specific institutions, but first we provide a framework which describes the relationships among institutions.

The formulation and adoption of economic policies involves the selection of priorities among economic targets or goals, often through political conflict. This is equivalent to finding a collective expression of preferences to guide economic activity. The implementation stage of

---

For example, within a set of profit-maximizing enterprises, the risk-averse may want regulation or insurance to protect themselves from catastrophe while the risk-lovers seek the promotion of speculative opportunities.

3. The existence of demand means that someone is willing to pay a particular price for some good. In a political setting, there may be many who would want some available good but lack the resources to obtain it. This means that political settings need not conform to the assumed characteristics of competitive markets but are characterized instead by collusion and concentration, unequal distributions of information, or provision of "public" goods (see chapter 1). This does not make economic reasoning inapplicable but does require less familiar analysis.

economic policy includes the selection and effective exercise of policy instruments to achieve preferred targets. The way in which preferences are articulated, aggregated, and eventually transformed into the selection of targets and instruments of economic policy depends on:

1. The internal structure, unity, and power of the political and economic institutions, and

2. The interrelationships among these institutions, in particular, whether these interrelationships are predominantly cooperative or adversarial. (Lindberg and Maier, 1983)

These two distinctions can be combined heuristically to give the four possibilities of Table 2.1. These terms describe particular relationships within countries. Major structures and relationships within each country are not the same. Internal structure and unity provide the possibility of "top-down" direction necessary to the implementation of centralized bargains. Cooperation describes the likelihood of achieving such bargains. These characterize a structure which cannot be changed or reconstituted *de novo* simply because that would be to someone's advantage. Institutions and institutional practices can be changed, but only at some cost. The cost arises because of bureaucratic inertia but also because many other actors have adjusted their behavior to the existing system. The institutional structure will be taken for granted in the case of most interventions. For this reason, it is a constraint.

The term *corporatist* describes any policy of cooperation among major private sector interests which are well organized. It includes the centralized collaboration of major business and labor organizations in wage determination in Sweden and the cooperation of government, finance, and industry in directive planning in Japan. Cooperation

TABLE 2.1   INSTITUTIONAL RELATIONSHIPS

Internal Structure	Relationship	
	Cooperative	*Adversarial*
Cohesive	Corporatism	Conflict
Fragmented	Weak planning	Local self-interest

among less structurally integrated institutions results in weak or indicative (that is, unenforceable) planning. Examples exist in France and especially the incomes policies of mid-1960s Britain. Where fragmented institutions are adversaries, the grass roots pursue self-interest while elites bargain and argue. An example is the behavior of private banks independent of a central bank in periods of conflict between government and central bank. Long periods of conflict between well-organized institutions are less common than fifty years ago. What follows sheds some light on why this is so.

LEVEL OF ECONOMIC DEVELOPMENT

Predominant patterns of political activity may be related to a country's level of economic development. There are characteristics common to industrial societies alone. Four important topics are the impact on political activity and economic outcomes of industrialization and finance, age of an industrial society and political organization, democratization and the demand for consumption, and openness of the national economy.

The social, political, and economic development of a country influences aspects of economic policy like taxation and public expenditure. Even a casual glance at the United Nations' yearbooks of *National Accounts Statistics* reveals that the public sector of developing countries is typically smaller than in industrial countries. Moreover, patterns of public expenditure vary. In less industrialized countries, transfer (particularly social assistance) payments are a smaller part of expenditures. In these countries, the public share of capital formation can be very much larger than in Western industrial societies. The structure of taxation has been shown to change as economies develop. As the technology of collection and available sources of revenue develop, the specific taxes on trade prevalent in early industrialization are replaced by direct taxes on individuals and broader forms of indirect taxation (Hinrichs, 1966; Musgrave, 1969).

Olson (1982) argues that stable societies with unchanged boundaries accumulate collusions over time. These collusions or "special interest organizations" reduce efficiency and aggregate income by achieving the power to distort market outcomes. These groups are inefficient because they make decisions relatively slowly and inhibit competition through restrictive practices, limiting entry into the labor force and adaptation to new technology. The normative content of the argument should be familiar.[4] Empirically, Olson argues that the European Economic Community (EEC) countries had high growth rates because membership of the EEC superseded established political jurisdictions. The small number of nations involved aided collusion. Age also retards growth rates in other industrial countries and the fifty American states.

Even in the restricted context of industrial countries, aspects of political development affect the economy. Democratization and increased participation at high levels of economic development alter demand for economic goods, with some form of consumerism becoming common (Galbraith, 1958). The existence of a welfare state entails the direction of national resources and income toward those with a higher propensity to consume. This may be in conflict with the need to promote investment to secure future economic growth. In the climate of declining growth rates, this conflict can become acute. O'Connor (1973) identifies the conflict between social expenditures needed to "legitimize" democratically elected governments with their constituencies and the function of the state to guarantee accumulation of investable profit for industry as the source of a "fiscal crisis of the state."

The openness of the national economy (the share of national product taken by exports and of national expenditure going to imports) influences political organization.

Given the structural features that tend to accompany economic openness—a high degree of unionization, relatively frequent government by Social Democratic and Labor parties, strong labor confederations, and, ultimately, a

---

4. The case for the inefficiency of collusions rests on the same grounds used to analyze other sorts of market failure in Chapter 1. Note, however, that Olson derives the existence of these collusive groups directly from the incentives of a decentralized, interest-group-based polity. He also argues that the consequences of monopoly are likely to be less damaging than of decentralized collusion. This argument occurs in other contexts (see Chapter 8) and will be discussed there.

large increase in taxation . . . the nations which tended to favor distributional equity rather than private accumulation were those with open economies. (Cameron, 1978, p. 1259)

In open economies the need to maintain international competitiveness leads to advantages from economies of scale in production and therefore more concentrated industries. Concentration in industry produces large-scale labor organizations, with consequences discussed below.

Large-scale international capital flows are another problem, more serious for those countries with sophisticated financial sectors. Unrestricted capital flows under a regime of fixed exchange rates (see Chapter 4) make an independent domestic monetary policy impossible. The availability of foreign funds inhibits the authorities' efforts to control the domestic banking system. Control is achieved by legal restraints on banks, but at a cost to the development of an open credit market. A small country with an open economy may be compelled to tie itself to a larger neighbor, eschewing internal flexibility for protection against monetary instability. Dutch monetary policy is deliberately and publicly tied closely to that of Germany. The Dutch thus trade domestic discretion for insulation against shocks provided by a larger partner. Under floating exchange rates, other European countries have done this as well, in the European Monetary System. A consequence of openness is increased concern with the balance of payments, exchange rate, or currency reserves as targets of economic policy and with the external world as a source of disturbances. (The distinction between internal and external influences on economic policy will be discussed in Chapters 4 and 6.)

MOBILIZATION OF THE WORKING CLASS

No feature of industrial organization has received as much attention as the extent to which labor organizations assert and defend their interests. Martin (1977) argues that the ability of party systems and other political structures to insulate industrializing elites from mass pressure is a critical determinant of economic outcomes. Greater mobilization and closer links between European labor and political parties are

reflected in the greater degree to which full employment and the welfare state have been maintained in Europe than in the United States. (p. 344)

The demands of workers should include higher wages, full employment, Social Security, and improvement in working conditions. Unambiguous findings about the effects of working-class mobilization have not emerged (Korpi, 1980).

Working-class mobilization could be influential through two channels: industrial leverage and voting. One measure of working-class power is extent of unionization. This varies from country to country. About 70 percent of the workforce is in unions in Sweden, nearly 50 percent in Britain and slightly less in France, 35 percent or so in Germany, and about a quarter of the workforce is unionized in countries like Japan and the United States (see Bain and Price, 1980). These figures conceal structural variation between cases where central organizations aggregate union demands and where unions are fragmented either in political allegiance or by industrial sector. For instance, the unions of France and Italy, though they represent a larger share of the workforce, are divided along religious and political lines. This reduces their ability to present a united front. In Japan, unions in the more concentrated sectors have gained considerable job security for their members. The weaker unions in the more numerous small industries have borne the brunt of "disinvestment," the transfer of investment resources to the more productive and profitable export industries. The German unions, though numerically smaller, suffer no important internal rivalries and have a long tradition of speaking for the working class as a whole. They also have a legal-institutional position which commits them to moderation.

The legally mandated policy of "co-determination" has placed union leaders on the boards of German business firms so that they can appreciate on the microeconomic level the relevance of adequate profits to support new investment. . . . The union leadership is well informed on the macroeconomic consequences of union action by the competent economists on their staffs. (Hodgman and Resek, 1981, p. 21)

By contrast in Britain, the Trade Union Congress includes the great majority of unions, and a substantial share of the workforce belongs to a union. Nevertheless, union power is more negative than positive. The unions have been able to block policies of elected governments but are less able to unite around a positive policy program, let alone secure the support and participation of their members in particular policy initiatives.

Union strength does not translate directly into the control of government by parties committed to interests of workers, except at the extremes of Sweden, where socialist parties dominate, and Japan, where they are absent.[5] This is so whether votes, parliamentary seats, or control over important ministries is used to reflect power. In Belgium, a high degree of union membership is not translated into stable voting for parties of the Left because of religious and political splits in the union movement. In Australia, despite both high unionization and a large and stable vote share, the Labor party has been largely excluded from any share in political power. On the other hand, in Switzerland (and to a lesser extent in Germany and the Netherlands), Left participation in cabinets has been high relative to modest levels both of unionization and Left voting.

Mobilization of the working class causes changes which are sporadic or transitory rather than sustained, compounding measurement difficulties. The income redistribution achieved by progressive rates of income taxation in the United States immediately after each world war was eroded by piecemeal adjustment in subsequent decades (Alt, 1982). Mobilization of the working class in the form of control over the executive produces short-term episodes of increases in transfer payments. However, it does not produce sustained increases in overall social expenditures or the size of aggregate public expenditures. Some evidence links working-class mobilization to relatively low long-run rates of unemployment and high rates of inflation, though the re-

5. Government policy affects union strength, so causation is not one way. This includes the effects of legislation passed by antiunion parties (right-to-work laws, restrictions on organized activities). If left-wing parties in government fail to secure working-class benefits, unions often become an institution of "antisystem" sentiment.

lationship really appears to distinguish the high unemployment rates of the United States and Canada from the low rates of Scandinavian countries and is period-dependent. (This is discussed further in Chapter 5.)

MOBILIZATION OF BUSINESS

Business or industry is more than just another political interest. The privileged position of business interests in Western industrial society is noted more or less ubiquitously.

Existing polyarchies are [dependent on the market system] and that only because, although they are libertarian, they are controlled undemocratically by business and property. (Lindblom, 1977, p. 169)

The advantages of business rest on control of capital and the difficulty of providing an alternative to market determination of investment.

Capitalist institutions have certainly proved to be a highly effective mechanism for organizing the capital formation required for industrialization. (Martin, 1977, p. 324)

The structural advantage of business for controlling investment compromises advantages in availability of funds, access to important information, and organizational ability.

The effort devoted to measuring the mobilization of workers is not matched in the case of business and industry. This would matter less if government was a passive arbiter among only two fundamental interests, labor and capital, and each increment of labor strength was ipso facto an increment of business weakness. However, this is an overly simple view. Business is itself internally divided between the interests of large and smaller units. The desires of productive industry are often at odds with those of service industries and commerce. The interests of consumers cut across the division between labor and capital. A harmonious relationship does not exist everywhere between industry and finance. Neither does conflict exist everywhere between industry and organized labor. Moreover, the state is not altogether passive. As we saw in the context of the New Deal, legislators and bureaucrats often pursue their interests independent of the desires of labor or capital. Moreover, public sector workers sometimes have group interests opposed to those of both labor and capital in the private sector (Dunleavy, 1980).

Olson's (1965) arguments about the costs and benefits of organization is of help in understanding the distribution of power among business organizations in a decentralized polity. If there are many companies in an industry, they will reduce their political contributions to collective, industrywide political efforts. Each company will hope to free-ride on the contributions of others. Collaboration is easier where few firms dominate an industry. The possibility of free-riding is reduced. Hence political activity should increase with concentration of the industry. There is some evidence that it does so in terms of political contributions (Pittman, 1977). Ambitious attempts to model the effects of firm size and market concentration suggest that among very large firms, the inhibiting effects of public visibility outweigh advantages of scale (Salamon and Siegfried, 1977; Coolidge and Tullock, 1980).

The power of business depends on its ability to present a united front. Antitrust legislation and regulation of American business owe as much to the hostility of smaller businesses toward more concentrated industries as to popular opposition to all business interests. Long periods of dispute over regulation exacerbate divisions within and between industries. The pressure for export competitiveness in open economies leads to more concentrated industries and possibly also to more cooperation between business and labor. In Japan, divisions within the business community are reduced by extensive ownership of smaller industries by larger ones. In Germany there is a long tradition of concentration in ownership.

Business power also depends on the organizations which represent it. In the United States, several large national organizations represent business, including the Chamber of Commerce, the National Association of Manufacturers, and the Business Roundtable. Each formed voluntarily and is well funded. Among the three they represent a substantial proportion of the American business community, and there are also dozens of smaller trade associations. In Britain, by contrast, the largest business organization, the Confederation (formerly Federation) of British Industry, formed in response to government pressure to provide a channel of coordination for World War I's production effort. It represents a smaller share of British industry and is not particularly effective.

Political strategies of business depend on the hostility between business and government. Vogel (1978) imputes the hostile attitudes of American businessmen toward their government to the absence of a major state role in the industrial development of the country. This is ameliorated by the tradition of fragmented interest group liberalism in government and the fragmentation of authority within the business community. Without the possibility of coordinating activities in a potentially beneficial "corporatist" strategy, business intervention is piecemeal. Businessmen fear and distrust the state because its power resources may be captured by someone else (politicians, labor, or other businessmen). The circulation between government and industry at high administrative and managerial levels in France and Japan reduces this distrust.[6]

Business power is expected to produce low rates of inflation, or at least relatively high unemployment, and to protect profits to encourage high levels of investment. Germany, Japan, and the United States have had comparatively low inflation rates, though in the latter two cases this has recently been less true.[7] At the same time, Japan and recently France have had high rates of capital formation whereas the United States has one of the lowest rates of capital formation in the industrial world. Britain has both a high inflation rate and a low rate of capital formation, consistent with weak representation of business interests. In any case, inflation and investment result from broader economic processes, of which an important aspect is the conduct of monetary policy by the banking authorities.

6. In the United States, similar circulation of personnel appears more frequently between industries and the regulatory agencies. This is argued to be a source of industry domination of these agencies.

7. Japan has historically had consumer prices which were allowed to increase rapidly while (exported goods) wholesale prices increased more slowly.

THE FINANCIAL SYSTEM

The central bank and financial systems of any country have two sorts of economic policy responsibilities. These are to ensure an adequate supply of finance or credit to facilitate economic growth and to manage the growth of the supply of money. (In Britain, the Bank of England has the further responsibility of marketing the government's debt.) These responsibilities are not always compatible, and the choices made by the monetary authorities are often highly politicized. This politicization results from the replacement of gold by government debt as the monetary base. The relationship between the central bank and elected political authorities has been the center of attention.

Parkin and Bade (1978) consider two measures of the independence of central banks from elected governments. One is whether a central bank is nominally the final authority over its monetary policy. In two of the countries they study (Switzerland and the United States) the bank is formally the final authority over policy. This was also the case in Canada before 1967. In Germany, the powers of the federal government over the central bank are restricted to the right to be represented in its deliberations and to delay upon request the implementation of central bank decisions. The central bank is also bound as far as possible to take actions consistent with the economic policy of the government. In all the other countries they study (Australia, Belgium, France, Italy, Japan, the Netherlands, Sweden, and Britain) the government is formally responsible for and may dictate central bank policy.

The other measure is the ability of the elected government to appoint the governing body of the central bank. Only in Switzerland and (possibly) Germany are appointments to these bodies substantially outside central government control. The long terms of directors in the U. S. Federal Reserve System insulate them from some political pressures. The two systems displaying most political independence (Germany and Switzerland) have the lowest long-run inflation rates (measured by exchange rate performance over a quarter of a century). The Netherlands is unique in having an explicit legal directive to its central bank to maintain price stability. It has the lowest inflation rate among countries with politically dependent banks. The diverse inflation performances of the other countries reveal that there are limits to the explanatory power of the formal constitution of the central bank alone. In fact, government-central bank relationships in most advanced industrial countries are similar. In every case senior decision-makers in central banks claim to feel political pressures. In every case they have consultative arrangements with political authorities in order to minimize episodes of serious disagreement. At most, the independent status of the bank provides a little insulation from direct pressure.

Woolley (1977) suggests that the autonomy of central banks vis-à-vis the rest of the banking system affects monetary policy. He suggests that this autonomy depends on the degree to which central banks possess complicated sets of policy instruments and whether control of these instruments is concentrated in one agency or diffused over several agencies. Concentration of instruments politicizes the central bank by making it a target of affected interest groups. Complexity of instrumentation politicizes the bank by making the effects of policy extend further into the banking system. Woolley's findings are restricted to countries in which there existed a well-developed open market for credit. In Japan, where private banks had no recourse to an open market for credit and were prevented from seeking funds from abroad, the Bank of Japan dominated the private banks through their dependence for funds on the central bank.

Comparisons of monetary policies require some sensitivity to the central banks' selection of instruments and targets. Most central banks attempt to guide the growth of the money stock through open market operations.[8] Only in a closed economy will this result in interest rate changes related to the growth of the money supply. Interest rates in open economies are more affected by external (world) interest rates but may be used to control international capital flows. Some central banks have rationed credit directly (France, Japan). In neither case do interest rates reflect allocation of credit. Rationing of credit has been used to redirect investment into productive industrial sectors, especially in Japan. There redirection is made easier by a high degree of

8. Wood (1981) argues that the responsibility for managing (selling) the government's debt has dominated the role of the Bank of England as manager of monetary policy.

bank ownership of industry and dependence of industry on bank finance.

Finally, political analysts presume that the likely policy preferences of finance are identical to those of business, namely, for the control of inflation, against government spending, and so on. This need not be so. Banks may not prefer lending to the private sector over the public sector. Bank profits are not necessarily reduced by high inflation. Private banks may desire stabilization of interest rates to reduce uncertainty in lending even if this precludes stabilizing the growth of the money supply.

POLITICAL INSTITUTIONS

How do institutions of industrial society interact with the democratic political process in the formation of economic policy? Most of this book examines specific models answering this central question. As a brief introduction, some of these studies of the politics of economic policy focus on institutions of government like constitutions and laws, legislatures, and bureaucracy. Others focus on parties, elections, and the electorate. They emphasize the incentives of political actors and how they are constrained by institutional structures.[9]

CONSTITUTIONAL-LEGAL STUDIES

Macrocomparative approaches stress the implications of decentralization and/or federalism for the conduct of a coordinated fiscal policy. For example, the division of responsibilities for the budget in the United States between branches of government and between the national and state governments limits discretionary fiscal action (Bach,

9. We omit that literature on the politics of taxing and spending. This "budgetary politics" literature views the budget as an allocative device and uses it either to investigate the power of various groups or institutions or to explicate aspects of the political process. The literature on budgeting makes it clear that macroeconomic considerations are often unimportant in the process by which budgets are made. This is an important point to remember. Only recently, and even then rarely, have political scientists considered the problem of the budget as an instrument of economic policy or discussed "economic" questions about the budget, like how large the deficit or surplus is and how large a share of national income is taken by revenues or expenditures.

1971). The federal German government shares with the eleven *Land* ("state") governments the responsibility for formulating economic policy. Unlike the American authorities, the Germans have evolved consultative arrangements, though they permit as much obstruction as coordination (Knott, 1981). These arrangements have turned the German tradition of centralization into a concentration of powers at the *Land* level, overcoming the problem of fragmentation in federal systems. On the other hand, a more highly diffused and open American political system permits policy initiatives like California's Proposition 13 and many other tax-limiting measures to emerge locally in a way inconsistent with a highly centralized system like Britain's. Actual instruments also vary. Countries with strong local authorities retain property taxes, and local authorities collect larger shares of revenue in federal systems (see Heidenheimer et al., 1983).

Procedural and legal differences also affect the ability of governments to conduct economic policies. Spending decisions are subject to referenda in Switzerland. Majority votes opposed to increased spending on programs automatically return spending levels to the status quo ante. The German constitution precluded the German government from having a budget deficit and therefore an active fiscal policy until 1967. Similarly, the postwar Japanese government did not use debt finance before 1963, though in recent years Japanese governments have shown substantial deficits. All these sorts of legal restrictions limit available government economic policies.

The distribution of power among various institutions also affects budgetary policy. (These will be discussed in detail in Chapters 8 and 9.) For example, a decentralized budget process aids special interests and hinders overall control of aggregate revenues and expenditures. Theories of bureaucracy allege that bureaucrats cause increased expenditure for the survival and expansion of their organizations. If legislatures purchase services from public bureaucracies at prices quoted by the bureaucrats, there will be a public sector larger than the electorate wants. This assumes passive legislators but shows the importance of the context in which an agency operates. Studies of regulation emphasize the discrepancy between agency incentives at the time regulation is introduced, when public attention is focused on agency activities, and the ordinary activities of the agency when only affected industries have the incentive to be informed and try to affect agency decisions. Others attribute public expenditure growth to legislative processes and incentives, especially where expenditures are allocated within representatives' constituencies. These theories usually assume some fiscal illusion in the electorate, a misperception of benefits supplied and costs incurred to finance them.

PARTIES, ELECTIONS, AND THE ELECTORATE

Party systems create the context of interaction between electors and elected politicians (Martin, 1977). Party systems thus influence the economic policies which emerge. This issue underlies Parts III and IV but deserves brief discussion here. If politicians maximize support by providing policies geared principally to the demands of a class-based core of supporters, there should be higher rates of increase in public expenditures and lower levels of unemployment among countries with extended periods of left-wing government. The demand for low unemployment is concentrated in the working class of industrial societies, who bear the brunt of it. Why is this model not generally applicable? First, there are other economic variables like inflation whose impact cannot be characterized in class terms. The cost of inflation hits those with money balances or nominal assets of an inflexible sort. Inflation also produces uncertainty and price distortions, that is, relative prices change arbitrarily. Powerful labor unions can protect themselves against inflation by bidding up wages. The costs of inflation may be feared as much as the costs of unemployment by those most at risk— the weakest or least organized workers and pensioners. So the actual vote-maximizing economic policy for politicians perceiving their support as class-based is unclear.

Moreover, this is an inappropriate model of many party systems. The fragmentation of party systems varies. Even where parties do promise consistent and distinctive alternative policy packages, government by coalition involves compromises. Some parties maintain internal cohesion by their monopoly on political advancement and important roles in the formulation and legislation of public policy. A different conception of support-maximizing politicians arises in a highly fragmented party system like the United States. Here there are multiple means of entry and advancement in politics and relatively little party discipline in legislation. Politicians can be thought of as strategic entrepreneurs who supply the public with whatever mix of policies appears at the time to command the widest degree of support. One possibility is that the policy which commands most support is always an expansionary one, and thus electoral democracies will be characterized by expansion of public spending. A further argument is that such expansions coincide with elections, though there is no strong empirical evidence that the frequency of elections is in any way related to rates of increase of public expenditure.

A central theme in the recent politicoeconomic literature is that vote-maximizing activities give rise to a sort of "political" business cycle. This theory is built on both the amnesia and myopia of the electorate. To make a short-term boom worthwhile in terms of votes requires that people forget all but the recent past in making vote decisions (amnesia). They also must have no independent vote-related expectations about government's likely future performance (myopia). If expansions always increase support, the electorate must be under some sort of permanent illusion that either benefits of policies exceed their costs or that someone else will pay more of the tax cost for a project while getting less of the benefits. However, economists have also used such illusions to explain the absence of government services, particularly defense. Suppose that project benefits are invisible relative to tax costs. Then the government budget would always be "too small" (Downs, 1965). These assertions of electoral amnesia, myopia, and illusion deserve empirical investigation. (They are discussed in detail in Chapter 7.)

SUMMARY

Major social, economic, and political institutions are constraints on policymakers. The concentration and scale of labor unions and business organization and the relationship between central banks, governments, and domestic banking systems all affect policy outcomes. Policymakers are also constitutionally constrained. The possible effects on policymakers of incentives to maximize their popular support have been raised. While institutions constrain political activities, they do not alone determine policies. There is another major constraint which has been left implicit until now—how the economy itself works. The next chapter deals with controversies about the operation of domestic economies, and Chapter 4 deals with the international context.

CHAPTER THREE

Macroeconomic Policy and Economic Theory

Political economics is concerned with what governments do and how successful they are. But how do we judge whether or not economic policies have been successful? Would we, for example, blame our government for inflation? The answer depends on how we think the economy works. Macroeconomic theories explain how changes in one economic variable cause changes in another. They say what the effect of a shock to the system will be, whatever its origins. Theory not only defines the feasible effects of government intervention on the economy. It also determines the extent to which some "good" or "bad" outcome is thought to stem from government policy. Any government has discretion over some aspects of policy but is constrained in others. Although policymakers' choice of policy instruments is constrained by institutional structures, different economic theories also imply different areas of discretion. The importance of understanding government discretion in terms of prevailing economic theories has increased in recent years as governments' economic policies have received close scrutiny and the state of the economy has affected their electoral fortunes.

The international economic environment changed dramatically in the 1970s. Most major countries had substantial increases in inflation and unemployment. In 1960, for example, inflation of consumer prices was 1.8 percent in the United States and 1.1 percent in Britain, compared with 13.5 percent for the United States and 18.0 percent for Britain in 1980. As recently as 1968, no major industrial country had an inflation rate much above 5 percent. In 1980 the overwhelming majority of industrial countries had inflation rates over 10 percent. This inflation was not the price paid for a higher level of real economic activity or real growth. In Britain, for example, industrial production was lower in 1980 than it had been in 1973. Most industrial countries suffered a large and steady upward drift of unemployment. All suffered at least a slowing down of their real growth rates.

Figure 3.1 shows the contrast between the growth decades of the 1950s and 1960s and recent inflationary experience. All these countries (others could as well have been included) have substantially lower real growth and higher inflation levels. In the earlier period, there was considerable variation in real growth rates, with predominantly low inflation. The later period shows variable inflation rates, but low real growth. (Unemployment rates are shown in Figure 5.2 in Chapter 5.) How can we account for this economic change? Did government respond to it, or even cause it? An answer requires a discussion of macroeconomic theory.

Macroeconomics concentrates on the behavior of broad economic aggregates by assuming for the most part that the economy is one big industry producing a homogeneous good. To facilitate analysis of growth, inflation, unemployment, and the balance of payments, it suppresses structural problems and concentrates on overall indicators like national income. National income is the sum of the values of all goods and services produced by an economy in a period of time.[1] The concern of macroeconomics is the total output of the economy as measured by gross domestic product (GDP) rather than the behavior of particular markets or firms. The role of "government" is central. Macroeconomics has sought ways in which government intervention can stabilize an economy by offsetting the causes of business cycles and

1. There are three measures commonly used. Gross domestic product (GDP) is total domestic output; gross national product (GNP) is GDP plus income from property owned abroad; and national income or net national income is GDP less an allowance for the depreciation of plant and machinery.

thereby maintain a higher average level of real output and incomes.

We cover several major stages in the evolution of macroeconomic thinking: Keynesian, Monetarist, and New Classical, along with other important contemporary variations and the issues which divide them. We describe the connection between economic theory and political values. Keynesian policies were "activist" while subsequent devel-

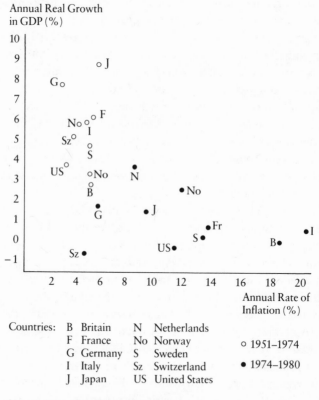

FIGURE 3.1. Real Growth Rates of GDP and Inflation Rates in Ten Countries, 1951–1974 and 1974–1980

opments suggest a more conservative policy stance. A commentary on the economic events of the 1970s and 1980s shows the different policy implications of the various schools of thought. How macroeconomic thinking was affected by changes in the international economic system is discussed in the next chapter. However, it is convenient first to outline the general view of economics before the 1930s.

THE CLASSICAL SYSTEM

Classical economics is the body of thought built up in the late nineteenth century on the foundation of work by Smith, Ricardo, and Mill, among others. It was principally a microeconomic system, in which there were many different goods and services. It emphasized the role of individual markets in determining what was produced and at what price products sold. At the center of the system, prices would adjust to changes in demand or supply to clear markets. If a product was in excess demand, its price would rise while in excess supply its price would fall.

The occurrence of "market clearing" is still a source of controversy with regard to the "New Classical" school of economics discussed below. It means that anybody with the money to buy a good can do so at the going market price if they wish or that there is no rationing. It also means that any supplier of a good who chooses can sell it for money at the going market price. The analysis assumes that *prices* adjust to clear markets and do so reasonably quickly. For example, at some price sellers may offer more goods than buyers will purchase. Lowering the price will both induce more purchases and perhaps reduce the numbers prepared to sell. At some price the greater demand and the lower supply will mean that the quantity on offer will just equal what purchasers wish to buy. This is the market clearing price. This adjustment of prices may work in many kinds of commodity markets, but there are other markets in which it may not, like the labor market. The observation of persistent "involuntary" unemployment supports the view that there is no ubiquitous tendency for wages (the price of labor) to adjust to eliminate unemployment.

The classical system presumed that the wage rate adjusted to clear labor markets, just as prices adjust to clear commodity markets. If there are unemployed workers, wages adjust downward until the supply is just equal to the demand. Firms will hire more workers if they can pay them less. There is some wage at which everyone who wishes to work *at that wage* will be able to find a job. Any involuntary unemployment must be because wages are too high, but in that event wages could be expected to adjust downward.

The only "macroeconomic" aspect of the classical system was the Quantity Theory of Money. This is really a monetary theory of prices. It says that the price level will be proportional to the stock of money in circulation. It is reasonable as a long-run proposition that the value of money will be the lower the more money there is in circulation. However, in the short term, it also implies that increasing the money stock has no "real" effects. All prices rise equally, but the physical quantities of goods produced and consumed are unchanged. There will be no changes in *relative* prices, the price of one good vis-à-vis another. In the classical system, only relative price changes have real effects. In this sense, money is neutral. The only potential macroeconomic policy is to control the price level through the money stock. Such monetary policies were not important prior to the twentieth century because money was generally based not on the liabilities of government but rather upon gold or occasionally the liability of some private bank. Money was not an issue of government policy.

Fiscal policy was not an instrument of economic control either. Theory gave no reason for changes in government expenditure or taxes to influence the real economy. A rise in government expenditure financed by borrowing would "crowd out" some private investment expenditure. The positive initial effect of the expenditure would be offset by the negative effect of borrowing. Only an urgent need to finance, say, a war made a prudent policy of government deficits financed by borrowing. The proper course for government finance was a balanced budget. The annual budget was designed to set tax rates so that revenue would just cover the cost of expenditures. The Keynesian revolution changed all this.

THE KEYNESIAN REVOLUTION

The worldwide Great Depression provided a period of substantial and persistent unemployment with no obvious tendency for wages to adjust rapidly to clear the labor market. In the Classical model, a wage cut was expected to solve the problem. Keynes's analysis presumed that market forces would not be an adequate automatic adjustment mechanism and gave government a central role in stabilizing the economy. The role of the budget as an instrument of control and the perception that governments are responsible for the state of the economy derive from this development.

Keynes's "General Theory," published in 1936, changed the focus of thinking about the economy. He pointed to the importance of "effective demand" failure. Unemployed workers would demand goods if they were employed, but they will not be employed until after demand for goods has risen. Workers have a "notional" demand for goods which would create more jobs if it were expressed. It cannot be expressed with money "effectively" until they have been employed (Clower, 1965). This problem of coordinating economic decisions is not solved by lowering wages. Although excessive wage rates can cause unemployment, this need not always be the cause of the problem. Keynes's analysis of a deep depression provided a plausible case where an economy could get stuck in a position of substantial unemployment which market forces would not quickly eliminate unaided.

Keynesian macroeconomic analysis focused on categories of aggregate expenditures. National output could be sold for personal consumption, investment, export, or government consumption. These combined expenditures determined total spending in the economy. Total spending determined the level of total national income. The existence of a depression meant that there were unemployed resources in the economy. There was thus no effective supply constraint, and so the only factor limiting production was demand. If more spending could be induced, more output would be forthcoming. Since total output equals total income, more spending increases national income. At least in early Keynesian models, aggregate demand entirely determined national income. If national income were below trend, it was because of a demand deficiency.

The personal consumption function was the central behavioral relationship in Keynesian macro models. This was the biggest component of total expenditure. At the simplest level, consumption was presumed to depend on the level of national income. It would rise with national income but not by as much. If incomes rose by $100 million, consumption might rise by, say, $80 million, and the rest would be saved. Two other aggregates were determined exogenously.[2] Investment depended largely on the expectations of firms. Exports depended on the income of foreigners. The last category to be determined, government expenditure, was exogenous to the economy but in the control of the policymakers. *The idea that came out of the Keynesian revolution was that policymakers should manipulate government expenditures to achieve a desirable level of aggregate demand.*

If aggregate demand in an economy is deficient, perhaps because of a decline in investment or exports, there will be a decline in national income and a rise in unemployment. The government can offset this by an active fiscal *stabilization policy*. Its instruments are tax rates and government expenditure. Government expenditure is a direct demand for goods. For any gross income, higher income taxes reduce private spending by leaving individuals less to allocate. Income taxes reduce the "disposable" income available for consumers to spend. Aggregate demand in the economy is increased by either lowering taxes (and thus raising disposable income and consumer spending) or increasing government expenditure. Both increase national income through the famous "multiplier," so named because in theory an increase in exogenous expenditure can lead to a larger increase in income. Suppose the government spends an extra $100. This is received as income by someone who spends some of it. This is received as income by someone else, and so on. Some income is saved each time, so the ripples even-

---

2. "Exogenous" means that the value of the variable is determined outside the model, that is, does not vary with, say, national income, which is determined inside the model. Sensitivity of investment to the interest rate later linked the real economy to the money market.

tually peter out. The multiplier is the ratio of the total increase in income to the initial expenditure.[3]

Economics textbooks talk indifferently about the choice between government expenditures and taxes as policy instruments. In political institutional terms they are very different. Much of this book is about how political pressures influence these decisions. Analytic economics often concentrates on government expenditure as the main instrument of fiscal policy. However, many government expenditures in reality are hard to change quickly. Civil servants cannot be hired and fired at will, and projects instituted with difficulty are protected by strong vested interests. For the most part fiscal policy is conducted through changes in taxes rather than through expenditures. (This argument is developed further in Chapter 10.)

Keynesian economics provided an intellectual justification for activist economic policies. Budget plans in this framework no longer simply set tax rates to finance expenditure. A budget deficit or surplus may be deliberately set to increase or decrease aggregate demand. Budgeting became an exercise of *economic control*, not balancing the books. The Kennedy/Johnson tax cuts of 1964 in the United States and the Barber budget of March 1972 in Britain are good examples of governments deliberately incurring deficits to stimulate the economy. The Jenkins period of 1968–1970 in Britain exemplifies deliberate engineering of a budget surplus.

Macroeconomics itself aimed to provide better quantitative formulations of the key behavioral relationships: consumption, investment, import and export functions. More accurate models would improve stabilization policy. The promise of the 1950s and early 1960s was not fulfilled. Keynesian models were increasingly unable to explain events like inflation. Keynesian models were modified to some extent in response to criticisms. There are two main groups of critics, monetarists and new classicists, though even here the dividing line is hazy. Roughly

3. This multiplier effect is only likely to occur in an economy with substantial unemployed resources. It would be a strange world, indeed, in which an increase in spending always called forth an increase in output (and incomes) which was always greater than the initial rise in spending. The size of the multiplier in simple Keynesian models depends on the proportion of additional income that is saved.

speaking, monetarists argue that important factors were omitted. The New Classical school, which evolved out of Monetarism, argues that the methodology of Keynesian macroeconomics was basically wrong.

THE MONETARIST CRITIQUE

The growth of monetarism was largely stimulated by the work of Milton Friedman and his disciples. They emphasized the importance of money and monetary policy in the economy. While Keynes had not ignored the monetary system, early Keynesians gave monetary policy a more or less passive role. They argued mainly that monetary policy (changes in interest rates and money supply) should accommodate fiscal policy (taxes and government spending). As we shall see below, before the 1970s no Western nation except the United States had the possibility of an independent monetary policy because it was obliged to maintain fixed exchange rates. That is why theories about the role of monetary policy developed largely in the United States.

The initial monetarist challenge to Keynesian orthodoxy proposed that the "demand for money" was a more stable behavioral relationship than the Keynesian expenditure functions. Money was normally defined to include cash plus bank balances. Monetarists argued that *on average* people try to maintain money balances as some stable proportion of their income, though this varies somewhat with interest rates. If the demand for money were stable, changes in the supply of money would affect spending. Monetarists argued that Keynesian models ignored this effect. The policy implications of such models would be incorrect, leading to mistaken and possibly damaging interventions.

As well as the importance of monetary policy, Friedman stressed the difficulties of using it for "fine-tuning" the economy. Monetary policy worked with a "long and variable lag" so that the timing of the effects would be uncertain. This severely limits its use for stabilization purposes. If the timing of the impact of policy is uncertain, the state of the economy may have changed by the time the effects of an intervention are felt. Intended countercyclical policies may turn out pro-cyclical, exaggerating the business cycle. Stabilization policy could be destabilizing. According to Friedman, the solution was to abandon the use of monetary policy for stabilization purposes. The money supply should instead grow in line with the trend growth rate of the real economy. This would ensure at least that no destabilizing influences came from monetary policy.

The debate between monetarists and Keynesians remained academic until the end of the 1960s. Events changed all that. Inflation became an important and growing problem. Monetarists were able to explain inflation more convincingly than Keynesians. Early Keynesian models assumed the price level fixed. If the price level was variable, these models could determine the price level or real income but not both. Their initial problem had been to explain depressions, in which prices did not rise but actually fell gradually. It was convenient to assume the price level constant and so explain "real national income." In the 1950s the Keynesian analysis was extended to determine real income *and* prices simultaneously.

This was done with the Phillips curve in 1958, a trade-off relationship between the rate of inflation and the level of unemployment. Lower levels of unemployment are associated with higher rates of inflation and vice versa. Governments could choose to use aggregate demand policies to reduce the level of unemployment but only at the cost of a rise in the rate of inflation. The trade-off was thought stable, so a lower level of unemployment could be achieved *permanently* with a stable (though higher) level of inflation. There could be benefits in some inflation associated with greater economic activity levels, higher employment, and higher real incomes.

Monetarists believed that the only long-run effect of the expansion of monetary demand was higher prices. The only acceptable rate of inflation was close to zero since inflation was costly. Inflation, at least to the extent it is unexpected, distorts the efficient working of the market economy by adding "noise" to price signals. Friedman (1968) criticized the Phillips curve. The theory of the Phillips curve was rooted in labor markets. The rate of increase of money wages was presumed to become greater with more excess demand for labor. Unemployment was simply a way of measuring the latter. Friedman argued that *real* rather than *money* wages respond to real pressure in labor markets.

Unlike money wage increases, a real wage increase compensates for changes in the value of money. For example, if inflation is 10 percent and money wages rise 20 percent, then real wages rise 10 percent. If labor market conditions permit a real wage rise of, say, 10 percent and inflation is expected to be 10 percent, this will dictate a money wage rise of 20 percent. The money wage rise exceeds the real wage rise by the *expected* inflation rate.

This may seem like a harmless modification, but in fact it was devastating. There is no longer a single Phillips curve. There is instead a different curve for each *expected* rate of inflation. For any level of demand in labor markets, higher expected inflation means higher increases in money wage rates and thus higher prices. If the current inflation is greater than expected, expectations will be revised upward. Only at a level of unemployment where expectations are fulfilled is the rate of inflation stable. This is called the "natural" level of unemployment. Because of expectations, inflation *accelerates* at any level of unemployment below the natural rate. Above the natural rate of unemployment there is decelerating inflation. Only at the natural rate does existing inflation persist.

Consider Figure 3.2. The original Phillips curve was a single trade-off between inflation and unemployment like PC_1. Unemployment could be reduced at the expense of higher inflation. A government could achieve zero inflation by manipulating aggregate demand so that there was U_N of unemployment. If, on the other hand, it was prepared to tolerate inflation of, say, $\dot{P}_1$, it could reduce unemployment to U_1 permanently. Under the revised analysis, however, this outcome (labeled B) is not stable.

Suppose PC_1 is the Phillips curve for an expected inflation rate of zero. If unemployment is U_N, then inflation will indeed be zero. If unemployment is reduced to U_1, inflation will turn out to be $\dot{P}_1$. Expectations were incorrect and will be revised upward. The Phillips curve for the next period will be above PC_1. Then, even if unemployment stays at U_1, inflation will rise above $\dot{P}_1$. Continued upward revisions of the Phillips curve mean that inflation accelerates as long as unemployment stays to the left of U_N. To the right of U_N the reverse is true. Inflation will be less than expected. Expectations will be revised

downward, and the Phillips curve will shift down. Inflation will de-
celerate. At U_N inflation will be stable. But U_N, the so-called "natural
rate," is consistent with zero inflation only if zero inflation was expected. If some inflation were expected, unemployment at the natural
rate generates that rate of inflation. Returning to stable zero inflation
requires spending time reducing expectations to the right of U_N.

The macroeconomic policy implications of these ideas are now well
known, if not always endorsed. It is undesirable to boost aggregate
demand to run the economy below the natural rate. Moreover, it is not
possible to do so for long. Eventually the economy will explode into
hyperinflation, or long periods of high unemployment will be needed
to purge inflation from the system. Bringing inflationary expectations
down is probably harder than pushing them up. An economy with no
inflation can do no better than set aggregate demand to achieve the
natural rate. Any other economy must tolerate unemployment above
the natural rate until inflation comes down to an acceptable level.

These are the main implications of the Keynesian-Monetarist de-

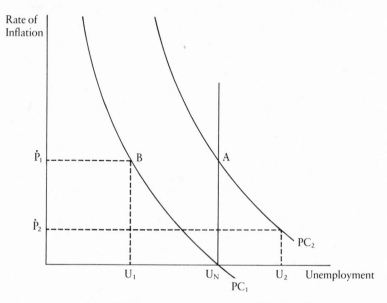

FIGURE 3.2. The Expectations-Augmented Phillips Curve

bate for macroeconomic policy. Keynesian economics encouraged activist macroeconomic policy. Fiscal policy was to regulate the economy. Whatever budget deficit turned out was presumed financeable without major difficulty. Short-run considerations were paramount. The longer term was left to look after itself. Monetarism was much more conservative. Concern for long-run problems dominated short-run considerations. Monetary policy should be set by rule rather than by discretion. Countercyclical fiscal policy may be cautiously used, but budget deficits must never inhibit the authorities' ability to control the money supply. The need to control inflation dictated the dominant role of a tight monetary policy. Keynesians, on the other hand, were typically more concerned with the problem of rising unemployment.

THE NEW CLASSICAL VIEW

Leading exponents of the New Classical school are R. Lucas, R. Barro, T. Sargent, and N. Wallace. Their work grew out of monetarist macroeconomics with clear parallels in classical economics. Much of the work of this school is in the tradition of the free marketeers discussed in Chapter 1. Its proponents claim to represent a radical departure from the Keynesian macroeconomic tradition, even though it had incorporated many of the insights of monetarism. Consider, for example, the words of Lucas and Sargent (1978):

In the present decade, the U.S. economy has undergone the first major depression since the 1930s, to the accompaniment of inflation rates in excess of 10 percent per annum. These events have been transmitted (by the consent of the governments involved) to other advanced countries and in many cases have been amplified. These events did not arise from a reactionary reversion to outmoded, "classical" principles of tight money and balanced budgets. On the contrary, they were accompanied by massive governmental budget deficits and high rates of monetary expansion: policies which, although bearing an admitted risk of inflation, promised according to modern Keynesian doctrine rapid real growth and low rates of unemployment.

That these predictions were wildly incorrect, and that the doctrine on which they were based is fundamentally flawed, are now simple matters of fact, involving no novelties in economic theory. The task which faces contemporary students of the business cycle is that of sorting through the wreckage, determining which features of that remarkable intellectual event called the Keynesian Revolution can be salvaged and put to good use, and which others must be discarded. . . . *our interest will be to establish that the difficulties are fatal: that modern macroeconomic models are of no value in guiding policy and that this condition will not be remedied by modifications along any line which is currently being pursued.* (p. 69)

The basis of their criticism is that Keynesian models are built around behavioral relationships which involve many arbitrary restrictions. For example, consumption is normally thought to depend on income but not on many other things which sometimes affect spending. These relationships are estimated from statistics for specific historical periods and used to "forecast" how the economy will respond to certain policy changes in the future. Lucas (1976) argues that this procedure is invalid. In principle, there will be different parameters for *each possible policy*. Estimates based on past policies are next to useless in forecasting responses to future policies. For example, suppose the best estimated relationship over the recent past gave the result:

$$\text{Consumption} = 200 + 0.8 \text{ income.} \tag{1}$$

Under Keynesian methodology this equation would be used to forecast consumption with different levels of income. According to Lucas, these estimates reflect special features about the sample period like the government policy of the time. These special features may not exist in the future, and there is no reason for estimates to continue to hold. A new methodology is necessary.

Models should deduce behavior from general principles of optimization. Then models would incorporate explicitly all possible environments or circumstances the actor faces. Such models are said to be "policy invariant." If a different policy had been in force during the sample period, the estimated behavioral parameters would still be the same. Requiring policy invariance restricts the range of permissible behavioral assumptions. Actors must be seen as rational optimizers, consistently making choices which maximize their objectives given their constraints, subject to all the information at their disposal. These actors interact in markets such that prices are determined which clear markets. In this sense the models are "equilibrium models." In contrast, Keynesian models explicitly assume nonclearing markets. This assumption of market clearing most obviously links the New Classical and Classical schools of thought.

The research line being pursued by a number of us involves the attempt to discover a particular, econometrically testable equilibrium theory of the business cycle, one that can serve as the foundation for quantitative analysis of macroeconomic policy. There is no denying that this approach is "counterrevolutionary," for it presupposes that Keynes and his followers were wrong to give up on the possibility that an equilibrium theory could account for the business cycle. (Lucas and Sargent, 1978, p. 59)

One dominant feature of models in the New Classical tradition is the widely used assumption of "rational expectations." *Rational* expectations will on average be correct. Any errors in expectations will be random (formally, serially uncorrelated with a mean of zero). If errors were not random, there would be additional unused information available to improve the forecast, contradicting the rationality of expectations. Everything systematic can thus be learned and therefore anticipated. For example, if the authorities have a rule to determine the money stock, this rule will be learned by private sector actors and rapidly incorporated into their price-setting behavior. An extension of this argument shows that in at least one class of models correctly anticipated monetary policy will have no real effects. It is simply discounted into the behavior of prices. Only "surprise" events or mistakes in expectations have real effects.

This approach does not readily explain the persistence of unemployment and indeed the existence of a regular business cycle. Extra assumptions have been used to explain these phenomena. One is incomplete information about the general price level. Suppose your money wage has risen, but you do not know whether all other prices have risen. You will not know whether your *real* wage has gone up or down. If you think it has gone up, you may supply more labor and output will rise. If you find out that all other prices have risen, you will return to your original position. During the learning period there will be a cycle in output. Cycles also arise if such "mistakes" lead to the installation of new machines. Such decisions are hard to reverse, and the effect on output will last a long time.

This approach reinforces monetarist strictures against active monetary stabilization policy. The Monetarist case was that "long and variable lags" made accurate stabilization impossible. The New Classical argument is that *any systematic policy will quickly come to be anticipated*. The position of fiscal policy is less clear since changing marginal tax rates will have real effects. However, any anticipated aggregate stimulus is generally presumed to be discounted into higher prices rather than output. Any macroeconomic policy intended to provide a stimulus to real output does so only to the extent that it "surprises" actors in the system.

This New Classical approach is still at an early stage of development and so is hard to assess fully. Many are not convinced by it, and considerable intellectual problems remain (Hahn, 1982). Since New Classical economics assumes market clearing, it has relied on some other ad hoc assumptions like arbitrarily restricted information or adjustment costs to account for phenomena like persistent unemployment. It is far from clear that this is superior to the Keynesian assumption of nonclearing or incomplete markets. The policy implications of the New Classical school are highly conservative. Their case is that systematic stabilization policy is anticipated and thus *cannot* affect the deviation of actual real output from its trend, capacity, or "natural" level. Systematic macroeconomic policy has no effect on the real economy.

ALTERNATIVE PERSPECTIVES

We have characterized three major phases in the evolution of macroeconomics. A wide variety of positions do not fit easily into our three boxes. Familiarity with some of these diverse views will be needed to understand what follows.

MODERN KEYNESIANS

Keynesian economics is not just a developmental stage in macroeconomics which has largely been superseded. Most professional economists would probably describe themselves as "Keynesians." *Modern Keynesians* (like James Tobin or Franco Modigliani) have clearly been influenced by the criticisms of other schools. They would regard the level of output of the economy relative to "potential" output as the result of aggregate demand policies. They would be unlikely to regard the distinction between monetary and fiscal policy as critical. They differ most from monetarists on how to control inflation. Monetarists claim that controlling monetary demand through the money supply is the *only* way to control inflation. To a modern Keynesian the inflation rate is relatively insensitive to such control. Reducing inflation significantly requires substantial unemployment and lost output because the pressure for high money wage rises is sustained by strong labor unions. It is consequently preferable to maintain higher levels of activity and to attempt to control inflation by means of an incomes policy. Incomes policies attempt to impose ceilings or other controls on the rate of increase of wages either by legal restraint or by voluntary agreement. However, most previous incomes policies (at least in the United States and Britain) failed to have more than small or transitory effects.

POST-KEYNESIANS

Modern Keynesians are very much part of the mainstream tradition of macroeconomics. A small but vocal group of post-Keynesians regard the mainstream to be on the wrong course. Leaders in this group include Paul Davidson, Hyman Minsky, and G. L. S. Shackle. Their ideas come from what Keynes "really said" rather than from the model of an economy as developed by Keynesians (and indeed monetarists). Their central view is that any economy can be understood only in the context of its own time-dependent institutional framework. (This sentiment is echoed in Chapter 6.) Actors make decisions at discrete points in real time. At the time decisions are made the future is uncertain. It is not just "risky" in the sense that probabilities could be attached to future events but so uncertain that there is no scientific basis for applying a probability calculus.

Therefore, the most crucial economic decisions must, by their very nature, be made largely in ignorance and uncertainty. In this uncertain world, it is ephemeral expectations, unpredictable waves of optimism and pessimism, and "animal spirits" which decisively influence investment, and therefore income and employment as well. (Crotty, 1980 p. 22)

To a post-Keynesian any view of a macroeconomy as stable or smoothly adjusting toward equilibrium even in the long run is inappropriate. The real world is characterized by instability and disequilibrium. The role of "government" as stabilizer and equilibrator on an active and ongoing basis is vital. Post-Keynesian ideas are thus strongly at variance with those of monetarists and new classicists who see the market economy as stable with the government as a major source of shocks.

SUPPLY-SIDE ECONOMICS

Supply-side economics is by no means an intellectually coherent doctrine.[4] It comprises three separate propositions, none of which need be held by all members of the school. First, high tax rates are a disincentive to work and effort. Since government spending must be financed by taxes (on average), smaller spending and, therefore, lower taxes are necessarily beneficial. Government spending does not just involve diversion of resources from the private to the public sector but also includes transfers like Social Security within the private sector. Little precise supporting empirical evidence is available on this subject (Keeley and Robins, 1979). Second, it has been argued (notably by Arthur Laffer) that lower tax rates could generate higher tax revenue. Cutting taxes will so stimulate economic growth that even at lower tax rates the tax take from the new higher incomes will be higher than before. This cannot generally be true as it would mean that the economy is unstable, for successive reductions in tax rates would produce unbounded growth.

The third proposition of supply-side economics is that an extensive government role in the economy is inimical to productive investment. The government is not seen primarily as the controller of aggregate demand, as Keynesians and monetarists alike see it, but rather as a

4. Most of its proponents would simultaneously regard themselves as monetarists or new classicists. Nevertheless, they also hold ideas which are not normally associated with either of these two schools.

competitor for resources that could be used in the private sector. The presumption is that private sector resource use is more efficient than government resource use, so slower productivity growth results from higher government resource use. While Keynesians see greater government expenditure as stimulating output by increasing demand, a supply-sider sees harmful effects in the diversion of resources into the public sector.

The possible conflict between public and private resource use has been extensively discussed under the name "crowding out." *Crowding out* describes a reduction in private sector output caused by an expansion of public sector output. In Keynesian models the multiplier meant that increased government expenditure generated larger increases in national income. The increase in output or income of the private sector exceeded the value of the resources shifted to the government, and the private sector wound up better off. Although this analysis was appropriate with considerable slack in the economy, not long into the postwar period it became clear that resource constraints were real. Available unemployed resources were not infinite. Close to full employment, the economy would behave differently, reducing the beneficial effects of expansionary fiscal policy. At full employment it *must* be true that a switch of resources into the public sector will reduce the resources available for the private sector. With fewer resources, private sector output must fall.

Crowding out effects operate through several different channels.[5] For example, if expenditure is financed by tax increases, the nature of the tax determines who bears the burden. If expenditure is financed by borrowing, and interest rates are forced up, the main burden falls on private sector investment. If the expenditure is financed by money printing, this leads to inflation, and those holding nominal assets, including money, suffer. Building macro models in which the economy tends toward a "natural" level of unemployment or a "natural" rate of output encourages the notion of crowding out since government

5. A major stimulus to the academic discussion of crowding out, especially in the United States, was Anderson and Jordan (1968). A more recent discussion is Brunner and Meltzer (1976). A specific version of the crowding out thesis was developed for Britain by Bacon and Eltis (1976), who argue that nonmarket sector absorption of market sector surplus has crowded out market sector investment and exports. See Hadjimatheou and Skouras (1979) for criticisms.

expenditure is typically not expected to improve the trend rate of growth of the economy.

Government expenditure will lower the underlying growth rate if it involves the diversion of resources into inefficient and unproductive uses. If government provides assistance for uncompetitive industries, enterprises in which the government becomes involved must show poor returns relative to the rest of private sector industry. Even if some public ventures are profitable, enough will lose money to provide ammunition for those opposed to government intervention. It is even easier to demonstrate the irrelevance of government if one grafts policy onto a model in which the private sector behaves optimally already. In such an exercise, government can only make things worse. This, however, amounts to proof by assumption rather than a genuine demonstration of the effects of policy.

POLITICS AND ECONOMIC THEORY

Economic theories indicate the likely effects of various courses of action. By defining the choices policymakers have, they represent a constraint on economic policy. All these theories also say something about the appropriate role of "government" in the economy. This is no accident. The portrayal of government is central to the intention of each school in the debate between Keynesians and monetarists. There is thus a close relationship between the choice of economic perspective and political values. But the political implications of choices in economic theory also depend on the institutional context.

This debate between Keynesians and monetarists has been carried on principally in the United States and Britain, the countries where Keynesian economics was most influential. It takes its form from the institutions of these countries. A government following a Keynesian strategy is autonomous. It does not require the close cooperation of business in planning investment strategy, as in Japan. It does not require centrally organized sectors of business and labor to implement national agreements over wages, as in Sweden. Keynesian economics is an activist strategy for a decentralized polity with adversarial interests of the sort discussed in Chapter 2. In other institutional settings, the search for an activist policy leads to a "command and control" strategy involving some sort of directive planning aimed at labor markets and control of investment.

Keynesian ideas took root in the United States and Britain through replacement of older generations in government positions by people trained in the new tradition. The British Treasury in the 1940s and 1950s was slowly "converted" to Keynesianism, though the process accelerated when Keynes was invited into the Treasury as adviser during World War II (Winch, 1969). In the United States, the evolution of policy owes more to the desire of various administrations to bring in economic advisers sympathetic to the more or less activist lines of the policy they intended. Keynesians came to Washington in the 1960s under Kennedy and Johnson. Monetarists arrived in 1980 under Reagan. These gradual changes also reflect economists' political activities. Keynes was a great pamphleteer and letter writer. Friedman's columns in *Newsweek* carry on the tradition. Woolley (1982) points out that these are the visible tip of a major campaign by monetarist economists to pressure the Federal Reserve, Congress, and the administration.

Nevertheless, it is an exaggeration to assume that all political beliefs of an economist can be deduced from his choice of theory. It is possible for monetarists as well as Keynesians to be convinced of the ultimate importance of full employment. However, a monetarist will not believe that an active stabilization policy is a means by which full employment can be achieved. Rather, he will believe that a money growth rule is the only government policy compatible with long-run full employment. So while political beliefs and the mode of economic analysis do not perfectly determine each other, they are strongly related. No one should really be surprised by this, though it does mean that great care has to be taken in assessing the import of seemingly "scientific" economic theories for practical policy.

MACROECONOMIC POLICY IN THE 1980s

At the outset of this chapter, we saw that during the late 1970s the world changed from one in which most countries had economic growth and some inflation to one in which there was high inflation with very little growth. It is thus hardly surprising that in the second half of the 1970s, the fight against inflation became a priority in many industrial countries. It was also widely accepted that the upward trend in inflation was closely related to an upward trend in money supplies. Because of its relative size, the expansionary monetary and fiscal policies of the United States after about 1963 were particularly significant. Both the domestic "War on Poverty" and the external war in Vietnam were involved. The exchange rate regime of the time, in which all major countries fixed the exchange value of their currencies to the dollar, exacerbated the situation. As the U.S. balance of payments went into deficit, many central banks had to buy substantial amounts of dollars to avoid appreciation of their own currency against the dollar.

These substantial outflows of dollars had two major effects. The direct effect was that most countries found themselves with abnormally large balances of dollar reserves. The indirect effect of those reserve purchases was upward pressure on domestic money supplies because dollars taken into reserves are "bought" by issuing domestic currency. Pressure on the dollar was such that on August 15, 1971, the dollar was, in effect, devalued. This led subsequently to the decision to let the major exchange rates "float," so the international currency market determines them on a day-to-day basis. In many countries, floating initially reinforced an already inflationary situation. Central banks found they had substantial reserves at the same time as the need for reserves was reduced. Where reserve shortages had previously dictated cautious macroeconomic policies, it was now felt that expansion was acceptable. Internal policies added to the inflationary pressures coming from the United States. The clearest example is Britain, which introduced a highly inflationary monetary policy in September 1971 and a strongly expansionary fiscal policy in the budget of March 1972. This is why the inflationary experience of Britain was even worse throughout the subsequent period than that of the United States.

It is to be emphasized that this build-up of inflationary pressures came well in advance of the 1973 oil price rise. Indeed, all commodity prices rose at this time, *with oil among the last,* though others subsequently fell and oil did not. The fourfold oil price rise added to the subsequent inflationary experience. It is an exaggeration to suggest that it was the principal cause of worldwide inflation. The worldwide inflationary experience produced widespread acceptance that the proximate cause was excessive expansion of monetary demand over several years. A few extreme Keynesians (mainly in Britain) would disagree with this, emphasizing cost pressures from a trade union wage push and commodity prices, especially oil.

Most governments, however, came to accept the Monetarist story that inflation followed excess monetary expansion. The experience of Britain seemed clear-cut,[6] as indeed did that of Germany and Switzerland in the opposite way. The latter countries pursued policies of strict monetary control and had below-average inflation rates. Switzerland, in fact, achieved a steady *decline* in its inflation rate in the immediate post-oil crisis period. Germany maintained low inflation throughout the period. In Britain inflation reached 25 percent in 1975. Even in the United States, inflation came close to 20 percent for a short time in 1980. At the end of the decade, Britain and the United States elected governments committed to the eradication of inflation. The inflationary experience of the 1970s explains the general upsurge in conservatism among macro policymakers.

Agreement about the mistakes that stimulated inflation is not matched by agreement about the appropriate remedies. Old-style monetarists who believe in "long and variable" lags favor a very slow tightening of monetary control. Since they believe monetary changes hit output first and prices only with a longer lag, tightening monetary policy too fast would generate a serious depression first and only subsequently slow inflation. The New Classical school would favor an (announced) fast reduction in the rate of monetary growth. This should reduce expectations of inflation and bring down inflation itself rapidly. Keynesians favor incomes policy to control inflation while maintaining a high level of economic activity because unemployment

6. Monetarism arrived in high places in Britain in the mid-1970s, not with the Thatcher administration in 1979. Labor Chancellor Denis Healey (1974–1979) adopted a Monetarist line of policy in 1975–1976, announcing monetary targets and saying publicly that the long-run target of full employment would have to be deferred in the interest of the short-run need to control inflation.

has become unacceptably high as a result of tight monetary policy. Choosing among these strategies requires both a choice of view about how the economy works and a judgment of the relative costs of lost output and inflation. Whatever the choice, the British experience suggests that to expel inflation from the system is a slow process and that the costs in terms of lost output are high.

SUMMARY

The evolution of macroeconomics provides the intellectual basis to justify various policy stances. Classical economics provided no basis for policy activism. Keynesian economics gave the government budget a central role in stabilizing the economy. Monetarism and New Classical economics successively reduced the scope for such stabilization policies. During the 1950s and 1960s, there was a clear and dominant (Keynesian) consensus about the appropriate framework for viewing the economy. There is much less of a dominant framework now. Whatever happens in the near future, the expectations of effectiveness of macro policy created by early Keynesian euphoria will remain severely diminished. Policy activism there may be. But its goals will be limited by the fear of inflation and the now widespread belief that macroeconomic policy at best can do little to generate long-term real economic growth but at worst can do economic growth serious harm.

CHAPTER FOUR

International Political Economy

Nations have to live together as members of the international community. This is the third major constraint on domestic economic policy. Policies adopted in one country have effects in others. International obligations limit the range of policies available to a country. Chapter 3 mentioned how worldwide financial developments affected domestic macroeconomic policies, and we shall extend below our discussion of the international financial system. The fact that national economies trade with each other has more than financial implications for policy. We have assumed so far that the central government is solely responsible for the legal and institutional environment of its own economy and that all decisions of a "governmental" nature are made by the individual national governments. Since many economic transactions take place across national frontiers, we need to discuss the issue of state intervention in this broader context.

Trade policy reflects the ability of governments to dictate the terms on which goods will be permitted to cross their frontiers, in either direction. What goods may cross frontiers, in what volume and at what rate of tax? The standard economic analysis of commercial policy compares the effects of intervention with "free trade." The impact of policy cannot be understood without the theoretical analysis of gains to nations from trading rather than living in isolation. Nations can be shown to benefit from trade when they concentrate on producing more of the good for which they have a *comparative advantage*. This is demonstrated in the appendix to this chapter. (Any reader unfamiliar with this analysis should read that before proceeding further.) Politically, nations with different comparative advantages can exploit gains from trade. They will attempt to do so by bargaining or some other form of political cooperation. Without cooperation, it is quite possible that potential gains from trade will be lost.

The role of the state is ambiguous in the international setting. Specific firms or individuals do not care in principle whether their trade is conducted in the same country or in another. For the central government, however, internal and external relations are entirely different matters. The state sets laws governing behavior within its own boundaries but has no such powers outside them. Domestically, it is the central arbiter. Internationally, it represents the sectional interest of its own citizens. In the international sphere a government's decisions reflect or intend to reflect the interests of its own constituency rather than the interests of the whole world. Indeed, in many cases policies will be intended to benefit the domestic economy *at the expense* of some known or unknown economy overseas.

However, most external policymaking has to contend with the existence of conflicting domestic interests. The structure of international trade and finance reflects efforts by nations to secure gains from trade through cooperation. However, domestic adjustments are needed to capture such gains. These adjustments will benefit those in the industry with the comparative advantage (more will be produced) and hurt those in the industry in which the trading partner has the advantage. These sectoral costs and benefits have to be set against the presumed overall gain from the growth of trade. These cross-cutting advantages and disadvantages exemplify the conflicts between internal and external objectives. A currency devaluation raises the price of imports to consumers but makes export industries more competitive overseas. A tariff on imported cars makes them more expensive to consumers, but domestic car producers profit from the artificial protection of their home market. Internal and external goals conflict in more general ways. For example, a government may have a policy of stimulating competition in its domestic economy. It also wants to protect the domestic economy from foreign competition. This protection may increase the monopoly power of domestic producers who can shelter behind tariff walls.

Policy outcomes in these cases involve states' pursuit of national advantage, the relative priorities attaching to goals of commercial and financial as opposed to other aspects of foreign policy, adjudication of domestic group conflict, and the balance of power in the international system. International power politics is important in setting up and policing "the rules of the game." For example, the United States and Britain between them established the Bretton Woods system (see below), and the United States had a dominant role in subsequent monetary developments. Economic power varies considerably between nations (and sectors of nations). It is more complicated than simply having the most power lying with the richest country. Resource endowments, import dependence, market structure, availability of substitutes, and many other characteristics will vary from product to product. A big country like the United States, which is able to exert leverage in many of its markets, may nonetheless be vulnerable to, say, an oil price cartel.

Our selective discussion of international institutions proceeds by economic analysis of the underlying issues. The first part covers commercial policies, that is, governments' attempts to influence trade. Even as narrow an area as tariff policy spans a broad range from the "highest" politics of international negotiation to the "lowest" politics of seeking favorable treatment from a domestic tariff commission. In international monetary affairs, the design of the "system" is of more direct concern. The existence of these institutions reveals how the international economic system diverges from a free market without having a specific sovereign government. Their economic effects show how the international economic system constrains domestic policy. Politically, these institutions are important attempts to make rational decisions at supranational levels, even though the ultimate coercive power lies at the national level. Their value as attempts to cooperate in controlling what would otherwise be a structureless external environment may exceed their strict "economic" benefit to participants.

INTERNATIONAL TRADE

We include four sorts of institutional trade arrangements in the international economy. Each of them has different purposes and effects and therefore creates different problems for domestic authorities. The first is commercial policy, which includes mostly tariff questions, and is the most familiar area of international economic policy. Our comments are restricted to the possibility of improving terms of trade and how they depend on cooperation among nations. Katzenstein (1978) gives good examples of the politics of commercial policy in several countries. The other arrangements we consider are customs unions, cartels, and commodity stabilization schemes.

COMMERCIAL POLICY

Many reasons have been used to justify the imposition of tariffs. These justifications are usually *temporary*. They include protecting a newly established industry until it becomes competitive, avoiding harm to domestic industries from "dumping" foreign products below cost, and protecting employment during structural adjustment (Sodersten, 1980; Caves and Jones, 1973). Tariffs imposed for temporary reasons have often turned out rather permanent. However, a convincing long-term case for tariffs can rest only on "terms of trade" arguments.

Terms of trade is a common name for the relative price of imports and exports. Policies which improve a country's terms of trade make it better off because the value of the things it produces rises relative to the value of the things it buys. However, the gains will not necessarily be shared equally. Those members of the economy who become worse off could in principle be compensated, but there is no guarantee that they will. A country's ability to influence its terms of trade depends largely on its structural position in the world economy. For example, a small country producing a homogeneous primary commodity[1] cannot influence the world market price of its output. It also probably cannot influence the price of its imports. A country which is large in some market can influence market prices by changing its own supply or demand. This is a common reason for imposing tariffs. Free trade may lead to the most efficient worldwide allocation of resources. However, an individual country that can influence its terms of trade can do better for itself than the global free trade outcome. It does so by acting like a monopolist.

Consider a country which exports one product and imports another. Suppose it is "big" in both the market for its imports and its exports. Now, if its government wishes to improve the country's terms of trade, it can do so *either* by restricting the supply of exports onto the world market *or* by restricting the flow of imports into the domestic market. Export restriction is a reduction in supply which raises the world market price of the good. It may also reduce the domestic price since some goods that would have been sold overseas will now be offered on the domestic market. Restrictions allow a wedge to be introduced between the domestic and foreign price. More commonly, governments restrict imports by introducing a tariff or quota. This reduces demand for the imported good, lowering its world market price, even though the *domestic* market price including the tariff may rise.

It is thus possible for trade restrictions to improve the position of a country relative to free trade. Its improvement is at the expense of its trading partners. However, if one country imposes a tariff on imports from another, the other will now gain by retaliating with its own tariff. Such retaliation and counterretaliation is an aspect of what is known as a *trade war*. The problem is that once a set of tariffs has been put in place, it is not in the interest of any country to reduce its tariffs *unilaterally*. This is true even though a global return to free trade would probably benefit all. Only *cooperation* in negotiated mutual

1. These include iron ore, rubber, or wheat. Since different producers produce a more or less identical output, a small supplier has to take the market price as given. By contrast, a supplier of differentiated manufactures will have more discretion over the price of his product since there is nothing else quite like it.

tariff reductions can improve the situation. Postwar attempts to nego-tiate mutual tariff reductions at a global level have been conducted since 1947 in the framework of the General Agreement on Tariffs and Trade (GATT).[2] GATT is today the only generally accepted inter-national agency setting out rules for the conduct of trade and providing a forum for tariff negotiations. The GATT has been associated with two major rounds of tariff reduction negotiations, the Kennedy round of the 1960s and the Tokyo round of the 1970s.

CUSTOMS UNIONS

Global negotiations for tariff reductions are thus extremely com-plex and time-consuming. They involve many diverse countries. As a result, many countries favoring freer trade have formed subgroups to promote free trade among themselves. The biggest of these is the European Economic Community (EEC), set up in 1957 when the governments of France, West Germany, Italy, the Netherlands, Bel-gium, and Luxembourg signed the Treaty of Rome. Britain, Denmark, and Ireland joined the EEC in the mid-1970s. Greece joined in 1981, and Spain and Portugal are negotiating for membership. The EEC has grown quickly as an economic unit. The combined gross domestic product (GDP) of its original six members was about one-third that of the United States in 1957. By the mid-1970s, it was two-thirds of the U.S. GDP. The extra members who have joined in the 1970s make the combined product of the EEC nearly as large as that of the United States.

The EEC is meant to be an area of free mobility of goods, labor, and other factors of production while at the same time providing greater coordination of monetary and fiscal policies. Such a customs union is halfway between free trade and each nation having tariffs. Members of the union remove tariffs vis-à-vis other members and adopt the same

2. Shortly after the war it was proposed to set up an agency of the United Nations, to be known as the International Trade Organization (ITO), which would be responsible for issues such as tariffs. ITO never came into being because it was rejected by the U.S. Congress. The members of the preliminary committee set up to draft the ITO charter held a tariff negotiating conference in 1947 in Geneva and agreed on a number of tariff reductions and on a multilateral trade treaty, the GATT.

external tariff against nonmembers. Membership of a customs union may be better or worse than either free trade or a system of national tariffs. Lower internal tariffs lead to some gains from "trade creation," but there is a loss from "trade diversion." Some trade previously conducted with third parties is now diverted to within the union.[3] These effects offset each other, and it is not possible to say in general which is larger.

A particularly important EEC institution is its Common Agricultural Policy (CAP). There is universal acceptance of the need for some kind of government support policy for agriculture because of the strategic nature of the industry and the likelihood of severe production cycles. Agricultural policies have usually been intended to stabilize the incomes of farmers. Two different methods have been used to achieve this goal. One relies on fixing the market price, as in the CAP. The other guarantees a price to farmers but sells output at whatever price the market will bear, as in the old British price support system. U.S. agriculture policies have involved aspects of both systems. Recent dairy industry support is of the CAP type. The methods have different effects.

Figure 4.1 represents demand and supply of some homogeneous agricultural output. DD is the quantity demanded in the domestic economy, and SS is the quantity supplied by domestic producers at each price. OW is the world market price at which the cheapest imports can be obtained. Suppose that in a price support policy the government wishes to raise the price received by domestic farmers but not the market price. It can do this by guaranteeing a price, say, OS. The output (ST) produced is then sold at the world market price OW. A net subsidy must be paid to farmers of amount WSTU. Production quotas are commonly used to limit the liability for subsidies. However, the subsidy is financed by general taxes. The market price of food remains as low as possible, given world market conditions.

A price-fixing system like the CAP raises *the market price* for domestic producers and consumers above the world price. This requires

3. Trade creation involves gains from trade. Trade diversion means an efficiency loss to the extent that the third party was a more efficient producer, but the joint external tariff means that more trade will now be conducted within the union.

exclusion of lower-priced imports. Suppose the price is fixed at OC in Figure 4.1. (This is higher than the market price would have been even without imports.) Production will be CP, but demand will only be CA. The authorities must buy up the excess AP. If they did not buy it, excess supply on the market would cause the price to fall. Butter mountains, beef mountains, and wine lakes are now common in Europe, and cheese mountains exist in the United States. They are the excess of production over demand that results from this price support system. Moreover, the subsidy to farmers is no longer financed by general taxes but is paid *by the consumer* in higher food prices. Annual discussions of price levels are politicized by the conflict of interest between consumers and producers.

CARTELS

Industrial nations with differentiated and diversified products to sell have the opportunity to improve their terms of trade through

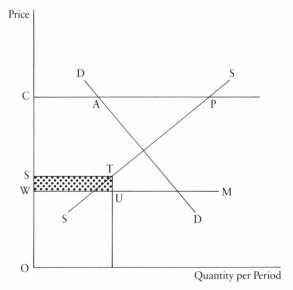

FIGURE 4.1. Agricultural Support Policies

tariffs and possibly through customs unions. A small exporter of homogeneous primary commodities has fewer options. There is little to be gained from a customs union with similar countries and little likelihood of influencing the world price of its exports by acting alone. A substantial debate exists around this issue of "unequal exchange" (Emmanuel, 1972). The only serious possibility for a small primary producer to influence its export prices is to coordinate with enough other exporters of its product so that *jointly* they may influence the market price. Such cooperative price fixing arrangements are generally known as *cartels*.

The most famous cartel of modern times is the Organization of Petroleum Exporting Countries (OPEC), which raised the price of oil over 400 percent in 1973–1974 and again over 100 percent in 1979. OPEC had existed for some years before to no avail. Another successful cartel was the International Bauxite Association. Other active groups include Cafe Mondial, the Intergovernmental Council of Copper-Exporting Countries, the Association of Natural Rubber Producing Countries, the Union of Banana Exporting Countries, and the Association of Iron Ore Exporting Countries. A problem of cartels is that it is usually difficult to preserve accord over a long period. Once the group has succeeded in raising its market price, there is always an incentive for an individual producer to increase revenue by undercutting the others. Behrman (1978) quotes a study by Eckbo which found that among fifty-one recent commodity cartels, the average duration of formal agreements was 5.4 years and the median was 2.5 years. A large number of such agreements are clearly not very successful.

GLOBAL COMMODITY SCHEMES

On their own, producer countries face difficulties in trying to control the markets for their goods. There has consequently been discussion throughout the postwar period about a possible commodity stabilization scheme supported by both producer and consumer countries. Most of these discussions have taken place in the context of the United Nations Conference on Trade and Development (UNCTAD).

The call for a "New International Economic Order" arose in a meeting of the General Assembly of the United Nations in the spring of 1974. A concrete proposal emerged from the group of seventy-seven (which had grown to 112 by then) less developed nations in the so-called Manila Declaration of February 1976. At the center of the UNCTAD debate was the proposal for an integrated commodity program financed by a common fund. The scheme had two explicit objectives. The first was to improve the terms of trade of developing countries to ensure adequate growth of the purchasing power of their earnings from commodity exports. The second was to reduce fluctuations of prices and thereby reduce the instability of incomes in developing countries, as well as reducing uncertainties for consumers.[4]

The UNCTAD IV conference adopted a resolution in favor of an "Integrated Program for Commodities." However, by 1981 nothing of substance had been instituted. The world summit meeting at Cancun made no measurable progress. In 1979 the Brandt report strongly endorsed the UNCTAD scheme. UNCTAD V, which took place in 1980, recognized de facto that stabilization through market intervention was a forlorn hope. Emphasis shifted to helping producers improve their "supply side" by increased productivity and greater diversity of product. The commodity stabilization scheme looks all but dead for two political reasons. One is that the United States, Britain, Germany, and Japan (among others) have governments that believe that market forces should be left alone. The other is that the technical difficulties in setting up something like the EEC Common Agricultural

4. Initially the scheme concentrated on seventeen commodities, which accounted for about three-quarters of the nonpetroleum commodity trade of the developing nations. Ten of these (cocoa, coffee, copper, sugar, cotton, jute, rubber, sisal, tea, and tin) were defined as "core" commodities (the others being bananas, bauxite, beef and veal, iron ore, rice, wheat, and wool). A stabilization authority was to be established with finances of $6 billion. This "common fund" was to be funded by subscriptions from importers and exporters alike (except for poor nations):

This fund would serve a catalytic role in stimulating new commodity stockpile arrangements by ensuring adequate finances independent of the particular financial difficulties of the individual countries participating in a specific commodity agreement. The common fund would also pool and reduce risks and have more bargaining power in international capital markets than could a set of individual funds for the same commodities. It also would require smaller financing than the aggregate of a set of individual funds because of differences in the phasing of cycles across commodity markets. (Behrman, 1978, p. 23)

Policy on a global scale are formidable, and the likely benefits of any feasible scheme are small.

A further problem is itself sufficient to raise serious doubts about the value of such schemes. The triple goals of price stabilization, income stabilization, and income raising cannot be adequately met by *any* single scheme. The real aim of raising incomes may be frustrated by any scheme which stabilizes prices. Income stabilization and price stabilization policies may have opposite effects. Suppose an agricultural producer has some years of abundant harvests and some years of lean harvests because of factors like the weather, which also affect other producers. In lean years supplies are scarce and the market price rises. In abundant years it falls. In lean years, although he produces less, he gets a higher price. In abundant years he gets a lower price. As a result his *income* is more stable than the volume of his output (indeed, income may even be higher in lean years than in abundant years). Under a policy to stabilize prices by holding them down in lean years and up in abundant years, his income would fluctuate with his output. It would be low in bad years and high in good years.

INTERNATIONAL FINANCE

The international monetary system allows us to trade with people in countries which have a different currency. The "trade" it allows means not just buying and selling goods and services but also borrowing and lending, so a full range of economic activities spills over national frontiers. A single currency is the legal money in each nation, like the dollar in the United States and the deutsche mark in Germany. Once we trade outside our own "currency area," the settlement medium is open for negotiation. If the seller of a product is paid in his local currency (not generally true for commodity exports), the buyer of the good has to buy that currency before he can pay for it. Foreign exchange markets must thus exist to facilitate goods trade, at a minimum. The core of the international monetary system is the markets within which currencies are exchanged and exchange rates determined.

Not every nation-state need have its own separate money. In the pure gold standard system, which existed for a short time in the late nineteenth century, each local money was gold or convertible into it. International trade payments caused no problem because the ultimate acceptable currency, gold, was the same everywhere. Trade with someone in the same country was the same as trade with someone abroad—both could be paid with gold. This is not the monetary system we have today.

THE BRETTON WOODS SYSTEM: THE "LIQUIDITY PROBLEM"

International financial discussions in the 1950s and 1960s were dominated by so-called "international liquidity," the total stock of gold and foreign exchange reserves held by central banks. Central banks needed reserves of foreign currency to stabilize exchange rates. This became an "official sector" problem in the system of the early postwar period. Earlier, international debts were settled by shipments of bullion or with major "colonial" currencies like sterling. There was no concern about the stock of international liquidity as such. The concern with international liquidity arose from the interwar episodes of hyperinflation in Central Europe and the Great Depression of 1929–1933. Particularly in the 1930s, many countries pursued substantial trade restrictions, and there were several competitive devaluations. To some extent these problems were seen as monetary, and there was a desire to set up institutions to make their recurrence less likely.

It was generally believed that international cooperation could produce a more stable environment than trade warfare. The end of the war presented an opportunity to design a new international monetary system. J. M. Keynes of Britain and H. D. White of the United States played a key role. Their plans had similar aims, though they were different in substance. Both saw monetary arrangements and trade as being closely interdependent. (See International Monetary Fund, 1969, p. 41.) A conference in July 1944 at the Mount Washington Hotel, Bretton Woods, New Hampshire, produced proposals which led to the establishment of the International Monetary Fund (IMF) and what came to be known as the Bretton Woods system. The central provision

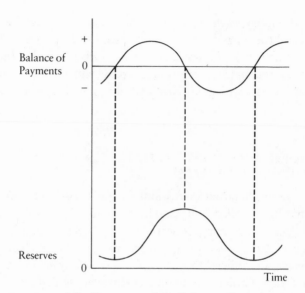

FIGURE 4.2. Reserves and the Balance of Payments

of this system was the commitment by all member countries except the United States to "peg" or fix their currencies' exchange rates to the value of the dollar. *Pegging* meant that each central bank was committed to buy its own currency with foreign currency (dollars) at a fixed price not more than 1 percent from the quoted "par" value. For its part, the United States agreed to maintain the value of the dollar in terms of gold. Keynes foresaw that these commitments required the availability of adequate liquidity.

Liquidity was important because the mechanism of pegging exchange rates required central banks to hold reserves of "key" currencies (especially dollars) for intervening in their own foreign exchange markets whenever their exchange rates deviated too much from announced "par values." Reserves were in effect a buffer stock[5] enabling stable exchange rates to be maintained across a trade cycle. The typical expected pattern is shown in Figure 4.2. During a period of

5. This is analogous to the stock of any commodity held by an intervention authority which is built up in times of surplus and run down at times of deficiency. The price is stabilized as a result.

surplus the central bank buys dollars with domestic currency to stop the domestic exchange rate from rising. During the following period of deficit, reserves are run down by buying domestic currency with dollars. The *international liquidity problem* is to ensure that at any time central banks as a group have sufficient reserves to survive normal cycles in the balance of payments without trade restrictions or devaluations. If the size of balance of payments surpluses and deficits increased with world trade, growing world trade would require growing balances of reserves for any given level of security.[6]

In practice, growing dollar balances provided most postwar growth in reserves. Triffin pointed out the dangers of this in 1960 in his book *Gold and the Dollar Crisis:*

The gold exchange standard *may,* but *does* not *necessarily,* help in relieving a shortage of world monetary reserves. It does so only to the extent that the key currency countries are willing to let their net reserve position decline through increases in their short-term monetary liabilities unmatched by corresponding increases in their own gross reserves. If they allow this to happen, however, and to continue indefinitely they tend to bring about a collapse of the system itself through the gradual weakening of foreigners' confidence in the key currencies. (p. 67)

As the volume of dollars held abroad rose relative to U.S. gold reserves, belief in the convertibility of dollars into gold at the required price would weaken. As a result of this diagnosis a new reserve asset, the Special Drawing Right (SDR), was introduced. It was intended to become the principal reserve asset of the international monetary system and thus to provide for growth in international reserves without additional dollar balances. The initial allocation of SDR 9 billion took place in 1970–1972 with a further allocation of SDR 12 billion in 1979–1981. SDRs were allocated to IMF members in relation to quotas, so the richer countries got most.[7] However, the initial issue of SDRs did not save the Bretton Woods system. The general commitment to fixed exchange rates was abandoned.

---

6. Whether this relationship between world trade and reserves should be linear (that is, reserves grew in strict proportion to trade) or not has been a matter of some dispute, but need not detain us.

7. For a critical assessment of the SDR, see Chrystal (1978).

The severity of the fixed exchange rate constraint on all countries but the United States can only be fully appreciated with the benefit of hindsight. Under Bretton Woods, only the United States could have a discretionary domestic monetary policy. For example, any attempt by Britain to increase the supply of pounds faster than the demand for pounds would eventually cause the British authorities to repurchase the extra pounds with dollars or other reserves. If they did not, the excess would cause the pound's exchange rate to fall. In general, any country other than the United States that embarked on an expansionary policy rapidly ran into balance of payments problems, indicated by reserve losses. It therefore had to reverse those policies. The position of the United States was different. Since all countries pegged their currency values to the dollar, it was unnecessary for the United States to intervene in foreign exchange markets. The expansionary policies of the Kennedy and Johnson administrations led directly to the collapse of the entire system.[8] Its maintenance, as it turned out, had depended upon the United States following restrictive or conservative economic policies.

> But the United States was simply not prepared to contemplate adjustment measures beyond the occasional tightening up of restrictions on capital markets. The reluctance to subordinate demand management policy to external needs was particularly well-founded in the case of a country with an economy as closed as that of the United States. (J. Williamson, 1977, p. 38)

The events of 1970–1973 completely changed the world monetary environment. There was both a substantial increase in the stock of dollars held by central banks and a switch to floating exchange rates by the major industrial countries. (Domestic consequences of these changes were discussed at the end of Chapter 3.) These changes altered the international liquidity problem. It was initially felt that there was

8. The specification of a full set of circumstances surrounding the collapse of Bretton Woods (whose immediate cause was the Nixon administration's decision to suspend convertibility of the dollar into gold) must include the change in the relative economic power of the United States and other major countries, the lack of familiarity with alternative exchange rate regimes, as well as aspects of domestic interests and priorities; see Bergsten, 1975; Odell, 1982.

an excess of liquidity rather than a shortage. The 1973 oil price rise confused matters by making an issue of the distribution as well as level of world reserves. As a result, the dominant topic of discussion in the mid-1970s was the "recycling" of OPEC surpluses. Most of this recycling was achieved through the money markets. By 1978 the OPEC surplus had all but disappeared. The inflation of the previous decade was felt to require a general increase in IMF quotas plus a new allocation of SDRs. Another major rise in the price of oil in 1979–1980 appeared to cause particular adjustment problems for the developing world.

The existence of floating exchange rates is an important element in understanding countries' comparative inflationary experience since 1973. Inflation *is* the change in the value of a currency when measured by its purchasing power over a typical basket of goods. In the 1950s and 1960s when the values of all major currencies were fixed to the dollar, it was impossible for inflation in any country to deviate significantly from the U.S. inflation rate. This is because a traded good will tend to have the same price in all countries when converted by the exchange rate, after adjustment for tariffs, local taxes, or transportation costs. Suppose a pound is worth a dollar. A good which costs $10 in the United States should also cost £10 in Britain. If it doesn't, a profit can be made by buying the good in the cheaper market and selling it in the dearer market, which will tend to equalize prices in both markets. An increase in the dollar price should cause the sterling price to rise. This is how other countries imported American inflation under fixed exchange rates. Figure 3.1 in Chapter 3 indicates clearly how small the differences in inflation rates among countries were. Any deviations mainly reflect the construction of price index numbers and the effects of nontraded goods on the price index.

Once a country's currency floats, its inflation rate is no longer tied to U.S. inflation. Now a change in dollar prices can be offset by a change in the exchange value of the other country's currency as well as by changes in its price level. In general, a country with higher inflation than the United States will find its currency depreciating against the dollar. The price index and the exchange rate are, after all, alternative measures of the same thing—the value of a money. It is a mistake to conclude that "floating causes inflation." A more reasonable statement would be that floating is more permissive of inflationary policies.

EUROCURRENCIES: VICTORY FOR THE MARKET?

Because we are concerned with the international context of government policy, we have talked almost entirely about the "official" sector of the international monetary system. The official sector is not exclusively "where the action is." Since the early 1960s, the Eurocurrency markets have grown to replace the official sector as the core of the international monetary system.

Eurocurrencies are bank deposits in a currency anywhere in the world except its home country. The Eurodollar market, for example, is anywhere but the United States.[9] The largest Eurodollar center is London, but other activity goes on in Singapore, the Cayman Islands, Hong Kong, Paris, Zurich, and elsewhere. These markets for deposits and loans are not small. Dollar deposits in London have for several years been considerably greater than the entire British sterling money supply. Eurocurrency markets are substantially "offshore." This means that they are not regulated by any government. One of the reasons that London is so important is that while banking in sterling is strictly regulated by British authorities, they have made no attempt to regulate business done in other currencies. Euromarkets are now so large that governments can hardly influence interest rates and exchange rates determined in these markets short of massive intervention. This is one main reason that major exchange rates float.

The size of these markets has freed governments to borrow foreign currency from them as well as from the IMF. In fact, Eurocurrency markets are a greater source of finance than the IMF to "official" borrowers. In the "crisis" following the 1973 oil price rise, these market channels coped fairly easily with the "recycling" problem. The Eurobanks effectively borrowed from surplus (OPEC) countries and lent to the deficit countries. The international financial system could

9. In 1981 a change in U.S. regulations permitted the establishment in New York of an "offshore" market in nonresident deposits.

not have coped without this. However, by now many countries (especially poorer ones) have accumulated substantial debts. Their interest payments represent a drain on national resources. Some argue that there is a serious danger that a major default could trigger off a worldwide financial collapse. Would governments be prepared to bail out the banks in that event? To what extent should they require the eurobanks to accept some regulations in return? These are important issues, but at present the eurocurrency system remains almost entirely unregulated.

FOREIGN EXCHANGE MARKETS IN LESS DEVELOPED COUNTRIES

The less developed countries have a special economic policy problem, dictated by their position in the world economy. Very few of these countries allow their exchange rates to float. Indeed, their trade and financial policy position is different from that of an industrial country. The less developed countries are not the only ones whose currencies do not float, as Table 4.1 indicates. At the latest count there were ninety-three countries pegging their currencies to either other individual currencies or currency baskets. Many of those not formally fixed have exchange rates pegged on some basis, perhaps to an unknown "basket" (weighted average) of currencies. The exchange rates of the currencies of some major industrial countries are linked in the European Monetary System (EMS), which specifies a maximum range of deviation between the member currencies. All other floats are at best "dirty," with official intervention from time to time.

Nevertheless, there is a clear difference between the exchange markets of industrial countries and developing countries. Developing nations have not "chosen" to spurn floating. They have structural considerations which effectively remove floating as an option available to their authorities. The currencies of most developing countries are not fully convertible, not regularly traded in an open market. McKinnon (1979) suggests a reason.

Governments in less developed countries often lack the internal political power and the accompanying fiscal and administrative capability to allocate domestic resources directly by centralized fiat in the manner of the communist centrally

TABLE 4.1   EXCHANGE RATE ARRANGEMENTS OF IMF
COUNTRIES

| | No. of Countries | |
Exchange Rate Pegged to	*June 30, 1975*	*Sept. 30, 1982*
U.S. dollar	54	37
French franc	13	13
Pound sterling	10	1
Spanish peseta	1	1
South African rand	3	2
SDR	5	16
Other basket	14	23
Jointly floating (Snake/EMS):	7	8
Floating or other intervention formula	18	41
Total	125	142

Sources: International Monetary Fund, *Annual Report* (Washington, D.C., 1975);
International Monetary Fund, *Survey* (Washington, D.C., October 25, 1982).

planned economies. Nevertheless, these same governments are usually not
enamored with the idea of decentralizing economic decision making through
the unrestricted use of equilibrium prices and free markets. Rather, the
government has a domestic plan and, perhaps, planning agency; its political
office is seen as a mandate to control or influence as much economic activity
as possible. However, the strongest instrument for internal economic control
that can be freely manipulated by LDC governments is often the market for
foreign exchange—where the clearing of international payments can be fairly
easily brought under a single authority. Since imports and exports usually pass
through centralized ports and border-crossing stations, they are more easily
monitored and taxed by a weak governmental authority than is commerce in
the domestic hinterland. (p. 41)

Control over trade necessarily involves control over domestic access to
foreign exchange.

Clearly, if all domestic firms and individuals were free to spend the domestic
currency for foreign goods—using commercial banks as unrestrained financial
intermediaries—the government's control would be undermined. Therefore,
the clearing of foreign payments usually devolves on the *central bank* in

LDC's. . . . Hence commercial banks are not free to create a unified market for foreign exchange, either spot or forward, as they might do with a floating convertible currency or one floating within given exchange margins.

Willy-nilly the central bank is cast in the role of announcing exchange rates for the various categories of transactions . . . and then providing the necessary foreign exchange to those traders satisfying the rules and regulations. (p. 42)

Thus, in the cases which involve severe foreign exchange controls, there cannot be a fully operative foreign exchange market. A more general problem is that the exchange rates of the industrial countries have fluctuated considerably since the advent of floating, despite their diversified trade composition and sophisticated financial systems. The foreign exchange markets of developing countries would be extremely thin. It is thus hard to believe that they could be anything but highly unstable if they attempted a free float. Israel's currency, long pegged to sterling and later to a basket, has exhibited major instability since floating. In this sense most developing countries may not be "optimal currency areas." In practice, therefore, their central banks have little choice but to announce a price at which they will buy and sell foreign exchange to traders, thereby "pegging" the exchange rate. Given pegging, whether financial restrictions sustain trade controls or trade controls are necessary to maintain exchange rates is unclear. If central banks are obliged to peg exchange rates, restrictions on foreign exchange holding, capital flows, and trade are necessary weapons for those endowed with inadequate reserves.

The role of international financial institutions, notably the IMF, has changed considerably. The IMF was created to help industrial countries maintain fixed exchange rates. These countries no longer need this help either because they are floating or because they have their own "local" arrangements like the EMS. Less developed countries now desperately need the kind of help the IMF was set up to give. They have become its main customers. However, at least a voting majority of the industrial nations are opposed to any major new expansion of IMF credit like an allocation of SDRs. They believe that such an expansion would further fuel inflation. They are even more strongly opposed to biasing future allocations of SDRs in favor of developing nations. This fundamental difference of attitude cannot be reconciled in existing institutions without an outbreak of magnanimity (wisdom?) among the leaders of certain major nations. What is unlikely to change is that an institution now most needed by one group of countries is controlled by another group.

SUMMARY

Like analysis of markets in general, "free trade" and "perfect competition" provide yardsticks of desirable outcomes in the economic analysis of commercial policy. Welfare economics presumes that governments try to correct "market failures." In a trade framework, governments are a major source of distortions. A country uses its monopoly power to improve its terms of trade. Tariffs benefit the initiating country and harm others. Each government is constrained by the commercial policies of others. The financial system also constrains the options available to policymakers. It is especially important to understand the role of the Bretton Woods system and its breakdown in the postwar period.

The international context affords nations substantially different scope for discretionary policy actions. A country like the United States has considerable room to maneuver. It has a dominant voice in international organizations and international treaties. It is "large" in the markets for the things it buys and sells, and it can use this "power" to influence market outcomes in desired directions. A typical small developing country has no such options. It has little effect on the structure of institutions and none on the markets for the things it buys and sells, or even in which it borrows. In between these two extremes is a range of countries which influence the international economy to a greater or lesser degree. The governments of these countries have a political problem of adapting to changing constraints imposed by their country's position in the international economic structure.

APPENDIX: COMPARATIVE ADVANTAGE AND GAINS FROM TRADE

Suppose two countries can both produce only two products, say, bread and shirts. Each country has a given technology and fixed resources. Thus, there is a maximum of bread and shirts that can be produced. Suppose country 1 concentrates all its resources on shirt production. Then it can produce a maximum OB units of shirts (see Figure 4.3) but no bread. If it put all its resources into bread production, it could produce a maximum of OA units of bread but no shirts. It could spread its resources between the two industries and produce some combination. Combinations of possible outputs may be characterized as the line AB for country 1 and XY for country 2. There is no strong reason that these "production possibility frontiers" should be straight lines. Their shape depends on technology. It is more likely that each will be concave toward the origin, but this does not affect anything essential in the argument.

In the absence of trade, the complete set of consumption possibilities for country 1 is the triangle OAB. For country 2 it is the triangle OXY. Assuming nonsatiation of wants (people would like more if they could get it) and full employment of resources, the economies will actually produce and consume at some combination given by a point on the frontiers AB and XY. Here the internal price ratios of these two goods will be given by the slopes of these frontiers. It should be clear that bread is more expensive in country 1 than it is in country 2 (relative to shirts). This is because with its resources country 2 can produce more bread relative to shirts than can country 1. In isolation neither country can consume above and to the right of its existing production possibility frontier. However, by rearranging production

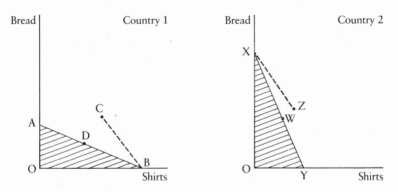

FIGURE 4.3. Gains from Trade

and *trading*, it is possible for *both* countries to become better off in the sense that both can now consume more of *both* goods.

Suppose that prior to trade country 1 produces and consumes at point D (any other point on AB would suffice). Suppose country 2 produces and consumes at point W on XY. The possibility created by trade opening up between the two countries is that domestic *production* patterns may differ from domestic *consumption* patterns. An economy will produce more of its exported goods and less of its imported goods than it consumes. Now let us suppose that each country specializes in the production of the good it produces relatively cheaply. Country 1 produces only shirts (OB of them), and country 2 produces only bread (OX of it). The countries then trade with each other so that country 2 exports bread in exchange for the exports of shirts from country 1.

At *any* international trade price ratio *between* the two different pretrade price ratios (that is, between the slopes of the lines AB and XY), both countries will be able to move to points such as C and Z at which each is consuming more. The net gain to all has come about by each country specializing in the production of the product in which it has a *comparative advantage*. This specialization must represent only a shift away from the pretrade production position. This idea involves concentrating on what you do relatively well and trading with someone who is relatively good at producing something else.

PART THREE

Government, the Electorate, and Economic Policy

Decisions about economic policy are made in the political arena by incumbent elected politicians. An informed analysis of economic policy decisions requires an understanding of both how the economy is believed to work and the institutional context in which the decisions are made. Three aspects of this framework are discussed in the next three chapters. Their order is not of great significance since they are mutually interdependent. For example, the importance of Chapter 6 arises partly from the failure of models in Chapter 5. These models depend critically on other results discussed in Chapter 7. Chapter 5 critically analyzes theories in which the electoral ambitions of incumbent parties or politicians determine their economic policies. Chapter 6 outlines the policy problem in an optimizing framework, with some warnings about misuse of the framework. Finally, the importance of the state of the economy for the popularity of governments and the "economic" or choice theoretic analysis of voting behavior are the subject of Chapter 7. Each of these chapters corresponds to one of the views of the state of Chapter 1: Chapter 5 to the exploitative state, Chapter 6 to the productive state, and Chapter 7 to the protective state.

CHAPTER FIVE

Political Business Cycles

Economic phenomena are commonly cyclical. Since economic fluctuations may cause hardship and uncertainty, much research has been devoted to their origins. Some academics have, naturally enough, wondered if economic cycles could be tied to political cycles. Early investigations relied on a mixture of observation and commentary and, unsurprisingly, reached no strong conclusions. More recent efforts have tried to derive a politically induced business cycle from theories that assume governments make economic policy with an eye on economic conditions at election time. This implies that certain economic indicators will fluctuate over time so that peaks (or troughs) in the series are synchronized with elections. They are consequently known as *political business cycle* models. They purport to show that at any given time the level of aggregate demand or general economic activity depends at least in part on how long there is until the next election. It is curious that the literature on political business cycles is widely invoked, even though there is little evidence for the existence of such cycles.

If political business cycles exist, economists need to know about them to understand the economy fully. Furthermore, political business cycle models usually imply that economic outcomes are *suboptimal*, that is, the public is worse off than if there were no manipulation of the economy by the government in pursuit of reelection. The most extreme version of the political business cycle model is the one where electoral manipulation of the economy creates an "inflationary bias" in democratic systems.

Political business cycle theories also have a number of political implications. First, economic conditions affect election outcomes. Otherwise, governments would not gain electorally from manipulating the economy. These models frequently assume that a high level of economic activity, whether measured by low unemployment or fast real growth, increases the popularity of governments. Second, many assume that the electorate is *myopic,* or short-sighted, in evaluating economic conditions. An extreme version is that the electorate is concerned only with economic conditions at the time of elections. A more common assumption is that the electorate has no expectations about the future. The electorate does not fully understand the economy.[1] Finally, politicians are taken to be *self-seeking manipulators* who mortgage the future for current electoral advantage. They show no concern for the welfare of the citizenry or their own long-term reputations. Whether evidence supports these theories is, of course, another question entirely.

COMMON CORE OF THE MODELS

All political business cycle models have a common core, though they can be subclassified. There are three common arguments:

1. Governments aim to win elections. In order to win elections, they attempt to maximize votes.

2. Among economic outcomes, electors have preferences that are reflected in their voting behavior.

3. Governments can manipulate the economy to improve their chances of reelection.

These statements are controversial. Take the first. It would be surprising if politicians had no concern for winning elections, but this

1. Note the contrast between this view, characteristic of political business cycle models, and the views of rational expectations theorists discussed in Chapter 3.

need not be their only or dominant motivation. Moreover, elected politicians are not the only actors who affect policy outcomes. The power of bureaucracies and the influence of party systems and the media constrain politicians. The assumption that citizens vote their economic policy preferences is also controversial (see Chapter 7). Finally, the degree of control over the economy is questionable, given uncertainties of timing and effects of interventions. These need not deter politicians from attempting an election-oriented economic policy, though they may impede its successful execution.

Table 5.1 represents variations in political business cycle models as dichotomies. How governments form policy is one difference. On the one hand (II, IV), *responsive* governments adopt the policy preferences of their supporters. *Strategic* governments (I, III) calculate policy to provide the greatest number of potential votes. This calculation may disregard the preferences of their own supporters. Strategic governments may appear responsive by attempting to shape popular preferences to the government's own policy preferences.

The second distinction relates to popular preferences. Some models (I, II) assume that popular preferences for economic outcomes are *fixed* for each individual elector, possibly by socioeconomic class. That is, electors' preferences do not evolve, and so available majorities do not shift. Other models (III, IV) assume the electorate has *varying* preferences. They vary because people change their minds about policy, whether or not politicians' persuasion causes the change. The formal consequence of varying popular preferences is some uncertainty about the "demand" for economic outcomes. The underlying assumptions

TABLE 5.1   MODELS OF POLITICAL BUSINESS CYCLES

Electorate Preferences	Government Capability	
	Strategic	*Responsive*
Fixed	I	II
Varying	III	IV

have major empirical consequences. We take the quadrants one at a time. In each case we review first the theory, then evaluate the evidence.

MODELS OF THE POLITICAL BUSINESS CYCLE

QUADRANT I: STRATEGIC GOVERNMENTS, FIXED PREFERENCES

Theory

Quadrant I contains models that assume strategic governments and fixed electoral preferences. The best known of these models is after Nordhaus (1975). It is built around a Phillips curve analysis and deals with unemployment and inflation but is in fact quite general. It applies to any intervention whose effects come only with a lag. Such policies can be exploited by a government, provided it understands the economy and the electorate does not. Strategic governments exploit an asymmetric distribution of information resulting from institutionally defined incentives. Decisions are taken for short-run gains, and long-run adverse consequences are ignored.

It is worth discussing Nordhaus's model in some detail. It has two central conclusions. One is:

Under conditions where voting is an appropriate mechanism for social choice, democratic systems will choose a policy on the long-run trade-off [between unemployment and inflation] that has lower unemployment and higher inflation than is optimal. (p. 178)

The other is:

The unemployment rate must be falling over the entire electoral regime. . . . immediately after an election the victor will raise unemployment to some relatively high level in order to combat inflation. As elections approach, the unemployment rate will be lowered. . . . (p. 184)

Because obvious difficulties surround an "immediate" postelection rise in unemployment to some high level, the second implication is weakened in empirical tests to be that unemployment should rise in the first half of an incumbency and fall in the second half.

In the model, an expectations-augmented Phillips curve relates inflation and unemployment:

$$I_t = f(u_t) + cv_t. \tag{1}$$

I_t (the rate of inflation) is a function of the contemporaneous level of unemployment (u_t) and expected inflation (v_t). The expected rate of inflation is a function of the difference between inflation and previous expectations. Expectations rise whenever actual inflation exceeds that expected. There is a short-term Phillips curve (see Figure 3.2 and the discussion in Chapter 3) labeled S in Figure 5.1, and a long-term

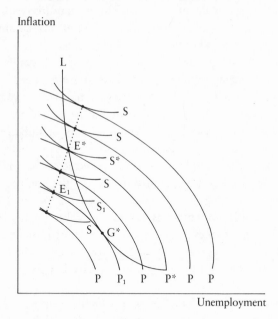

L	Long-run Phillips Curve
S	Short-run Phillips Curves
P	"Iso-vote" Curves

FIGURE 5.1. Expectations-Augmented Phillips Curve in the Nordhaus Model

Phillips curve, labeled L.[2] The slope of the long-term curve is *steeper* than that of the short-term curve, though not vertical in the Nordhaus analysis. In the long term, inflation is responsive to unemployment because of the cumulative impact of expectations. In the short term, the inflationary cost of reductions in unemployment is relatively small.

On the political side, a government that has been democratically elected and has wide economic policy powers can use these powers to choose a level of unemployment for the economy on the short-run curve but *not* to alter the short-run trade-off during its incumbency. Incumbent politicians choose policies to maximize their votes at the next election. They are assumed to know the preferences of voters. Voters evaluate policies at the end of each incumbency on the basis of levels of inflation and unemployment. The evaluations result in incumbents receiving some proportion of the vote at any combination of unemployment and inflation. The proportion decreases as unemployment or inflation increases. The line connecting all combinations of inflation and unemployment giving rise to *some* specific vote percentage can be called an "iso-vote" line (examples are drawn in Figure 5.1). These "iso-vote" lines are assumed to be quasi-concave.

The government searches for combinations of inflation and unemployment that are *optimal* with respect to the popular vote function, subject to the economic constraint reflected in the Phillips curve. Nordhaus argues that the government chooses the point on the *short-run* Phillips curve tangent to the highest available "iso-vote" curve. In other words, unemployment is set to the value giving the highest possible number of votes. If S_1 is the relevant short-term Phillips curve, then E_1 is the point on the highest "iso-vote" curve. The government chooses E_1 as its policy, knowing it will receive P_1 percent of the votes and could do no better.

If E_1 lies to the left of the long-term Phillips curve, it represents a combination of unemployment and inflation that can be sustained only

2. In Figure 3.2 there was a natural rate of unemployment, which implies that there is no unique long-run trade-off between unemployment and inflation. This would be depicted in Figure 5.1 by a vertical line. The long-run trade-off in Nordhaus's analysis is not vertical, though the cumulative impact of expectations means that the inflationary cost of reducing unemployment is greater in the long run than in the short run.

in the *short term* and will ultimately produce higher levels of inflation. The short-term Phillips curve must shift *up,* giving more inflation at any level of unemployment. Thus, E_1 will not be feasible at the next election. A new tangency point will be chosen. This will continue until the chosen policy E^* on the short-term Phillips curve S^* also lies on the long-term curve. If the first choice had been to the right of the long-term curve, subsequent choices would converge on E^* from above rather than from below.

There is a point G^* on the long-run curve which gives the maximum long-term level of support to the government. This is the most popular combination of inflation and unemployment *sustainable indefinitely.* E^* was reached by a series of decisions in which the future was entirely discounted and only the present considered. Thus, the government steers the economy to a higher level of inflation than if it chose the most popular point on the long-run trade-off.[3] This yields the first implication, that long-run inflation rates in democratic societies are higher than socially optimal. However, it follows not just from electoral considerations but also from economic management being treated as a series of short-run decisions, with the long term being discounted entirely.

The second implication is that unemployment must be continuously falling through the election period. This arises from discarding the static treatment outlined above in favor of a continuous model.[4] Now

3. Nordhaus refers to a social welfare optimum point in between E* and G*, implying that some rate of discounting the future *is* appropriate, but he does not clarify why or how much.
4. It is just as well that the first treatment of the problem is discarded. In no recognizable institutional framework do governments make one policy choice per incumbency. The static and continuous models are not logically inconsistent. The short-term/long-term Phillips curve is present in both. In the continuous model, the short-term curve has slope b whereas the long-term curve has slope b/1 − c (steeper if c is less than 1). There is also one major intervention per incumbency, driving up unemployment after the election rather than taking an optimal choice along the short-term Phillips curve. In the continuous model, it is less clear where the suboptimality arises. The "extra" inflation does not come from inconsistencies between short-term and long-term trade-offs. The inflation that results from lowered unemployment comes only after some delay, allowing the creation of a "window" during which unemployment and inflation are temporarily low. Because this window occurs when the welfare function is most heavily weighted and because the increase in unemployment (and inflation from the previous low unemployment) come later in a more discounted future, the system produces more

treated as a continuous optimization problem (see Chapter 6), attention is switched from decisions of government to the behavior over time of unemployment and inflation. Nordhaus does not show that the implication of higher long-term inflation follows from total future discounting in the continuous model, but it does. Nordhaus substitutes a specific welfare function (by an arbitrary but important assumption, it is quadratic in unemployment but linear in inflation) for the specification in Figure 5.1. He supplies an actual function for the f(u) in equation (1) above (linear so that $I_t = a - bu_t + cv_t$). The problem is to maximize $-u^2 - dI$ (the welfare function, with two negatively valued economic states), subject to the constraint that $I_t = a - bu_t + cv_t$, where the welfare function is considered to be weighted more heavily close to the election but to carry no weight at all beyond the next election. It is then possible to deduce the optimal movement of unemployment over time. Its rate of change is shown to be everywhere negative *within* each election period. Since the rate of unemployment does not fall forever, it is raised immediately after each election and falls continuously until the next. Just how it is raised or how its continual fall is ensured is not clarified.

Unemployment falls throughout the incumbency because the future is totally discounted. Nordhaus himself points out that expectations of inflation in the economic evaluation underlying voting decisions alters the cycle and pulls the system toward the "golden rule" point or long-term vote-maximizing outcome. This myopic discounting of the future is very important since it guarantees that the government incurs no electoral penalty from inflation after the election.[5] *Myopia* describes a process in which expectations are derived entirely from observations of the past. Myopia has nothing to do with amnesia, the rate at which

---

inflation than if the weights were evenly distributed throughout time into the indefinite future. Some of the cycle, as well as the extra inflation, arises from Nordhaus's wholly arbitrary choice of making inflation linear but unemployment quadratic in the welfare function.

5. The Nordhaus model does not say whether myopia is a desirable characteristic of government policy, simply the way governments make decisions, a feature of the electorate in evaluating economic policies, or a feature the government imputes to the electorate's evaluation, or what. It is simply present in the system.

people forget the past. Any rate of memory decay is compatible with the myopic expectations Nordhaus uses in his model. Myopic expectations always underestimate accelerating inflation. This allows the government to escape any penalty at election time for the inflation which is about to occur. Any expectations which include extra information, whether about the tendency of inflation to accelerate at election time or about the role of unemployment in generating inflation, will undo the cycle if people vote their expectations as well as their observations of past inflation. Myopia in Nordhaus's model makes the question of expectations moot, for even if people did vote their expectations, these expectations contain only past observations. Of course, empirical support for the Nordhaus model would be evidence that people actually do vote myopically.

Evidence

Nordhaus does not present any estimates of his model. No suggestions are made about the origins of the welfare function, why it is quadratic in unemployment but linear in inflation, how its weights could be determined, or whether the actual values in the economic constraint matter. The only empirically contingent point is whether or not unemployment rates conform to the pattern implied by qualitative analysis of the continuous model, namely, that they should always fall. Thus, the model focuses entirely on the behavior of unemployment rates, not on the behavior of governments.

Nordhaus looked at interelection rates of unemployment in nine countries. He found the expected pattern of unemployment rates rising in the first half of incumbencies and falling in the second half in only three of the nine, Germany, the United States, and New Zealand. The substitute proposition that unemployment should simply be higher in the first half of incumbencies does no better. This formulation picks up support largely from the trend of declining unemployment in the United States in the 1960s. Other attempts also fail to find significant differences in unemployment rates between years of incumbencies (Golden and Poterba, 1980).

Moreover, of the nine countries, two of the three where the cycles appear to exist, Germany and the United States, have among the *lowest* long-term inflation. Germany is lowest of all in average inflation from 1951 to 1974, and the United States is second lowest (see Figure 3.1). It is true that the assumption that the government treats economic policy decisions with a short-term horizon only entails that inflation would be higher than the "optimal" inflation produced under less extreme discounting of the future. It would be odd if those countries where inflation was higher than "optimal" were also those with the lowest inflation rates. Even if electorally induced cycles produced some extra inflation in these countries, they do not appear to have suffered from it. So the Nordhaus model fails in this additional sense. Its principal *suboptimality*, extra inflation, is also inconsistent with the evidence.

Do governments operate with a one-election time horizon? Alternatively, is the weight attached to economic conditions beyond the next election zero? G. D. MacRae's (1977) model empirically tests the assumption of myopia, contrasting it with the "strategic" hypothesis that governments maximize support over an indefinite time horizon. MacRae suggests that of four American administrations, in two cases policy was characterized by the assumption of electoral myopia and in two cases by strategic behavior. Alt's (1979) replication of the MacRae model for British administrations since 1951 produced no evidence at all of a political business cycle of either description in two of five administrations. In two of the other three cases, the indefinite time horizon hypothesis outperformed the myopic hypothesis, and in the final case both were equally plausible. British administrations may thus occasionally have practiced giving the electorate what the government thought the electorate wanted. There was no evidence that governments had ever attempted to steal reelection by taking advantage of the lag with which inflation follows reduced unemployment.

QUADRANT II: RESPONSIVE
GOVERNMENTS, FIXED PREFERENCES

Theory

Quadrant I assumed that a government was free to choose any combination of unemployment and inflation and derive support from it. Electors had fixed preferences for unemployment and inflation, but changes in economic outcomes would make them change party allegiance. If people are not so flexible, then political authorities cannot be unconstrained strategic agents. Their actions will be largely constrained by the preferences of their supporters. Authorities can still be optimizing and indeed vote-maximizing. The optimal decision will assume that the best they can do is to implement programatically a set of policies on the basis of which they were elected.

Such "programatic" behavior on the part of the political authorities in a competitive electoral system can be rational. It requires at least that each party's supporters have different but stable preferences over some policy alternatives. If a party's supporters can find alternative parties within the system to implement their preferences, responsiveness becomes likelier. Followers enforce it if they do not switch parties but abstain if their party did not implement their preferences, accepting short-term defeat in return for longer-term adherence of the party to its supporters' goals. The changes of economic priority which arise when there are partisan changes in incumbency will produce a "political business cycle." In this case, economic conditions will change after rather than before elections. The cycles will have a periodicity which is at least one interelection period long.[6]

Hibbs (1977, 1979, 1982a, 1982b) proposes a model of the political business cycle along these lines. Each country faces a Phillips curve trade-off between unemployment and inflation. The trade-offs faced by all countries are sufficiently similar to allow one to characterize long-run outcomes among countries as choices along such a trade-off curve. Left-wing parties' programs should place greater emphasis on providing high levels of employment. Countries with greater long-run socialist or left-party participation in government should have lower

6. We should note at this point that there is a model, owing largely to the work of Frey (1978) which subsumes both quadrants I and II and also provides a criterion by which to decide which sort of behavior the government will adopt. In particular, he argues that governments which feel secure about their reelection prospects will be responsive whereas governments which are not secure will become strategic. Because the model is couched in terms of the instruments of policy and in fact has no clear implications for cyclical movements of the outcomes, it will be more convenient to discuss it in the context of systematic models of economic policy (Chapter 6) and expenditures and revenues (Chapter 10).

long-run unemployment and higher inflation than countries predominantly governed by right-of-center parties.

Hibbs presents evidence that this is so. For instance, in the 1960s Scandinavian countries, with predominantly socialist governments, had average annual inflation rates around 4 to 5 percent and unemployment rates of 1 to 2 percent whereas the United States and Canada, with little or no left-wing control of government, had inflation rates of 2 to 3 percent but unemployment rates around 5 percent. Such long-run characteristics could also result from economic-structural variations. Therefore, Hibbs provides a model of unemployment in both the United States and Britain which shows that partisan changes in incumbency in each country are accompanied by the predicted change in unemployment rate. The long-run or steady-state rate of unemployment under the Democrats is approximately 2.5 percentage points lower than under the Republicans. There is a similar kind of difference in unemployment rates between Labor and Conservatives of slightly less than 1 percent. Support for socialist parties is strongest among those in working-class occupational grades. Preferences for reduced unemployment and indeed the incidence of actual unemployment are greatest in these occupational classes. (We return to this point in Chapter 7.) The working class is most hurt by unemployment and possibly less hurt by inflation. Their policy preferences for reduced unemployment at the cost of inflation correspond to their objective interests. They support left-wing parties which implement policies reflecting these preferences. Both short-run and long-run outcomes reflect these partisan differences.

Evidence

Hibbs's empirical conclusions have been widely, if not always fairly or usefully, criticized. The "cross-national Phillips curve" is a useful heuristic device, but it is not clear what economic theory underlies an international trade-off. Under the Bretton Woods system, no country could have lower long-run inflation than the United States unless either its currency appreciated against the dollar or its nontraded (service) industries' prices rose slower than those in the United States. Although there is a clear contrast between the extreme cases Hibbs discusses, it is less clear how much information the curve gives about differences between countries in the middle of the curve. Moreover, it is a time-bound creature. As Figure 5.2 shows, the same countries displayed no systematic trade-off between unemployment and inflation over the next decade. This reflects varying domestic responses to major shocks and indeed changes in inflation under floating exchange rates (see Chapter 4). Perhaps the fixed exchange rate period of the late 1950s and 1960s was the only period in which countries actually can be seen as having had a choice along an inflation-unemployment frontier of the sort Hibbs describes.

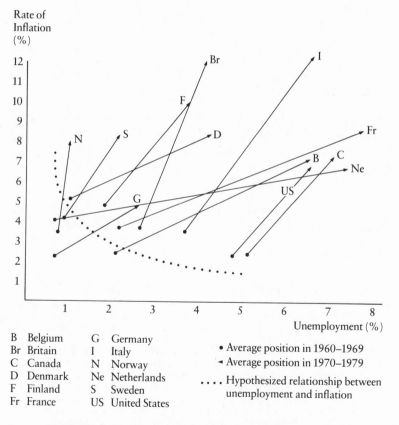

B	Belgium	G	Germany
Br	Britain	I	Italy
C	Canada	N	Norway
D	Denmark	Ne	Netherlands
F	Finland	S	Sweden
Fr	France	US	United States

• Average position in 1960–1969

◄ Average position in 1970–1979

. . . . Hypothesized relationship between unemployment and inflation

SOURCE: OECD, *Main Economic Indicators, 1960–1979.*

FIGURE 5.2. Inflation and Unemployment in the 1960s and 1970s

Nevertheless, the underlying rank ordering of 1970s unemployment rates in Figure 5.2 is still much as it was in the 1960s, though Belgium and France have higher levels of unemployment. Hibbs is probably right to interpret these unemployment rates as reflecting structural characteristics and long-term labor market policies as well as the cumulative effects of short-term interventions.

N. Beck (1982) reestimates Hibbs's model of American unemployment rates and finds smaller differences between the parties, though the qualitative differences remain. Part of their dispute is technical.[7] However, differences in unemployment rates are greater between some incumbents of the same party than between many incumbents of opposite parties.

In the postwar United States, only Truman and Johnson look like the Democrats described by Hibbs; similarly, only Ford really fits Hibbs's Republican pattern. Looking at the unemployment rates only, it would be quite hard to tell that Carter was a Democrat. . . . (N. Beck, 1982, p. 91)

It is surely no coincidence, given the changes in economic theory and institutions in the 1970s (described in Chapters 3 and 4), that at the same time Carter was not acting like a traditional Democrat, the British Labor government in the late 1970s abandoned low unemployment as a target in favor of controlling inflation.

I do not think this [increase in unemployment] will be reduced for some time. . . . as long as we try to squeeze inflation out of the economy . . . this is one of the consequences we have to bear. . . . (Prime Minister Callaghan, quoted in the *London Times,* January 26, 1977)[8]

---

7. Beck argues that Hibbs may have misspecified the underlying process of unemployment rate changes, thereby obtaining estimates of the adjustment speed of unemployment which were excessively slow. On the other hand, Beck omits the effects of wars, which are hardly economic policies, and his discussion appears to confuse instantaneous and cumulative impacts of partisan changes.

8. We believe there was a major policy shift in this period, even if one does not always wish to take politicians' pronouncements at face value. Some might argue that Callaghan's statement was a strategic announcement in the light of Labor's need to shore up the support of the financial community in order to secure a massive loan from the IMF in 1976–1977. It seems at least as likely, given that under a floating exchange rate regime the need for such a loan is questionable, that Labor's seeking a loan with tight economic policy conditions attached from the IMF was a strategic attempt to shift the blame for contractionary policies onto a third party.

Party commitments to a core of policies are not invariant over long periods, certainly not in the face of major changes in economic theory and the international context.

Even the party differences in Britain are not well established by Hibbs's model. There are only three changes of incumbency in Britain in this period: 1951 (Conservatives take over), 1964 (Labor), 1970 (Conservatives). Estimates of party differences in his model depend largely on unemployment trends at these critical times. Britain is a small open economy. Its level of economic activity responds to world (or U.S.) trends. The U.S. economy was in an upswing after 1964 but was slowing down in 1952 and 1971. The first two postwar British Labor administrations were in office at the same time as the Truman and Johnson administrations, which Beck finds to be the two American administrations which most successfully produced low unemployment. If wars are removed from the American unemployment series, should not the effects of the U.S. economy be removed from the British series?

Hibbs argues that the rise of unemployment in Britain after 1966 should be ascribed to the reform of social benefits enacted in that year, which made earnings-related benefits available to the unemployed, reducing the personal economic cost of unemployment. Although this reform may have had some effect, 1966–1970 was also a period in which the Labor government had a consistently deflationary economic policy. This policy produced in 1969 and 1970 the last budget surpluses in recent British history and the highest levels of government revenue relative to national income and expenditure since 1955.[9] Ignoring the effects of this deflation—which the Wilson government acknowledged publicly but claimed was necessary to restore balance of payments equilibrium—weakens Hibbs's case. Reducing the supposed impact of social benefits on unemployment rates diminishes the estimated interparty differences.

Looking only at indicators like unemployment risks missing politi-

9. This underscores the problems which accrue to Hibbs's decision to model the effects of party changes as occurring only at the beginning of incumbencies. The effects of any major policy changes (midterm U-turns) at other times are absorbed more by the parameters of the underlying economic series and less by the party impact parameters.

cal interventions whose effects were canceled out before working through to the ultimate targets. The Kennedy administration, as Beck notes, had little effect on unemployment but made an effort to reduce it. Their early strategy was built around the investment tax credit rather than orthodox Keynesian policy. Only after this policy failed to reduce unemployment were the Johnson tax cuts passed. Actual interventions require looking at the instruments rather than the targets of policy with models in which policymakers react systematically to the economy (see Golden and Poterba, 1980; and see Chapter 6).

Parties' goals change even if the British parties maintain more ideological coherence than the "impermanent coalitions between the various sectors of society, with elections offering a choice between temporary alliances," which Beck describes in the American case. The next two quadrants discuss models of the political business cycle where popular preferences vary. First, however, a word in defense of Hibbs's model. Members of the British electorate differ along class and partisan lines over the importance of unemployment and inflation as issues, whether it is worth reducing unemployment if the cost is increased inflation, and what means should be used to fight inflation (Alt, 1979). In all cases Labor supporters display greater aversion to unemployment. We doubt whether any account of the steep rise of British unemployment from 6 to 12 percent between 1979 and 1981 will be written with no mention of the change to a Conservative incumbency. Thus, there is still some power in Hibbs's account even if his estimates do not clearly establish interparty differences in the earlier period of fixed exchange rates and consensus in economic management.

QUADRANT III: STRATEGIC GOVERNMENTS, VARYING PREFERENCES

Theory

Electors may vary in their preferences according to circumstances, the presentation of circumstances in the media, or even in response to government persuasion. Tufte's model of the political business cycle contained in his book *Political Control of the Economy* (1978) exemplifies this case. We drop for the moment the idea that govern-

ments are constrained to respond to the preferences of a core of supporters. Suppose instead that governments have the latitude to carry
out strategic macroeconomic manipulation. However, assume there
are a variety of preferences which they could satisfy rather than known
penalties being attached to particular outcomes.

Nothing as specific in its parameters and terms as the Nordhaus
model is put forward. Indeed, Tufte has at different points in his book
three distinct ideas about the political business cycle. In part of his
work he uses Hibbs's fixed preference/responsiveness model. At another point he suggests a decision rule of "attack whatever problem the
electorate considers most important" which is identical to Mosley's
varying preference/responsiveness model (next section). His central
assertion is that incumbent politicians seek to win elections by staging
the most favorable possible conditions with respect to two key economic variables: real disposable incomes (that is, personal incomes net
of taxes in constant prices) and the rate of unemployment. There are
"accelerations" of real disposable incomes in election years. In the
United States this gives a two-year cycle. Real disposable income always grows more quickly in the (even numbered) election year than in
the year before. The rate of unemployment declines over the twelve to
eighteen months before a presidential election. This is expected to
produce a four-year cycle.

Electors are sufficiently discerning to respond to rates of change
rather than levels. Popularity accrues to a *decline* in unemployment
and *faster* real income growth in the election year regardless of previous levels. Policy choices do not require the optimizing calculations
of the Nordhaus and MacRae models. Rather the model assumes that
politicians have sufficient policy instruments to make any situation
better in the year before an election. How do they do it? Tufte suggests
two ways: taxation (particularly tax rates) and transfer payments.
Exactly how these instruments are controlled is not elaborated, though
in one place Tufte describes how a strong president can affect the
timing of veterans' benefits and Social Security payments.

Since cycles in economic aggregates are observed rather than deduced from first principles of behavior, Tufte mobilizes a lot of quantitative evidence. He argues that: (1) accelerations of real disposable

income occur more frequently in election years than nonelection years
in nineteen of twenty-seven countries studied having elections between
1961–1972; (2) such accelerations were more common in the United
States in election years from 1946–1976, at least provided the Eisenhower years are ignored;[10] (3) unemployment levels have been lower
at election time than twelve to eighteen months before in six of eight
recent presidential elections (again the Eisenhower incumbency—1956
and 1960—is deviant); (4) there are only a few years in which both
unemployment and inflation have declined, but most of these are presidential election years; (5) increases in real disposable income in the
United States are, on average, largest in election years when an incumbent president stands for reelection, slightly smaller in midterm election years, smaller still in presidential election years with no incumbent
standing, and smallest of all in years with no election; (6) within-year
increases in Social Security benefits tend to occur in election years
whereas beginning-of-year increases occur in nonelection years; (7)
unusually large increases in veterans' benefits occur in the fourth quarters of election years; (8) "windows" are created between Social Security increases in benefits (timed for before the election) and contributions (timed for after the election), with the 20 percent increase in
benefits in October 1972 and consequent increase in contributions in
January 1973 a prominent example; (9) transfer payments tend to
"heap" such that in presidential election years with a strong president
in the White House, there are peaks in payments for the last month
(sometimes October, sometimes November) whose check would arrive
before the election; and (10) the amount of currency in circulation has
tended (again outside the Eisenhower years) to increase faster in the
two years before a presidential election than in the two years after.

Evidence

Tufte's simultaneous concern for the outcomes and instruments of
economic policy is a strong point. He deals not only with electorally
timed movements in unemployment and incomes but also with how
politicians bring these cycles about. The problem with Tufte's results
is that more formal studies do not find the expected cyclical patterns.

10. Without omitting the Eisenhower years, "accelerations" become a fifty-fifty
proposition both in and out of election years.

One weakness is his observational method. Many of Tufte's observed periodic contrasts require an "all other things being equal" assumption which cannot be sustained. Furthermore, many of his propositions rest on categorical judgments of what are quantitatively very small differences.

For instance, adding up cases in Tufte's Table 1.1 shows that (across all countries) income accelerations are a fifty-fifty bet in non-election years but occur in fifty-eight of ninety or 64 percent of election years. But several of these countries do not have fixed election periods. If such governments choose to call elections at favorable opportunities, growth will coincide with elections. This does not entail political control of the economy. Only a dozen such cases make the overall difference between election and nonelection years disappear. Whether the unemployment series supports or rejects the hypothesis of declining rates before elections and rising rates after is frequently a marginal choice. For instance, Tufte claims post-1972 as a confirming case, although unemployment actually fell for a few months after the election, stayed below October-November 1972 levels for eighteen months, and only rose above them in September 1974. In the same way, he counts the *February* 1968 Social Security increase as "within-year" but the *January* 1965 increase counts as "beginning of the year." Long trends in unemployment cloud the picture further. Unemployment in the United States declined (because of fiscal policy and the Vietnam War) more or less continuously from 1961 to 1969, confirming several preelection cycle expectations on the way. His evidence on transfer payments is equally shaky. His "windows" certainly exist, but most of the largest ones occur far away from election times (Winters et al., 1981). While 1972 exemplifies "heaping," his figures for 1964 and 1970 do not conform to published Commerce Department data, and 1962, the only other supporting case, involves an extremely small difference in monthly levels of benefit (Brown and Stein, 1982). Finally, nearly all the expected relationships failed to materialize between 1976 and 1980. Real incomes fell before the election. Unemployment fell continuously after the 1976 election and through 1979 but rose before the 1980 election.

Not all of Tufte's evidence can or should be discredited. Sometimes there is observable evidence of a cycle and sometimes not. The Eisenhower and Carter years are disconfirming cases. The Nixon years (especially 1972) and less clearly but possibly the Truman years (especially 1948) in the United States and the Conservatives' 1955 budget in Britain appear to be supporting cases. The Kennedy-Johnson years offered sustained rather than cyclic economic expansion. Care must be taken to demonstrate the existence of electoral cycles independent of trends. The Ford years are overshadowed by response to the oil crisis of 1973, though 1976 like 1964 does not refute the hypothesis of an electoral business cycle. Preelection stimulation of the economy could be a strategy which may or may not be adopted, but no theory says why the strategy sometimes is and sometimes is not adopted.

Something which occasionally works is an unsatisfactory model of the politics of economic policy. Eclecticism is part of Tufte's problem. He has at least four behavioral rules for the authorities (support your core clients, do whatever the public finds most important, get unemployment down for the presidential election, and get real incomes up for any election) with no lexicographic ordering among them. Conflict between them is clearly possible. Whatever happens can probably be interpreted as supporting one of these rules.

Finally, Tufte's account is also institutionally inconsistent. He stresses presidential influence rather than Congress's. Four presidential elections come closest to sustaining his case—1948, 1964, 1972, and 1976. In at least three of these—1948, 1964 and 1976—tax changes rather than transfer payments created the economic stimulation. The 1964 tax cut came in an election year because Congress resisted the tax cuts Kennedy sought earlier. In 1976, the tax cut which passed Congress was larger than the one President Ford had sought. In 1948, a Republican Congress passed the tax cut over Democratic President Truman's veto! If Congress is sometimes so important, why not the rest of the time?

QUADRANT IV: RESPONSIVE
GOVERNMENTS, VARYING PREFERENCES

Theory

Suppose we drop the assumption of strategic governments and assume that governments only respond to conditions and popular preferences but that these preferences vary from time to time. Mosley's (1976) political model of economic policymaking allows motivations of policymakers to transcend the prescriptions of economic advice. His model involves "satisficing." *Satisficing* models, in contrast to *optimizing* models, have at least one of three main characteristics: information is taken to be limited and costly, preferences over alternative outcomes are partial and not necessarily transitive, and the desire for goods is satiable and may reflect subjective levels of aspiration. There are conditions under which such behavior is nevertheless still optimal decision-making. Though Mosley does not develop this point, we will return to it in the next chapter.

In Mosley's model the government and electorate are crisis-averters. The government does not fine-tune or steer the economy toward long-term goals. The actual workings of the economy are only relevant when some economic variable goes into "crisis." Crises only reflect negatively valued states. The electorate is aware of the economy (or so the government assumes) only when things are sufficiently bad. Such concern adversely affects the government's reelection prospects. Governments do not benefit by doing particularly well in economic management. The only political purpose of economic policy is thus to steer the economy out of crisis. Mosley claims his model describes accurately how governments actually involve themselves in economic policy. In his model governments consider at most one target at a time, unlike the simultaneous optimization of the Nordhaus model. Any relevant target is identified by popular concern, which varies with the severity of bad economic conditions. Intermittent interventions characterize policymaking, which is geared neither to core constituency preferences nor the electoral calendar.

British bank rate, tax rate, and public investment changes identify crises from 1946 to 1971. Changes of more than £100 million in tax revenues (at 1946 prices) or deviations of more than 50 percent from trend (investment) or 20 percent from trend (bank rate) are the thresholds. Years in which at least two of these three instruments had above-threshold changes are defined as crises. Mosley selects unemployment and the balance of payments as the targets which caused changes in the instruments. The selection rests on regressing changes in taxes and public investment on deviations of unemployment and the balance of payments from trend. Mosley (1978) extends the model to the electorate by considering whether government popularity is particularly affected by economic crises. If government popularity is only affected by economic crisis, it is appropriate for the government to follow a satisficing strategy. We will discuss formal aspects of this model in Chapter 7.

Evidence

Mosley's model contains an important insight into the sporadic nature of interventions and the variability of popular preferences. Cycles could arise from government (possibly rationally) pursuing a strategy of considering only one target at a time and for a substantial period. Such behavior is indeed optimal under reasonable assumptions about politicians' intervention costs and the uncertainty of popular demand for economic outcomes (see Chapter 6). Cycles could then follow directly from optimizing behavior but without Nordhaus's extra assumption that the government tries to exploit an information advantage or Hibbs's assumption that politicians rigidly serve the fixed interests of their core constituencies.

Mosley starts from observed interventions. His empirical problem is therefore to estimate the decision threshold. Deviations from trends do this badly. Consider the case of "threshold" levels of inflation. Mosley regresses inflation on a time trend and claims the fitted values give levels of inflation which were satisfactory at the time. But only the high levels of inflation of the mid-1970s make many of the earlier years appear not to be crisis periods. Trend values of British inflation calculated over a period including the 18 to 25 percent levels of 1974–1976 are going to be substantially higher across the 1960s than would be the case if the trend calculation stopped even in 1973. For instance, the inflation rate in the final quarter of 1964 is 4.4 percent. This is above the trend value of inflation for that quarter calculated from 1955 to 1964, which is 2.3 percent. Indeed, inflation at the end of 1964 exceeds its trend values until the calculation period includes 1974. But in Mosley's model inflation was only satisfactory in 1964 because of the higher inflation experienced ten full years later! Satisfaction cannot reflect events many years ahead and should be affected by what has happened recently. A moving average of recent inflation levels would be a better guide to satisfactory levels. Any such formulation produces a different set of crises from Mosley's. An a priori model of "acceptable standards," without which there are no testable predictions, is needed.

SUMMARY

No one could read the political business cycle literature without being struck by the lack of supporting evidence. There must be cases where politicians have undertaken electorally motivated interventions. It is difficult to imagine politicians not exploiting some extra information or other resources. But while this clearly happens, and happens particularly clearly in some cases, such cycles may be trivial in comparison with other economic fluctuations. Incumbents may be able to give themselves significant advantages relative to challengers. But the ability to intervene economically is only one of many possible incumbency advantages. The existence of such advantages may not make anything worse overall or in the long run.

Available trade-offs as well as the goals of different administrations appear to vary considerably, contrary to fixed preference models. Models of movements of the ultimate targets of policy like unemployment have not been empirically confirmed. On the evidence we cannot say whether this is because the authorities did not attempt a political business cycle or tried but failed. This distinction requires looking systematically at how policymakers respond to their economic environment. The next chapter discusses models which explain economic policy as a systematic set of responses to economic conditions, built around the core of policy optimizing.

CHAPTER SIX

Policy Optimization and Reaction Functions

The full set of factors which influence economic policymaking can only be understood in a framework that can distinguish between hypotheses about the goals of policy. Policymakers have goals for the state of the economy, whether their concern is the level or the stability of aggregate economic activity, employment, or prices.[1] The fact that electoral-cyclical considerations are not dominant does not mean that policy is not systematic, particularly where a Keynesian policy is pursued. But the choice of goals available to policymakers is not unrestricted. "Uncontrollable" facts of life like economic structure, dependence on particular commodities, and position in the world economy are important constraints on policymakers' discretion. The extent to which policy reflects their chosen goals can only be estimated with a model which formally expresses policy as a problem of constrained choice.

A popular representation of such governmental economic policy choices is known as a *reaction function*. Reaction functions typically

1 . The study of public policy must encompass intentions and actions as well as outcomes. Traditional case studies of public policy often explain actions by showing that they appear reasonable in light of the intentions of and obstacles faced by policymakers. How preferences associated with particular interests were articulated and organized into political actions is a standing concern. Two of Allison's (1971) three models of the policy process—rational and bureaucratic politics—are directly counterposed notions of how to conceive of the preferences which affect policy outcomes.

relate some instrument of economic policy like expenditure to its own past values and those of other economic targets like inflation and unemployment. The equations in Cowart (1978) and Frey and Schneider (1978a, 1978b, 1979) are all reaction functions. A recent study of American monetary policy reactions is Abrams, Froyen, and Waud (1980).

The reaction function approach is attractive as a simple way of representing how economic policy instruments are adjusted in response to goals of policy. Reaction functions are not an ad hoc specification of the policy process. They have a long intellectual pedigree in the area of policy optimization. Reaction functions share the analytic problems of optimization. Understanding of the strengths and limitations of the optimizing approach is important since most applied policy analysis is a special case of it.

AN EXAMPLE

Underlying the reaction function approach is the idea that when some economic conditions (the "targets") differ from their ideal levels, the authorities change other economic variables (the "instruments") in order to improve the situation. Ideal values are rarely incorporated explicitly in published models. In the standard form, instrument x_i at time t is a linear function of its own past values and the contemporaneous values of the economic targets y_j (of which there are $k-1$):

$$x_{it} = a + b_{i1}x_{it-1} + \sum_{j=2}^{k} b_{ij}y_{ijt}. \tag{1}$$

The coefficient b_{i1} of the lagged dependent variable is sometimes interpreted in the literature as an adjustment speed parameter. Its value will normally be between zero and one. Values of b_{i1} close to one mean that the instrument does not change much from period to period. A coefficient close to zero means that the current value of the instrument is not closely related to last period's value. The remaining coefficients are often presumed to reflect the preferences of the authorities since they show how the instrument changes with respect to changing values of the targets.

An example of a monetary policy reaction function for the United States may help. Abrams, Froyen, and Waud (1980) estimate one from monthly data for March 1970 to March 1977. The interested student should read the original, which has far more in it than our example. Their analysis is built around a reaction function. The following result is typical.

$$R_t = 2.049 + 0.82R_{t-1} - 0.339U_t + 0.016P_t + 0.093M_t + 0.059D_t \qquad (2)$$
$$\quad\;\; (3.052) \quad (15.5) \quad (3.071) \quad (0.297) \quad (3.311) \quad (3.873)$$
$$R^2 = 0.974$$

where the instrument R_t is the federal funds rate[2] and R_{t-1} is its value lagged one period. U_t is the deviation of unemployment from its desired level, P_t is the rate of inflation, M_t is the deviation of the money supply growth rate from its target level and D_t is the percentage effective devaluation in the exchange rate of the dollar. Figures in parentheses beneath coefficients are the absolute values of t-statistics. As a rule of thumb, if these values are greater than two, then the coefficient concerned is significantly different from zero. There is thus a significant relationship between R_t and all the other variables except the inflation rate P_t. Their results show that interest rates are depressed by high unemployment and increased when money growth is above target and the dollar's exchange value falls.

Reaction function models can be used in comparative research. Black (1981) estimates carefully specified equations for monetary policy in ten industrial countries for 1964–1979. He shows that with few exceptions policy weights on inflation are inversely related to domestic inflation rates. A high policy weight on inflation is associated with lower inflation. In his equations, weights on inflation were inversely related to weights on unemployment, except in Canada, the Netherlands and Britain. The first two countries pursued policies tied to those of larger neighboring trading partners (the United States and Germany). British monetary policy apparently responded only to external targets like currency reserves, the balance of payments, and the inflation rates of its trading partners.

2. The federal funds rate is an interest rate set by the Federal Reserve Bank. Its level is presumed to affect the level of all other interest rates, and its role is similar to that of central bank discount rates in other countries.

These analyses have considerable potential explanatory value, particularly if attention is paid to the political and institutional framework of policy. However, it can be difficult to say more about results like these than that there is some relationship between changes in, say, interest rates and the other variables. Cowart (1978) and Frey and Schneider (1978a, 1978b, 1979) tried to interpret the coefficients of target variables in these reaction functions as if they reflected the preferences of the authorities directly. But equations like (2) are not evidence about the preferences of the authorities without more information about the structure of the economy. But evidence about preferences is precisely what is sought.

THE REACTION FUNCTION APPROACH

The beginning of this chapter raises two issues. One is how far economic outcomes result from policy interventions. An answer requires measuring the economic consequences of observable policy actions (see Blinder and Goldfeld, 1976). Our present concern is the other, the extent to which outcomes systematically reflect intentions. Relevant outcomes include the example of comparative inflation rates. Do different countries' combinations of inflation and unemployment result from happenstance, economic constraints, or conscious strategy on the part of political authorities? Political analysis of such outcomes is ambiguous without a model of the process by which outcomes are generated, and the structural relationship between them.

Measures of economic policy outcomes cannot be *presumed* to reflect the preferences of political and administrative authorities. First, not all outcomes are feasible. Second, the constraints are complex, involving relationships among many variables. Treating outcomes as if they reflect unconstrained preferences overstates the discretion of the authorities and gives an unrealistic expectation of what policy can achieve.

Formal models of economic policy like reaction functions provide a framework within which to disentangle constraint from intention. These models have two components: (1) the intentions or preferences of the government and (2) a statement of "how things work" or a set of constraints describing the relationships among economic variables.

Both components must be included in empirical work. A review of policy optimization (see Stokey and Zeckhauser, 1978, pp. 22–44) will clarify the theoretical underpinnings of reaction functions. Reaction functions have the strengths and weaknesses of the optimizing model, which also deserves discussion as a tool of policy analysis. The rest of the chapter discusses limits on inferences from reaction functions and ways in which the framework can incorporate aspects of the politics of economic policy.

POLICY OPTIMIZATION

The optimizing model portrays economic policy as made by a unified authority with clearly defined preferences.[3] This authority has discretionary control over some instruments (for example, the level of expenditures or interest rates) and uses this discretion to steer the macroeconomy in "desired" directions. It can be used normatively to translate a given set of preferences into policy choices, given how the economy is thought to work. It can also be used in the opposite way, to analyze the authorities' behavior, by assuming they engage in optimizing behavior using the same model available to the analyst. The study of outcomes under the assumption of an optimizing authority with known preferences allows investigation of the constraints on policy. This analysis of government economic policy choices was developed by Tinbergen (1952) and Theil (1968).[4]

BASIC CONCEPTS OF THE OPTIMIZING MODEL

A few basic distinctions and definitions are needed before further discussion. A model is an explicit statement of systematic relationships. Values of some variables are taken as given within any model.

3. This places it squarely in what Allison (1971) calls the "rational actor" approach to explaining policy outcomes. It should be added that the optimizing model is usually used in a normative way. By formalizing the structure of the economy and goals of policy, it can be used to offer advice as to the best course of policy.

4. The techniques had earlier been applied to consumer theory and the theory of the firm, and the optimization problem of the government was seen as being no different in principle.

Such variables are called *exogenous*. Variables whose values are determined (even if subject to error) by the relationships specified in the model are called *endogenous*.

The optimizing model contains two sorts of relationships, an *economic constraint* and an *objective function*. The constraint is a set of equations linking the economic variables to each other.[5] Many values of the economic variables will be consistent with the constraints imposed by the structure of the economy. These values form a set of *feasible* outcomes. The objective function is sometimes called a *utility function* or *welfare function*. It provides a measure (utility) of the extent to which values of the economic variables are liked or disliked. These perceived costs or benefits associated with each variable may vary with levels of that and other variables. By associating a cost or benefit with each value of each variable in the system, the objective function provides a means of evaluating every *feasible* outcome. The central assumption of the optimizing model is that the chosen outcome will have the highest utility value of those that are feasible, subject to the constraints. For this reason the problem is described as one of *constrained optimization*.

Some economic variables can be directly controlled and others cannot.[6] No Western government has the power or scope of activity to hire or fire enough people (while controlling offsetting private sector behavior) to set the rate of unemployment to any desired level. The same is true of inflation. Governments cannot normally control private sector price setting either by legislation or net purchases or sales in markets, although this is sometimes done in individual sectors like agriculture. The authorities usually have goals for many of the uncontrolled variables such as inflation and unemployment, which are spoken of as

5. Some of the equations are *identities,* or definitional equalities, as in the case where the budget deficit equals expenditure minus revenue; some are *stochastic,* or subject to error, as would be the case for the equations summarizing, for example, the processes by which revenue and expenditure were believed to be generated.

6. There is a declining continuum of control from the actual instruments to the targets. Some analysts capture this continuum by drawing distinctions between *ultimate targets* (for example, GNP) and *intermediate targets* (for example, change in money supply), and between *nominal instruments* (for example, "interest rates") and *actual instruments* (for example, some precisely controllable rate such as the federal funds rate).

target variables. The economic policy problem is to steer the target variables toward these goals by using controlled variables such as tax rates (called instruments). The links between all the instruments and targets are given by the equations of the economic system or constraint.

THE FORMAL OPTIMIZING MODEL

(This section contains material which is more advanced technically than is assumed for the rest of the book. It may be skipped at a first reading. It establishes formally one point which the reader may be prepared to accept without proof, that the coefficients of a reaction function involve parameters of both the objective function and the constraints.)

The optimizing model of economic policy assumes that the government chooses the values of a set of instrument variables x in order to maximize some objective function W which depends upon the instruments and some target variables y. Formally the problem is:

Choose x to maximize $W = w(x,y)$ (3)

subject to $c(x,y) = 0$ (4)

where (3) is the objective function and (4) are the constraints determined by the general structure of the economy. If a solution exists for optimal instrument values x^o, it can be expressed as a function of the targets (y):

$$x^o = f(y).$$ (5)

This function depends upon the parameters of both w and c, the objective function and the constraints.

To illustrate this, suppose there is only one target and one instrument. For the sake of the argument, let us treat the level of prices (denoted P) as the target of policy and some measure of interest rates (R) as the instrument. The preferences of the policymakers reflect the difference between prevailing values of prices and interest rates and their ideal values. Assuming that policymakers react more strongly if they are further from their desired targets, we set up a quadratic loss[7] function reflecting preferences:

$$W(P,R) = a(R^* - R)^2 + b(P^* - P)^2. \tag{6}$$

The state of the economy is evaluated by the deviation of interest rates and prices from their desired values R^* and P^*. The evaluation requires taking the squares of both deviations, each weighted by (unknown) positive factors a and b. For simplicity, assume further that P^* and R^* equal zero and that prices and interest rates are related to each other inversely.[8] Thus, we have:

$$W(P,R) = aR^2 + bP^2 \tag{6'}$$
$$P = c - dR. \tag{7}$$

(7) is a constraint. It says that prices fall as interest rates rise. Their exact relationship depends on unknown positive constants c and d. Both P and R appear in the objective function (6'), but they are not independent of each other because of (7).

The optimization problem is simple. Many combinations of P and R are consistent with the constraint (7). One of these combinations of P and R will give a smaller value for (6') than any other. A rational authority faced with a choice would choose the combination of prices and interest rates giving the largest value of welfare or the smallest value of W. Finding that smallest value of (6') subject to the constraint (7) is called *constrained optimization*.[9] To optimize subject to a con-

7. Loss functions measure distress or negative values of utility. Thus, the problem becomes minimizing loss rather than maximizing utility.

8. We ignore here the extra problem that if prices are measured by an index including interest rates that there must be direct association between the two. Rather we assume that raising interest rates will contract economic activity and thereby lower prices. The example only illustrates the method.

9. An important point to note is what Theil calls the "inconsistency problem." Recall that utility or welfare—W in (6)—is affected by the extent that values of R and P deviate from "ideal" values which policymakers have for those variables. In general the optimal decision $R°$ for R is not equal to R^* for the simple reason that $P^* \neq c - dR^*$. If this inequality did not hold, the problem would not be one of *constrained* optimization, and policymakers would shoot straight for their ideal values, which would be attainable. The essence of the economic constraint is the implication that all ideal values are not simultaneously attainable, and thus the optimal decision may be thought of as an *optimal compromise* between R^*, P^*.

straint in simple cases, one can substitute the right-hand side of the constraint $(c - dR)$ for P in the objective function $(6')$ and choose the value of R which minimizes that function. So the problem is simply to choose R to minimize:

$$W = aR^2 + b(c^2 + d^2R^2 - 2cdR).$$

Differentiate with respect to R and set equal to zero:

$$\frac{dW}{dR} = 2aR + 2bd^2R - 2bcd = 0$$

rearranging:

$$R = \frac{bcd}{a + bd^2}.$$

If desired, we could now find the value of P that will result from this decision by substituting this expression for optimal R into (7), since P is a target, not an instrument. In more complicated cases, one proceeds by what is known as the method of Lagrangean multipliers.[10] The optimal value for the interest rate depends on *all* of a, b, c, and d. The

10. Here, one would set up the Lagrangean expression:

$$L = aR^2 + bP^2 - \lambda(c - dR - P)$$

where λ is the undetermined Lagrange multiplier. Minimize L with respect to R, P, and λ. The first-order conditions are:

$$\frac{\partial L}{\partial R} = 2aR + \lambda d \quad = 0$$

$$\frac{\partial L}{\partial P} = 2bP + \lambda \quad\quad = 0$$

$$\frac{\partial L}{\partial \lambda} = c - dR - P = 0$$

These three equations in three unknowns may be solved by substitution for R, P, and λ. The solution for R is $R = \dfrac{bcd}{a + bd^2}$ as above.

The solution for P is $P = \dfrac{ac}{a + d^2b}$.

The optimal value for R is positive because all the constants are defined as positive; and the optimal value is a minimum since the second derivatives of L with respect to P and R are both positive.

optimal decision thus reflects not only the parameters of the objective function representing preferences but also the parameters of the constraint. This is also a problem when inferring preferences from reaction functions. Notice also that in this specific case the optimal value of the instrument R is *uniquely* determined by the parameters of this "one instrument/one target" system. In more general cases it will depend on the values of the entire set of instruments and targets.

MORE COMPLEX VARIATIONS ON THE BASIC MODEL

This example can be extended in four ways. One recognizes that governments have more than one target of policy and more than one instrument. The second incorporates the existence of uncertainty. The third extension is the calculation of optimal instrument levels with regard to the values of the targets not only in the present period but over a longer time span. The final extension treats the underlying problem as one of maintaining an "inventory" in the face of uncertain demand.

The Extension to Many Variables

The problem is never as simple as the previous example. The authorities must at least be concerned about other targets like unemployment. Unemployment may be related in some way to the level of prices.[11] The objective function would thus contain a further variable, unemployment, and the constraint should contain an extra equation relating unemployment and prices (and perhaps interest rates). A full model of the economy (constraint) as well as any statement of preferences (objective function) will contain many variables. Nevertheless, this only changes the algebra and associated notation. For compactness, we need to employ matrix notation. Theil's model for the static case has m real-valued controlled (instrument) variables

11. Most economists would question the assumption of a stable long-run trade-off between unemployment and inflation. This does not mean that the relationship can be omitted. Rather, it becomes even more important to specify some relationship, probably involving expectations.

$x = (x_1, \ldots, x_m)$ and n real-valued uncontrolled (target) variables $y = (y_1, \ldots, y_n)$. The authority has a quadratic (for computational convenience) objective function defined over all $m + n$ variables:

$$w(x,y) = a'x + b'y + \tfrac{1}{2}(x'Ax + y'By + x'Cy + y'C'x) \qquad (6^*)$$

where the x and y actually represent deviations from ideals as in equation (6). The a and b are the intercepts of the marginal utility curves attaching to the instruments and targets, respectively. The matrix A contains parameters reflecting the change in the marginal utilities of each instrument with respect to changes in its own value and that of each other instrument. B does the same for targets so that, for example, the cost of one extra percent of unemployment is not independent of either the level of unemployment or the level of inflation. C gives the cross-product marginal utilities, denoting the extent to which the cost or benefit of a unit of any target depends on the levels of the instruments and vice versa.

The model also requires a constraint in the form of a linear equation system linking the y and x variables:

$$y = Rx + s. \qquad (7^*)$$

The matrix R contains the coefficients of the equations of the economic model, and s is all the associated constants and errors. Theil (1968, pp. 36–43) shows that (6^*) can be maximized subject to (7^*) with the resulting optimal x values for one period ahead depending on *all* of a, b, A, B, C, R, and s as well as the target value x^* and the target and actual values y^* and y. Again, the optimal decision rests on the parameters of *both* constraint and objective function.[12] The solution is of the form $x = f(x^*, y^*, y)$, which is the form of the reaction function.

Uncertainty

There is uncertainty about nearly all the parameters on which the optimal values x^o depend. It arises because the future must be estimated. Even the present values of some targets may not be known at

12. For a determinate solution to exist, a necessary condition is that there be at least as many independent instruments as there are targets. That is $m \geq n$.

the time decisions must be made. They need to be forecast. The goals or objectives on which the utility function depends may not be known to the forecasters. If the problem is treated as one of risk or probabilistic uncertainty, a solution may be reached by maximizing the expectation of the preference function. For one period ahead the solution is simple. Theil called this "certainty equivalence."

The Extension to Many Periods

However, many further problems arise if the authorities are trying to find a decision which is optimal over several future periods. First, a choice must be made on how far to discount outcomes further in the future. Second, some uncertainty reflects unexpected shocks, which occur in every period. The economic situation faced in the future will not be that which the authorities expected to face when decisions were made. This stochastic element of the economy presents the analyst with the serious dilemma of whether to model government decisions in terms of actual observed economic outcomes or in terms of the forecast values for these outcomes available at the time decisions were made. A dynamic economic model in which one of the variables in the constraint is a derivative or rate of change with respect to time complicates things further. An example is in Nordhaus (1975) where the constraint contains an equation for inflation, which is the rate of change of prices with respect to time. Multiperiod problems combining stochastic elements and dynamic constraints are called problems of *optimal control.* Their solutions define the optimal time paths of the instruments.

The Welfare Function as an Inventory Problem

The optimization model as it stands assumes that in any decision period the authorities will benefit by intervening. This is because intervention has no costs other than the direct welfare costs attaching to the targets and instruments of policy. But suppose we reconsider and assume instead that intervention is costly. Governments incur many costs when they intervene: their credibility may suffer, intervention may focus attention on the very problems they are trying to alleviate, and indeed many interventions require cooperation from others which will have to be paid for. In such cases, the optimal strategy may not be continuous optimization but rather sporadic interventions like those of Mosley's (1976) satisficing agents discussed in the last chapter.

This is an optimal decision-making strategy if the political authorities' problem is analogous to that of an entrepreneur who maintains an inventory to meet uncertain demand. Suppose the costs of carrying the inventory and of running out of stocks are convex (that is, characterized by increasing marginal costs). Suppose further that there is uncertainty attaching to demand for the product. Finally, assume that to reorder stock has both fixed and proportionate cost elements. Then, Arrow, Karlin, and Scarf (1958) show that the optimal strategy is not to reorder in every period. Rather it is to operate with two thresholds, an upper threshold S and a lower one s. If the inventory at any time is greater than s, no reordering is done. If the inventory is less than s, enough is ordered to bring it up to S. This result of the optimality of intermittent reordering rather than continuous updating holds even where there are delays in delivery.

A policymaker's inventory is the "capital stock" of good will required for the implementation of policies and the probability of being reelected. (Chapter 7 discusses models which treat popularity this way.) The good will stock depends on economic conditions during incumbency, which they can affect by economic intervention (reordering). Optimal policy then consists of intermittent policy changes if the assumptions of uncertain demand, convex carrying and shortage costs, and fixed reorder costs are reasonable characterizations of the politicians' situation.

The demand uncertainty is relevant in the political case if targets drift as when popular preferences vary over time. Shortage (insufficient stock) costs include the cost of losing the next election because some economic variable has gone beyond acceptable bounds. Fixed costs attaching to reorders (interventions) seems a particularly reasonable assumption. The costs of increasing the budget deficit in the United States include not only whatever electoral costs attach to the resulting deficit itself (variable costs) but also the transactions cost for the president of getting a bill through Congress. Similar fixed costs attach to dealings with strategic private sector agents like trade unions or the financial community. They arise when the goal is implementation or compliance with policy. Indeed, there may even be fixed popularity costs in intervening if intervention affects the credibility of government statements or popular concern over the state of the economy. Thus, under reasonable assumptions, such models of "satisficing" or intermittent intervention have more than descriptive appeal. They turn out to be optimal decision rules. The need to maintain the good will stock may still lead to intervention cycles in the economy which are political in origin but are no longer tied to the dates of elections.

The complexity of these models is increased by the need to specify the adjustment costs as well as the preferences. It is possible to make assumptions about the carrying/shortage costs, the probabilities of different levels of demand, and the reorder costs to derive the decision thresholds. However, it may be better to think of "satisficing" as optimal only "in principle." Empirical work should concentrate on whether such models actually offer good accounts of interventions. This will depend on the derivation of the decision thresholds, making the difficulty of inferring preferences from observable actions even greater.

REACTION FUNCTION MODELS

PROBLEMS OF INTERPRETATION

The optimizing model can be a tool for aiding a policymaker with quantifiable preferences to find the "best" decision satisfying certain constraints. Observed outcomes can also be treated as the results of optimal decisions, inferring from this what the preferences appear to have been (see, for example, G. D. MacRae, 1977). This inferential use of the optimizing model requires many assumptions and measurements in order to specify a model of the structure of the economy as well as preferences over all economic variables. Consequently, when poor results are achieved it is often unclear where the problem lies. Many use reaction functions to avoid specifying the entire economic model. A behavioral equation can be specified directly rather than by deducing behavior from a utility function and constraints. This specification also appears consistent with policy as incremental changes or partial adjustment rather than full optimization. Problems of interpretation unfortunately are not to be solved so simply.

Reaction Functions as a Special Case of Optimization

Pissarides (1972, p. 248) shows that if one solves (6*) subject to the constraint of (7*) above in order to isolate the optimal reaction x_i^o for any instrument x_i, the solution (where a, b, and C have been omitted) is

$$x_i^o = x_i^* + A^{-1}R'By^* - A^{-1}R'By. \tag{8}$$

In terms of (7), let $b_{ij} = A^{-1}R'B$; then (8) can be written

$$x_i^o = x_i^* + b_{ij}y^* - b_{ij}y. \tag{8*}$$

It is apparent that the optimal reaction (8*) and the simple reaction function (1) may be equivalent. They will be equivalent if and only if:

1. $x_i^* = b_1 x_{t-1}$; that is, the optimal values of the instruments are a constant fraction of last period's actual value for the instrument; and

2. $b_{ij}y^* = a$; that is, the ideal values for the targets are *constant*; that is, the goals of the authorities do not change with changing circumstances.

Thus, reaction functions like equation (1) above are not an ad hoc specification. The appropriate theoretical interpretation of the commonly estimated form of reaction functions is that they are a special case of the optimizing model. However, they are a special case which contains two hidden assumptions. One of these, the assumption that the ideal values of goals do not change, is highly restrictive. The difficulty of obtaining any information about politicians' ideal values may make this assumption inescapable. Both the connection between reaction functions and optimizing models and the extra assumptions in the reaction function model should be borne in mind when interpreting empirical results.

The Identification Problem

Reaction functions share a further practical problem of optimizing models. In order to reach the commonly estimated form (1) or (8*), b was set equal to $A^{-1}R'B$ in terms of (5*) and (6*). The coefficients of the targets in a reaction function thus *necessarily* contain the parameters of both the constraint (matrix R) and the objective function (A and B). This is why the coefficients of a reaction function do not directly give evidence about policymakers' preferences. The coefficients implicitly contain estimates of the parameters of both preferences and the economic constraint. *No inferences can be drawn about preferences* without first disentangling the underlying economic structural elements within the coefficients. The problem is that two things, preferences and constraint, are being estimated simultaneously from one piece of information. The terms of the constraint are needed to infer preferences. The preferences are needed to infer the constraint.[13]

Comparisons Across Time Periods and Countries

Even the simplest inferences about preferences become more difficult if comparative statements are made. Comparing weights on the same target across countries contrasts the parameters of the economic systems of these countries *as well as* the preferences of policymakers in those countries. Even within one country, the validity of comparing weights of two target variables at different times depends on the assumption that the trade-off between those two variables has been *stable* throughout the period. This limits using reaction functions to differentiate preferences of parties which succeed each other after long intervals, as in Germany in 1967 or Britain in 1964.

For example, directly comparing relative weights on inflation and unemployment assumes that the trade-off between inflation and unemployment *has not changed* in the period covered by the comparison. That assumption would be unjustified if the preferences of the British Labor government of the 1960s were contrasted with those of the Conservative government of the early 1970s. Comparison of prefer-

13. In a paper which is valuable for anyone considering reaction function estimates, Makin (1976) identifies a broad class of cases for which estimates of preferences can be separated out, given estimates of the underlying structural model. In general, whether there will exist a solution for the weights as ratios of each other depends on a number of factors, most notably (1) the number of targets and instruments in the system; (2) whether one includes cross-products in the objective function; that is, whether utility from target i depends on the state of target j; (3) whether one includes linear terms in the objective function; and (4) whether there exists a variety of relationships among present and lagged values of targets and/or instruments to help constrain the system.

ences between two incumbencies requires at least some formal stability tests on the constraints between those two incumbencies. This problem can only grow larger as more complex inferences are sought.

PROBLEMS OF APPLYING REACTION FUNCTIONS TO POLICY ANALYSIS

Hypotheses about political effects on economic policy are easy to graft onto reaction functions. Economists have typically estimated reaction functions over short enough periods to obtain stable and meaningful estimates of the behavior of the authorities. By contrast, political analyses seek causes of changes in the weights in reaction functions. The dynamics of these weights are used to test hypotheses about the impact of political conditions on economic outcomes. All the major models of Chapter 5 translate directly into hypotheses about the weights on economic targets in reaction functions. The weights may shift at election times if incumbents use policy instruments to support and defend their interests. Policy may change with the composition of ruling coalitions or as new interests are mobilized into political conflict. This requires clear description of governing coalitions and clear hypotheses about the expected consequences of coalition changes. Partisan changes are easily incorporated if they are not too frequent. Others—like the hypothesized dominance of status-quo-oriented interests in fragmented party systems or the preference for conservative policies arising from the privileged position of an independent central bank—are less easy to manage.

Fragmentation

Are policy objectives well defined? Does a uniquely defined objective function exist? *Fragmentation* describes political structural aspects of these questions. Party systems are fragmented if there are many parties and if forming stable majority coalitions is difficult (D. Mac-Rae, 1962). A government structure with very low levels of fragmentation is one with a unitary state, a weak parliament with high levels of party discipline, and a strong bureaucracy dominated by a cohesive elite resistant to interest group pressure. High levels of fragmentation are involved in a federal state, a separation-of-powers national government with weak political parties, or a divided bureaucracy subject to pressure from interest groups and the legislature.

The extent of fragmentation may differ with respect to spending decisions and taxing decisions. Consequently, either spending or taxing is more likely to be an instrument of policy than, say, the deficit. Certainly, the degree to which the deficit really constitutes an instrument of policy will vary from setting to setting. It is frequently argued that the process of adjusting revenues in the United States is less fragmented than the process of controlling expenditures, though adjusting tax rates is still a problem (Pechman, 1977; Okun, 1970). Therefore, policy responses may come more through taxes than spending. This certainly seems to be the case in Britain.

Fragmentation also affects policy timing. There is a lag between recognition of an economic condition and the response to it. Economists sometimes refer to this as the "inside lag" or "response lag." In general, the lower the degree of fragmentation, the lower should be the observed response lag. Various devices for nationwide bargaining may overcome the lags due to fragmentation. Such corporatist bargaining may facilitate contingent agreements about future policy. This, in turn, may permit a rapid policy response. Empirical studies must be careful not to overstate the actual level of fragmentation by ignoring corporatist devices.

Institutional Change

How can reaction functions handle structural changes in decision-making institutions? "Environment" changes alter the outcomes being forecast and acted upon by policymakers. Therefore, they also affect decision rules and behavioral relationships. Three types of changes in decision processes include adoption of a rule for the use of an instrument, emergence of a new instrument which may or may not be controlled, and regime changes which alter the actual instruments of economic policy.

1. Rule-following. What happens when policymakers follow a rule? *Rule-following* means, for example, that the money supply should grow by a fixed percentage each period or that the budget should balance. The rules affect the reaction function framework because the authorities' *discretion* is removed. The impact of rule-following depends on whether the rule which is followed exists for the "actual" instrument or not and whether it is assumed that the rule is exactly followed or exists as a guide or norm.

There are three possibilities. (1) If the rule is *for the actual instrument* and is exactly followed, then that instrument is no longer the dependent variable of a reaction function but becomes *exogenous*. It takes its place in the constraint as a limit on the scope for maneuver with respect to other variables. (2) If the rule is for the instrument but is not exactly followed, the reaction function can be estimated for deviations of the instrument around the rule. Each period's deviation from the rule is taken to be a function of the previous period's deviation from the rule plus other targets, and so on. (3) If the rule is *not for an actual instrument,* then, whether or not it is followed, a reaction function for the actual instrument can be estimated. It uses the information about the rule to measure the "ideal" points of the targets. Reactions for monetary instruments should be measured relative to the fluctuations of the money supply around its stated target rates of monetary growth (see McClam, 1978). The rules in this case are a guide; the information should be used, but policy is still discretionary.

2. Evolution and learning. Less tractable are cases where the available instruments change over time, where the working of an actual instrument adapts or changes, or where the government becomes aware of new theoretical developments. An example is the growth of an open market in government securities in Japan. The actual instruments of monetary policy in Japan since the late 1940s include various sorts of quantitative ceilings on interbank lending and bank liabilities. An open market in long-term government debt began to emerge after the large government deficits of the mid-1970s. There is no evidence that the government has begun to use this market seriously to control the money supply (see Royama, 1980), but the market is now available to a limited extent to private banks. It enables partial evasion of government controls. This presumably weakens the links between money supply growth and the actual instruments of policy. Unless the authorities compensate for this growth of the open market, parameters of a money supply reaction function would change. It is difficult to specify a priori what form these shifts would take. Even so, shifts in the reaction function coefficients would have little to do with changing intentions or preferences of the authorities.

3. *Regime changes.* The third problem is common, though more tractable. Consider the impact of a regime change, such as the shift to floating exchange rates. Some variables become discretionary, for example, foreign exchange intervention. This is the mirror image of the effect of adopting a rule, which removes an instrument of policy. In either case, the analyst should estimate a different function before and after the regime change. Regime changes may also alter the targets of policy. For example, currency reserves were probably a target of policy in Britain up to the change to floating exchange rates but not after.

Outcomes and Intentions

Reaction function estimates inevitably rely on "ex post" measurements of how things turned out. Inferring why policymakers acted as they did is hampered by the extent to which an outcome differs from what was expected or intended. This means more than that policy may be made consistently on the basis of wildly inaccurate forecasts. Not all apparent "reactions" reflect deliberate discretionary choice. Many large changes in the targets and instruments of policy arise "automatically" rather than through choice. An example is the decline of revenue in a period in which national income declines. Economists refer to such changes as *automatic stabilizers.* A reaction function cannot always distinguish this shift from one which is a deliberate discretionary response. Some instruments, like government consumption expenditures, do not have automatic components. If these expenditures vary with unemployment, the variation must be discretionary. The same is not true in the case of personal transfer payments because of the "automatic" rise in payments to the unemployed. A further example is *fiscal drag,* the tendency for revenue to rise as inflation drives personal incomes into higher income tax brackets. Is this discretionary policy in the sense of a deliberate decision? The answer hinges on whether policymakers are conscious of the consequences of inaction, that is, leaving tax brackets unchanged.

Instrument Availability

Errors arise in estimating the same reaction function in two countries because an instrument available in one country may be unavailable in the other. For instance, the use of open market operations as a monetary policy instrument requires a substantial private market for government securities. Some countries, notably Japan and France, have not had such a market through most of the postwar period. This rules out the possibility that open market operations could be an instrument of monetary policy. The meaning of interest rates in reaction functions will vary according to whether or not the central bank undertakes open market operations. Black (1981) gives examples of the diversity of instruments which must be chosen to represent monetary policy in different countries.

The fact that an instrument is available is not evidence that it is actually used. Selection of some targets (or rules) effectively removes some potential instruments from use. Thus, a decision to peg exchange rates excludes the domestic money supply from consideration as an independent target. Floating exchange rates free the money supply as a target (McClam, 1978; Volcker, 1977; Bryant, 1980). Policymakers themselves may have preferences about which instruments to use. American policymakers prefer not to use instruments of direct control such as selective credit allocation. The use of such instruments in France is not merely a reflection of the technical fact of their availability. Reaction function estimates can demonstrate only that something is not systematically used as an instrument, through the absence of systematic relationships with identifiable targets of policy. Reaction functions give no political insight into why some available instruments are not used, and political scientists must study this in other ways.

On-Off Policies

Not all policy choices can be easily modeled in the reaction function framework. Use of some instruments is reflected in discrete changes. Some policies, like price and wage controls, are either off or on. Estimation methods for categorical dependent variables may capture the on-off nature of their effects (Black, 1981). Some instruments are used only once, so these techniques do not help. An example from U.S. monetary policy is the use of special reserve requirements against money market mutual funds and against credit accounts imposed in October 1979 but since removed. The actions were unusual, but the controls were important in restraining the economy. Models must allow for such discrete events whether or not more than ad hoc procedures are available for dealing with them.

The Lucas Critique

Implicit in the reaction function approach is the view of the policymaker as sitting *outside* the economy pulling strings. Reaction functions presume that there is some systematic and stable relationship between the state of various parts of the economy and which string gets pulled and by how much. Lucas's (1976) "Critique of Econometric Policy Evaluation" raises the implications of the New Classical school of macroeconomics discussed in Chapter 3. The actors in the economy can learn about and anticipate the behavior of policymakers. As a result, a specific policy may have different effects at different times. In the optimizing framework this means that the constraints, the structural and behavioral relationships which describe the economy, cannot be taken as given independent of the values of the instruments chosen.

Two considerations reduce the force of this criticism somewhat. First, the interdependence of instrument and constraint is a matter of degree. For major policy changes it may be a serious problem, though no worse than the general problem of handling shocks, such as the oil crisis. In "normal" times interdependence may be of little importance. Second, adequate models must incorporate the efforts of actors and policymakers to learn about and anticipate each other's behavior. This is a further source of complexity, but not fatal to the optimizing framework itself.

SUMMARY

Reaction functions are the principal tool available for empirical economic policy analysis. We hope to encourage their use. At the same time, sophisticated and careful use of reaction functions requires appreciation of their limits. The main points that we have tried to establish are:

1. Virtually all forms of reaction function can be understood in the context of a policy optimization framework.

2. The coefficients commonly estimated in reaction functions reflect both the effects of the objectives of policymakers and the influence of structural constraints. Separating these two effects requires extra effort.

3. There are limits to the variety of political, institutional, and environmental *changes* that can be analyzed, particularly if the changes are concurrent or interact in complex ways. The technique is thus no substitute for familiarity with the workings of economic and policymaking institutions. Such knowledge is a prerequisite for the successful application of reaction functions to the study of economic policy.

CHAPTER SEVEN

The Economics of Voting

The analysis of economic policy is incomplete if the goals of policymakers are inferred without considering the interaction between the economy and the objectives of the electorate. Economic conditions have some impact on popular evaluations of incumbent governments. Evidence comes from surveys and voting results. People respond positively to governments under which they have prospered, measured by real personal disposable (net of taxes) incomes and possibly by unemployment and inflation. Many features of this simple observation require elaboration. Two questions predominate. First, do voters evaluate candidate promises or past performance when deciding about voting? Whatever the answer, how large is the role of observed economic (as opposed to noneconomic) conditions in this evaluation? The choice-theoretic or economic analysis of voting provides models in which to answer these questions. The issues raised by the economic theory of voting are relevant to broader concerns of electoral behavior and indeed of the representativeness and responsibility of governments.

As a typical example, Fair (1978) presents this equation for the vote share V_t of the Democratic candidate for U.S. president from 1916 to 1976:

$$V_t = 34 + 1.2\Delta Y_t + 0.7T_t + 3.5I_t + u_t \tag{1}$$

with all coefficients statistically significant and a standard error of 4 percent, which corresponds to explanation of about 70 percent of the variance in vote shares. There is a long-run time trend T in favor of the Democrats and an incumbency advantage I_t which adds 3.5 percent to either party's vote share when an incumbent ran for reelection.[1] Each percentage point of growth in real per capita GNP (ΔY_t) in the election year adds (symmetrically, subtracts if GNP shrank or the Republicans were in office) 1.2 percentage points to the Democratic share of the vote. This result is typical because economic conditions are found to have significant effects, though noneconomic factors are also important, and considerable variance is left unexplained. Fair's results are atypical in that they are estimated in the context of a particularly rich "retrospective" model. This allows testing rather than the assumption of a number of things to be discussed below. These include the lagged effects of past performance, effects of past performance of the presently nonincumbent party, and asymmetrical effects between good and bad times.

Similar results have been obtained for at least nine countries including the United States, Britain, France, West Germany, Australia, Japan, Denmark, Sweden, and Norway.[2] In general, lower inflation, lower unemployment, and higher rates of growth of disposable income increase popular support for incumbent elected politicians. Related models have been proposed for Switzerland and some Eastern European countries. Such studies confirm well-established ideas like the greater aversion of the Germans to inflation and the greater tolerance of Americans than the British for high levels of unemployment. However, diverse model specifications make comparisons difficult. The two principal findings are, first, that economic variables explain a minor share (perhaps a third, maybe half in a few cases) of the variation in popular support; and, second, that the results display considerable instability,

1. Fair's model also includes a test for advantage attributable to a candidate's personality independent of incumbency, which we mention below. We do not present t-statistics for the coefficients above since they represent combinations of separately estimated parameters.

2. For the purpose of this discussion we treat opinion poll results on vote intention and actual vote shares as (at least asymptotically or conceptually) equivalent. Good systematic reviews of the literature are readily available (Monroe, 1979; Paldam, 1981).

even within countries and over fairly short periods. Their instability, which means that estimated coefficients change from sample to sample, is the more troubling result.

The fact that economic variables do not explain more variance is readily understandable. First, economic conditions do not exhaust the political agenda, though there are places and times (like Britain in recent years) where they nearly do. Second, where the data are survey-based, they are subject to considerable measurement and sampling error. Third, as we shall see below, attempts to capture a variety of trends, cycles, and shocks are often arbitrary. Since the economic variables contain some of the same trends and cycles, they compete with these "exogenous" factors and obtain a reduced share of the explained variance.

Why should the results be so unstable? Part of the problem may be technical. Big differences in estimates can result from seemingly small differences in model specification, estimation techniques, and the definition of variables. Another problem may be preference cycles in the electorate. Paldam (1981) points out that if people prefer different parties on different issues, the overall level of support will change back and forth over time between the parties as the relative salience of different issues changes. Thinking about the problem this way stresses how mass opinion responds to the structure of the agenda set by competing strategic politicians. They will change the focus of public discussion to suit their electoral positions. Finally, one might go further and ask how the agenda is set. This means elaborating the impact of the media and spectacular or dramatic events on the public. All this suggests that the rewards will be greater from thinking more about the models and the voters' use of information than from studying more countries or perhaps searching for the marginal effects of a few more economic variables.

The fact that the relationship between economic conditions and political evaluation is unstable should not be a surprise. Look at the problem as one of information. What information about the economy is available? How is it obtained? How long are memories? How is conflicting information reconciled? If aspects of economic policy can be identified that should give rise to stable preferences or demands for a given social structure, progress could be made toward a stable model. We need a theory of the *demand*[3] for economic outcomes and a theory of *information* usage.

Two alternative types of choice theoretic model of economic influences on voting will be discussed. These are *policy* and *retrospective* models. The economic approach to voting is first defined. Then the basic properties of policy and retrospective models are outlined. In the latter, two important features are emphasized: the existence of hypothetical alternatives and the rationality of retrospective voting. The distributive impact of economic policy is considered as an element of demand for outcomes. Information requirements affect political evaluation both in content—knowledge, memory, myopia, the role of the media—and standards—collective criteria and thresholds. Finally, there is a discussion of shocks and cycles in the context of causality.

THE ECONOMICS OF VOTING

The "economic" theory of voting holds that voting is a choice between alternative candidates and that people make that choice by estimating what their "expected" utility might be under the alternative possible incumbencies. They choose (vote for) the candidate who offers the largest expected utility. The voter's decision is rationally self-interested in the sense that the voter makes efficient use of available information. The economic theory of voting does *not* presume that economic conditions are dominant determinants of voting. However, it would be surprising if they did not have some influence in a period when economic issues are widely held to be important and economic conditions commonly held to be the responsibility of governments.

The economic approach to voting is distinct from other approaches, including sociological and psychological approaches. The former discuss the voting behavior of social, ethnic, regional, or similarly defined groups. The latter treat voting as an affirmation of support or as the product of internal mental drives and desires. By contrast, the eco-

---

3. We mean demand here in the economic sense of preferences backed up by a currency (votes).

nomic approach treats the vote decision as the outcome of an explicit cost-benefit calculation. Within the economic theory of voting, what people actually consider in forming their estimates of expected utility is a matter to be determined empirically. Such a calculation is not confined to personal income considerations, though it would be odd if these were absent. Similarly, other economic considerations like inflation and unemployment may influence the calculation. Non-economic considerations such as the probability of war and peace also have a role. The theory demands only that there be a calculation about what will be the case in the future under the contending alternative candidates. Since expectations of utility are required, the next question is, "how are these expectations formed?"

Two pieces of information are available: what the candidates say they will do and what they have done in the past. There will be no information on candidates who have not served before. They may be closely identified with well-known political parties and their policies, which can serve as a substitute for information about the candidates in such cases. Contending approaches allow this sort of information to play different roles.

In *policy* models, electors choose candidates on the basis of what candidates say they will do if elected. Policy models focus on preferences of the electorate and whether a "median voter" exists. Assume an issue for which alternatives can be set out along a linear scale, such as the amount to be spent on some project. The median voter is the one whose preference is such that half the electorate prefer more and half the electorate prefer less. It was proved many years ago that if all electors had single-peaked preferences, then the preference of the median voter on a single issue is a stable policy outcome under majority rule. More complex models may have no such policy implications. When more than one issue is considered at a time, it becomes likely that there will be no unique ordering of possible outcomes that is the preference of a majority, so no stable equilibrium can be reached. How far control of the agenda (the order of voting on proposals) produces control over eventual outcomes where there is no dominant or stable equilibrium outcome is a major concern of recent public choice research (McKelvey, 1979; Shepsle and Weingast, 1982).

Policy models become "spatial" when positions on issues are treated as locations. Most spatial modeling has concentrated on the behavior of the candidates rather than on the electorate. Downs (1957) introduced the assumption that candidates are only interested in winning elections. Candidates formulate policies (promises) to win elections rather than win elections to implement a policy program. This plus the assumption that candidates comprehend perfectly the electoral consequences of any policy they adopt implies that competing parties will converge on promising the same policy on any single issue. The promise is the policy preferred by the median voter.[4] Provided there is a median voter, this result is quite robust. It holds even with further assumptions of programatic parties and uncertainty about the electoral consequences of chosen policies.

When there is no median voter, there will be no convergent platform guaranteed to defeat all others. Candidates would not have clear best strategies, and competing platforms would cycle indeterminately. If a candidate can trap an incumbent whose platform must be consistent with his past actions in office, there are again theoretical grounds for some convergence (Kramer, 1977). Further problems arise empirically if candidates cannot only offer promises of what they intend to do but also make claims about what the other has done. We return to this in the treatment of retrospective models.

Popularity functions are rarely policy models because competing parties do not continuously make appeals and propose agendas. This does happen at election times, but then there are few solid measurements of the electorate's preference structure and considerable uncertainty about candidates' foresight. This makes it difficult to detect whether electors are responding to competing policy packages. Jacobson and Kernell (1981) argue that the economy has an effect on the strategies of candidates. Good times discourage challengers—other things being equal—and incumbents design campaign spending strate-

---

4. One set of results deals with testing for the dominance of the preferences of the median voter in appropriate institutional circumstances. These tests are complicated to construct, but, for example, when expenditure decisions (a good case for one-dimensional ordering of single-peaked preferences) are considered in the context of direct democratic decisions (or possibly representation with subsequent referenda), median voter preferences are found to be carried out.

gies to maximize the image of economic competence they can project. The decentralized American party system diminishes the identification of a party with a particular ideology since parties attempt to be "catch-all" organizations appealing to as broad a section of the public as possible. It is also less likely where parties have highly variable records on particular policies. A series of recent models by Jackson (1975), Page and Jones (1979), Budge and Farlie (1977), and Markus and Converse (1979) all suggest reciprocal links between issues, partisanship, and popular preferences for candidates. The Markus-Converse model suggests that people are as likely to change their ideas on issues toward those of a warmly evaluated candidate as to change their candidate evaluation. All the models link long-term partisan feelings and positions on particular issues.

There are reasons to extend the two-party competitive model. Candidates have incentives to make their proposals ambiguous to appeal to as wide a range of opinion as possible (Shepsle, 1972). They will also delay taking positions as long as possible to avoid being outflanked by opponents. As a result, electors may not be convinced by candidates' popular appeals. Convergence is sometimes an unappealing strategy. A challenger may find it preferable to dissociate himself from the incumbent in hard times, letting the incumbent have all the blame for the bad times. This introduces a new element: the use of observations of performance to inform judgments about candidates' promises. Following Downs, we define policy models to allow observed performance to inform electors' judgments of the reliability of promises. To go further and allow observed performance to inform the expectations or utility judgments directly produces a different model: *retrospective voting*.

RETROSPECTIVE VOTING

In the retrospective approach, judgments about future utilities derive more or less directly from the performance in office of competing candidates or of previous incumbents of the candidates' parties. It jettisons the central assumption of the policy model, that judgments about future utilities are derived from the stated positions of competing candidates. Popkin et al. (1976) argue that the "public" nature of the goods that politicians provide and the costs of being informed about issues lead voters to use predictions of actual performance instead. These are derived from observation of "competence" in office and emphasize information which voters pick up "free" as part of their daily lives.

The most accessible retrospective model is Fiorina's (1981). His model, like those of Fair (1978) and Hibbs (1982a, 1982b), has three basic features:

1. The voter's decision is made by assessing developments (often, but not necessarily, economic) during an incumbency and assigning the credit or blame for these to the candidate or party in power. The evaluation of *observed performance* is a comparison between the incumbents' inherited situation and subsequent developments.

2. Voters can compare incumbents' performance with a hypothetical view of how well other candidates or parties might have fared in office at the time.

3. Discount weights are assigned to past and future events. Uncertainty discounts hypothetical calculations and future promises. Memory, or the rate at which people forget, discounts past performance.

Support thus depends on how well a party is perceived to perform in office, (1) discounted by how long ago this took place, (2) net of how well a competitor might have performed if in office at the time, and (3) discounted by the reliability of expectations based on past performance.

THE HYPOTHETICAL ALTERNATIVE

The *hypothetical* alternative to which the performance of the incumbent is compared is a big innovation of retrospective models. Fiorina describes it as a possible feature of voters' calculations which can be downplayed. In time-series models of approval and voting (Hibbs, 1982a, 1982b; Fair, 1978) party-specific memories provide the hypothetical alternative. Each successive incumbent's performance is accumulated, subject to the effects of limited or decaying memories. When there is a change of incumbency, the new out-party's performance record is frozen. It continues to be further discounted as it slips further into the past. This gives a general model:

$$V_t = d_{t-i} \cdot \sum_{i=1}^{\infty} g^i Z_{t-i} \tag{2}$$

where V_t denotes vote or approval ratings, Z is a set of economic conditions or other indicators of retrospectively observed performance, d_{t-i} alternates between $+1$ and -1 to indicate which of two parties was incumbent at time $t-i$, and g is a memory decay parameter (valued between 0 and 1) raised by one power for each period further into the past. (Fair's time periods are whole incumbencies rather than months or quarters.) After an election when party control changes, the accumulated performance of the out-party "reverses sign." The bad things for which it was blamed (for example, war, unemployment, inflation) are now credits for the new administration. The "out" party's good points (real growth) are debits to the new administration. The record of the nonincumbent party does not change while it is out of office,[5] though memory fades and the assessment of the new incumbent becomes more completely based on its own record.

For these hypothetical calculations to matter, three things must be true. First, the hypothetical calculation of one party's ability must not be simply a reflection or extrapolation of the perceived performance of the incumbents. Second, the performance of the incumbents should be affected by events which occurred within their incumbency, but these events should not affect the hypothetical ability of the opposition. Third, both sorts of calculation should enter into subsequent partisan evaluations. Is there any evidence for the existence of such hypothetical calculations? There have been both aggregate studies and surveys of individuals. Where aggregated models containing a hypothetical term are compared with models excluding the hypothetical term, the evidence does not distinguish between them (Hibbs and Vasilatos, 1981).

---

5. The hypothetical alternative, the guess about how challengers might have done if in office, is not really "hypothetical" if it is based only on challengers' accumulated previous performance. It becomes truly "hypothetical" if electors also make guesses about possible performance independent of this accumulated past.

The American surveys used by Fiorina do not contain any direct measures of such hypothetical calculations.

One British survey can be used to construct such a test. Alt (1983) analyzes assessments of Conservative performance in 1974 on the issues of prices and strikes. Electors were asked how well they felt the Conservative government had handled these problems and how well the Labor opposition would have handled them had they been in office at the time. There was not a close relationship between the perceived competence of the Conservatives and the hypothetical competence of the Labor party: one was not an extrapolation of the other. Events during their incumbency clearly affected evaluation of the Conservatives' ability. People placed on the three-day work week (ordered by Conservative Prime Minister Heath during a miners' strike) had a lower opinion of the Conservatives' ability. Their hypothetical opinion of the competence of the Labor party was not affected by these events. Partisanship changed in intensity and direction as much through hypothetical evaluation of nonincumbents as the perceived competence of the present incumbents. This aspect of retrospective models passes a prima facie test.

Including the "hypothetical alternative" will have little effect on findings for countries like Germany, France, and Japan, whose recent history has been largely under incumbents of one party, or bloc, for long periods of time. The effect of deducting approval of the losers' past performance is discounted by the amount of time passing since they were in power. In the case of Germany, the three-year Grand Coalition lasted long enough to allow most memories of Christian Democrat (CDU) "performance" before 1967 to fade. The Social Democrats' popularity when they formed the government after 1970 was largely unaffected by the comparison with earlier CDU performance.

RATIONALITY OF RETROSPECTIVE VOTING

In practice, policy and retrospective models represent two ways of making a vote decision. Policy voting exists to the extent that electors derive expected future benefits from policy promises. Observations of past performance appear principally as estimates of the reliability of promises. Retrospective voting downplays promises, and expectations of the future are based on extrapolation from past experience. The elector's problem is to evaluate content and reliability of these two sorts of information, available in varying degrees to everyone. The analyst's problem is to determine which strategy electors have chosen and why.

Retrospective voting will be more attractive where candidates' promises are ambiguous, whether for strategic reasons or because of the complexity of issues. Ambiguity is most likely in times of peace and prosperity. All candidates want to be associated with the status quo and therefore say similar things, as long as they assume the electorate sufficiently risk-averse not to gamble for even more by trying the "out" party in good times. Ambiguity is unlikely in times of depression and unpopular wars, for no one wishes to be associated with the status quo, and different candidates stress alternative means out of it.[6]

The attraction of retrospective voting also rests on characteristics of party and electoral systems rather than on the nature of the times or the strategy of politicians. It requires an identifiable alternative for whom to vote in the case of an unpopular incumbent. If real multiparty systems make it difficult to identify the alternatives, retrospective voting is inhibited. Disliking an incumbent's performance does not directly imply favoring a particular opposition party. Most multiparty systems rest on and reflect a complex set of underlying social cleavages and differing views about some central areas of public policy. Where these cleavages are durable, parties will be closely identified with policies (both in the past and in future promises) which supporters of some other parties would find difficult to support.

Parties do sometimes undertake policies which ignore their core supporters' interests both in two-party and multiparty systems. The British Labor government abandoned a full employment target between 1974 and 1979 in favor of a Monetarist approach to economics

6. There is no necessary relationship between one's evaluation of war versus peace (ends) and one's evaluation of performance with respect to appeasement versus brinkmanship (means). The choice of model does not rest on a means-ends distinction, for it is possible to make promises about future conduct with respect to either means or ends and, indeed, to like or dislike past performance with respect to either.

and an insistence on curing inflation first. The desertion of Labor by its traditional core supporters, noted as early as the 1960s, was evident in its defeat in the 1979 election (Finer, 1980). Particularly in multi-party systems, parties may exist for long periods without offending their core supporters. Then they will be closely identified with a set of policies which benefit their supporters. In these circumstances, voter defections because of poor performance must be reduced by the clear distributional costs of the election of some other party. A supporter of a party which has deserted its long-term commitments may not defect if another party is likely to serve him even worse. However, defection may appear attractive as a strategy to reinstate the original policy. Resolving this dilemma depends on several things, which we discuss as features of retrospective voting.

CHARACTERISTICS OF RETROSPECTIVE MODELS

What do these models show which is relevant to economic policy formation? We need to know more about the economic policy preferences of electors in order to aggregate individuals into groups with consistent preferences, which could then be a core of policies to which parties would make long-term commitments. Whether aggregation along socioeconomic lines is possible requires that we know more about the distributional impact of policy. Do different groups have a *demand* for certain sorts of economic outcomes? Voter preferences will also depend on information. The following sections answer questions about voters' information, like How long do popular memories last? Do expectations of the future have a role in otherwise retrospective models? Do people require simple standards to make political evaluations? Do they consider their own well-being or that of a wider group?

DEMAND FOR ECONOMIC OUTCOMES

Retrospective models assume a demand for economic outcomes. However, not all electors have a common stake in all outcomes. An individual's stake in one economic outcome may conflict with other interests and preferences. The link between macroeconomic outcomes and definable social cleavages is not close enough to allow people to recognize the distributional consequences of particular policies easily. Political parties thus cannot neatly aggregate popular economic preferences. They could if they were single-purpose interest groups pursuing a specific policy on behalf of their members. This is true more or less of all the economic variables associated with retrospective models—unemployment, inflation, real incomes, government expenditures, and so on.

Unemployment is the target of policy most closely linked to support cleavages. In the United States and Britain, the costs of high unemployment tend to have been borne by manual workers and in particular by nonwhite racial minorities. Effects of inflation are more complex. Inflation lowers the real value of assets and incomes fixed in money terms. The sufferers do not fit neat social classifications. Inflation redistributes to those in debt from those in credit unless prevailing rates of interest are high enough to reflect expected inflation and the expectations are correct. The costly outcome is thus *unanticipated* inflation rather than just inflation. Inflation benefits those who correctly anticipate it when others do not either by holding assets whose price rises by at least as much as general prices or by accepting wage settlements which protect real incomes. The costs of inflation have to be seen as uncertainty and arbitrariness: uncertainty because inflation makes any economic or financial decision more risky than otherwise, and arbitrary because the actual distributional consequences of inflation are difficult to pin down and anticipate. The redistributional impact of inflation seems to be accidental rather than the deliberate outcome of policy.

The distribution of preferences for other economic outcomes is ambiguous for similar reasons. One might expect taxation or changes in government spending to appear in these functions in some form. Of course, taxes are already netted out if *disposable* income is the variable chosen. Moreover, if people are voting their interests as consumers, taxes per se should not matter as much as either disposable income or their net position with regard to aggregate government taxing and spending. It is a formidable task to establish the class impact of government taxing and spending or a rationale for the dislike of taxation per se. However, Pissarides (1980) finds that high taxes affect government popularity in Britain, and Hibbs and Madsen (1981) attempt to link tax revolts to a perception of differences between pretax and posttax incomes, though their evidence is not strong.

There are some popularity functions disaggregated by class. Hibbs (1982a, 1982b) shows (using the model discussed above) for the United States that the sensitivity to unemployment of government approval is greater within the ranks of the manual working class than in the middle class. Approval is more sensitive to inflation in the middle class than in the working class. In Britain, the impact of inflation is even across classes, though again the impact of unemployment is greater among manual workers. For example, a sustained increase of 2 percent in unemployment would cost a government over six percentage points of support among nonmanual workers, but only three percentage points among nonmanual workers. Other studies (Schneider, 1978) are consistent with the expected greater impact of unemployment on the working class, though in no cases are the differences between classes very large. Disaggregation does not greatly alter the fit of the models. Nevertheless, the view of public opinion as responding to personal experience of changing economic conditions is supported.

INFORMATION

Content: Knowledge and Communication

A satisfactory theory of retrospective voting requires accurate popular perceptions of performance. Accurate perceptions are most likely when people have collected the required information as part of their daily lives (Popkin et al., 1976). People's economic information is therefore likely to be narrow, though it could be quite detailed on a matter of immediate concern, like farm price supports to a farmer. However, most retrospective models have to be estimated on data aggregated over considerable numbers of individuals. Thus, a popularity function should only include variables whose values were known by a sizable proportion of the population. Where broad indicators measure the perceptions of large groups, anything could be the case.

People could vote on the basis of complete misinformation about the rate of inflation or whether the country was in a recession. Indeed, one of the principal aims of campaign propaganda is to represent the existing state of affairs in the way most beneficial to the candidate.

The extent of popular knowledge about the economy is not well known. It is probably characterized by some inaccuracy and by processes of slow adaptation to changing circumstances. Any major shock which passes through the system will have some effect contemporaneously and will continue to have some effect later. Partly this is because the dissemination of information may itself be slow. People are also not quickly convinced that some belief has become obsolete. Almost throughout the 1970s sizable majorities of Americans believed that the country was in a recession (from *Public Opinion,* various issues). These majorities were only moderately altered by considerable swings in real growth rates. This perception of lasting recession is not necessarily irrational. Actually, there was little or no growth in the real income of the average American during the decade. More importantly, perceptions of economic states like prosperity and recession need not move up and down instantaneously with changes in observable economic indicators.

The relationship of political popularity and real incomes exemplifies a related problem. It may be sensible to assume that people do not suffer from *complete* money illusion (perceive money incomes as real). But how accurately do people perceive the relationship between money incomes and inflation? Clearly, politicians have an incentive to stress real gains. The headline in a popular Conservative newspaper, "Wages: You're Still Ahead," toward the end of the February 1974 election campaign was an attempt to spread belief that wages under the Conservative incomes policy were still increasing faster than retail prices. Even though this was true, it is unlikely that many were convinced. Inflation was widely considered to be the most important problem facing the country and one for which the Conservative government was partly blamed. In fact, in spite of persistent real growth, a large majority of the public appears to believe that their incomes are consistently falling behind prices. Exaggerated popular perceptions of inflation are one of the reasons for this.

Even if perceptions are biased, movements in opinion can still respond to changes in the economy. Empirical work on price expectations suggests that the process of expectation formation, even among financial specialists, is not sophisticated (Mullineaux, 1980). There is evidence of learning by updating past expectations in the light of recent information about price movements. Movements in expectations relate to the observation of transitory shocks. Different individuals may have very different learning rules (Jacobs and Jones, 1980; Figlewski and Wachtel, 1981). The literature leaves three further issues open: from where people get their information (does it come from personal experience, interpersonal communication, or the media?), the nature of the process by which observations of economic change are transformed into evaluations of performance, and how long the memory of particular disturbances lasts.

To address the last issue directly, Hibbs's model—equation (2) above—includes a memory lag parameter. This is the rate at which people forget past economic experiences. One can thereby estimate the period over which any economic event contributes to approval ratings. Tests on quarterly data for the United States, Britain, and West Germany give memory parameter estimates in the range of 0.8 to 0.85. This implies that less than a fifth of influence is contemporaneous. Indeed only about half the total effect of any event is felt within the first year. The full effect lasts four or five years. This is consistent with the estimates derived from simpler formulations involving lagged dependent variables.[7] Most such estimates give memory parameters of

7. To see why this is so, one must know how to transform the infinite series into the simpler lag formulation. The transformation goes as follows. If

(1) $y_t = bx_t + cy_{t-1}$, then

(2) $y_{t-1} = bx_{t-1} + cy_{t-2}$.

Substitute (2) into (1):

$y_t = bx_t + c(bx_{t-1} + cy_{t-2})$ or
$y_t = bx_t + bcx_{t-1} + c^2y_{t-2}$.

By repeated substitution for the final term, ultimately

$$y_t = b\sum_{i=0}^{\infty} c^i x_{t-i}.$$

0.5 to 0.9. Indeed, the one case which finds no memory (Fair) uses four-year observation periods. This is about the likely limit of popular memory.

Moreover, an event need not have its maximal impact contemporaneously. Some conditions require communication before becoming widely known. The effect of a particular month's unemployment figure may have an impact on mass perceptions, which is mostly reflected in opinion after several months have passed (Monroe, 1980). In models which reequilibrate after shocks, economic conditions (inflation rate, unemployment rate) have fairly long "half-lives" (MacKuen, 1980). Economic news does not simply have an instantaneous impact on opinion and then disappear. Enduring impact reflects continuing media discussion. Whether the media not only provides the information but even structures public response to it depends on the trustworthiness of the source and the political issues under consideration.

Content: Expectations and Myopia

In retrospective models, voting is based on evaluations of past performances, with little role for independent calculations about the future. Recall from Chapter 5 that myopic voting was a prerequisite for a political business cycle. *Myopia* denotes *short-sightedness* rather than amnesia or forgetfulness. That is, voters are myopic whenever they are unable to anticipate policy outcomes systematically. Do forecasts or expectations enter into approval ratings or popularity? On the whole, it appears that prospective judgments of economic conditions are important. Using individual level survey data, Kuklinski and West (1981) find that economic expectations are better predictors of voting than are past observations. Other studies using aggregate survey measures of expectations as well as forecast values of economic series show consistent results. Does this mean voters are not myopic?

An answer depends on both the role of expectations in evaluation and what information is reflected in expectations. With regard to the first part, expectations themselves have two distinct roles in evaluation. One is in part the evaluative calculation itself. People may alter their approval of a government because of what they think is about to happen. An example is the unpopularity of a president attributable to the likelihood of recession in the near future. Second, expectations cushion the severity of subsequent shocks. That is, the contemporary impact of, say, a recession will be partly reduced by having been widely forecast. Thus, just as it is unanticipated inflation, which is most damaging, it is bad "surprises" which are most harmful to the incumbent government. A forecast of bad times only partly reduces the ultimate impact. Until it actually occurs, it remains an uncertain prospect. Its realization brings some further penalty.

Expectations could have some role and yet voters still be myopic. The second question was whether expectations are based on more than just past observations of whatever is being forecast. Fiorina includes expectations in his vote equation but estimates them from the same retrospective information that influences voting and partisanship. While this does show that expectations at least *partly* based on past observations are relevant, it provides no information about the myopia of the individual voter. Voters can be myopic under a number of different assumptions about how expectations are formed. The formation of expectations is most commonly represented by a first-order adaptive process. In such a scheme, expectations are changed by some fraction of the error made last time:

$$(E_t - E_{t-1}) = a(P_t - E_{t-1})$$

where E_t is the current expectation, E_{t-1} was the expectation last period, and P_t is the outcome of what was expected last period.

Voters are myopic if expectations are adaptively formed under a first-order scheme. Expectations depend on a series of past observation with exponentially declining weights.[8] Here, no matter how long memories are (that is, how far back the last observations in the series), voters will continue to be myopic. They cease to be completely myopic only when expectations reflect further information *systematically* related to the future outturn P_{t+1} which they are trying to forecast at time t. The literature on approval gives us no information on whether voters

8. In this case, $E_t = aP_t + (1 - a)E_{t-1}$, but $E_{t-1} = aP_{t-1} + (1 - a)E_{t-2}$ so that E_t can be set equal to $aP_t + a(1 - a)P_{t-1} + (1 - a)^2E_{t-2}$. But this last term can be cast into a form involving P_{t-2} and E_{t-3} and ultimately by recursion E_t is given by an infinite series of past values of P. Therefore, people forming their expectations adaptively actually use no information other than that contained in past values.

are myopic. Studies which use exponentially declining lag weights to generate forecasts are imposing a structure in which expectations must be myopic. The same sort of adaptive functional forms have been used to explain survey series of expectations. Here again, although past values clearly have something to do with expectation formation, the critical question is whether *other information* is also used to form the politically relevant expectations.

The myopic voter is a feature both of retrospective voting models and much of the political business cycle literature. Nevertheless, expectations may not be myopic. First, the analysis of media and event impact on attitudes can be extended to the case of expectations. Expectations could contain not only past observed values of whatever is being forecast but also awareness of what has appeared in the media about the relevant series such as the predictions of professional forecasters. Indeed, price expectations contain major transitory variations independent of the trend assumed by the adaptive model (Jacobs and Jones, 1980). Economic theory also gives grounds for expecting certain other information to systematically influence expectations. Thus, under Monetarist assumptions money growth as well as past inflation should influence expectations about prices. We are still a long way from a satisfactory understanding of expectations formation, and thus answers in this critical area are tentative.

Standards: Individual and Collective Judgments

Do people judge the economic performance of the incumbent government on the basis of their own well-being or that of some wider group? Voting behavior is linked to measures of performance unrelated to personal experiences, like the close link between support for incumbents and the business conditions index (Kinder and Kiewiet, 1981). Similar results are common. The question is whether this overturns the rational self-interest postulate fundamental to economic theories of voting.

The answer is "probably not" since the purpose of thinking about whether or not you (or others) have prospered is to inform a calculation about the future. This is true whether it is a direct calculation of party preference or an evaluation of the reliability of various promises.

In general, the answer turns on the relative availability and usefulness of two different sorts of information. It may well pay a voter to vote to avoid a general shambles even if he cannot discern the links which lead from government policies to his own condition. If it were thought that one party would produce 20 percent unemployment, it would be foolish not to weigh that more heavily in assessing employment prospects than one's present employment position. The decision turns on the cost or availability of relevant information. The media routinely present a steady flow of information about general conditions and about the link between these conditions and government policy. Cost-effective use of available information may dictate that one use information about general conditions in forming an expectation about how one is likely to fare under competing alternatives.

Standards: Thresholds and Satisficing

The characterization of the average elector as someone who scrutinizes the newspapers for economic statistics is deficient. Perhaps people vote for incumbents whose performance is "satisfactory" according to some simple standard (Kramer, 1971). People may respond only to economic changes which are particularly large, or exceed some threshold of perception, or diverge sufficiently from what they expect or have grown accustomed to. Some effort needs to be made to incorporate the likely limits on popular observations and reactions in a model of political evaluation. Is public evaluation of an economic condition contingent on what they have become accustomed to, or what they have come to expect, or what they believe can be achieved?

The impact on approval ratings of a 1 percent increase in inflation rates could not have been the same in 1960 (when average inflation in the United States or Britain was only 1 or 2 percent per annum) and in 1980 (when the average was closer to 15 percent). The marginal cost of an extra one percentage point of inflation in 1980 should thus be smaller than in 1960, and so the penalty in approval ratings should be less. Some standard is required against which performance can be judged. On the other hand, it may be that if inflation is 2 or 3 percent, no one cares which it is, and so the extra percent has no impact at all because no one is paying attention. This requires the specification of a threshold below which economic changes or conditions are imperceptible.

Standards and thresholds are usually modeled as functions of the observed conditions. Thus, Mosley (1978) creates a threshold model of political support which is an analogue of his model for politicians' behavior (see Chapter 5). By using time trends for inflation and unemployment, he isolates years in which each of these variables were "in crisis." Economic conditions are expected to show larger effects on popularity in crisis years. There are a number of problems with the analysis, such as the use of exogenous cycles and the definition of crises. But one finding which does come through clearly is the absence of any connection between popularity and economic conditions in noncrisis years. Another example is the idea that voters are more likely to punish incumbents for poor performance than to reward them for good. While a theoretical case can be made, there is little empirical evidence of asymmetric responses.

Standards are usually introduced by taking some average of past observations under the assumption that people come to expect more or less what they have perceived. Indeed, if past observations are weighted with an exponentially distributed lag scheme, then such measures turn out to be the same as expected levels under a simple adaptive model of expectation formation. Approval will respond principally to economic conditions in periods in which the conditions are changing rapidly and adaptive expectations fall behind. While estimates of such models do not always offer a greatly improved fit over simpler models, they offer better estimates of particular effects. A good case is the impact of inflation on popularity in Britain after 1974, where unprecedentedly high levels of inflation did not have an effect on popularity commensurate with that derived in periods of lower inflation.

Exogenous Information? Cycles and Shocks

Even the earliest opinion studies recognized that economic fluctuations could only offer a partial account of popularity. Popularity or approval ratings had both cycles and short-term disturbances or shocks unrelated to the economy. For example, the very different initial levels of support which different incumbents have brought with them are never explained. This explains a good deal of statistical variation in popularity levels through time, but the initial support level is generally treated as an unidentified sort of residual difference between incumbencies. Jacobson and Kernell (1981) find that some of these differences result from elite strategies in response to the economic climate. For example, hard times may induce some incumbents to retire, while more attractive challengers may stand and find financial support, all of which will affect the eventual results.[9]

Early studies of approval ratings noted a common cyclical pattern within incumbencies. Generally, the ratings decline over time.[10] One explanation rests on the argument that the president puts together a broad coalition of supporters at election time and is forced through subsequent policy decisions to alienate groups of previous supporters, thereby losing support (Mueller, 1970). It is unlikely that presidents would deliberately undertake policies which offend supporters, though conflicting demands interfere with the possibility of actually delivering on past promises. Policies which attract as much new support as they lose might be available, however.

Election campaigns stimulate considerable initial support for new presidents, some of which is inevitably lost (particularly if one is considering approval rather than vote intention ratings). For example, a president whose policies gain new converts from the opposition at the same rate as they lose previous supporters will show declining poll ratings as long as his initial rating was *more than half* his maximum potential support. This model of decline only involves a long-term equilibrium support level generated by constant gain and loss rates and a maximum theoretical level of support (Salert, 1978). Indeed, the general pattern of declining support under such assumptions is quite robust. It can appear even where the gain rate exceeds the loss rate, provided initial support was high enough. If this sort of model is

9. In a very clever piece of econometrics, Fair (1978) at least identifies what part of the residual variance could be attributed to the presence of the same candidates in more than one election, but the "candidate" effects he estimates are far smaller than the usually very large and unexplained interadministration differences others estimate.

10. A simple interelection cycle of decline in support is one autoregressive pattern. It is not, by any means, the only such pattern, and its predominant appearance among all possible autoregressive patterns deserves explanation.

empirically correct, a president could gain net support during an incumbency only by starting out with low levels of support.

The general retrospective model can explain cycles in support endogenously. Whatever inflation existed under the past regime will be counted to the *credit* of the new regime. As time moves on, the diminished weight on these past observations reduces the credit whereas the increased weight on recent observations (even if unchanged) reduces the present support level. Even if economic conditions remain unchanged under the new incumbent, his support will decline from initially high levels simply because his rating increasingly reflects his perceived responsibility for prevailing conditions. Thus, a new incumbent could increase support only if conditions improved by enough to offset the fading memories of how badly the opposition had done. This interpretation will be strengthened if such cyclical patterns of decline after elections are absent either in a period of economic improvement or after reelection of incumbents.

Few expect economic variables to offer a perfect account of opinion poll fluctuations (for reasons of measurement error alone). At a minimum, there must be some role for fluctuations in response to major international events (for example, the seizure of hostages in Iran or the Falklands crisis) or major domestic speeches (Thatcher's immigration address of February 1978) and similar events. Indeed, the earliest systematic opinion studies included what were called "rally-round-the-flag" variables, denoting those events which appeared to sharply increase support for the president independent of any particular achievement on his part.

Can events be used to explain movements of opinion? One should not start from the assumption that each such event is unique. Prior restrictions must be placed on admissible classes of events. Each event must be assigned to a class, and the effect of events in that class has to be determined. MacKuen (1980, 1983) does just this. Events are specified a priori, grouped into classes of similar events, and each class is treated as having a common magnitude and duration of effect. It turns out that some events have very little lasting impact on the public's perceptions of important issues whereas a few (for example, the 1963 March on Washington in the context of civil rights) are much more important both initially and over a longer period. This model treats support as a function both of objective economic conditions and of dramatic events of symbolic importance. This moves the study of opinion poll popularity beyond the economic realm but in a way which is theoretically rigorous and consistent with the tenets of the economic approach.

SUMMARY

There is a relationship between the concerns of the previous chapters and the economics of voting. The political business cycle models of Chapter 5 all depended on the characterization of popular preferences or on the assumptions politicians made about those popular preferences. The optimization models of Chapter 6 conceived of government activities as reflecting weights attached to various targets of policy, but it was not clear where these weights came from. An important possibility is that the weights derive from attempts to observe and respond to the preferences of the electorate or to the desires and interests of that part of the electorate which forms a core of support for the incumbents.

Whether economic policy is made in the public interest or by a responsible government depends on whether the government responds systematically to the preferences of at least some part of the public. The desirability of their doing so depends in turn on whether public preferences can be characterized as consistent and well informed. If the public systematically perceives, evaluates, and responds to economic conditions as the output of government activity, a stable aggregation of popular economic policy preferences is possible. Only then can it be said whether policy is consistent with them.

PART FOUR

The Scope
and Growth
of Government

The appropriate role and size of government is one of the most controversial problems of our time. Previous sections have all had some bearing on this central issue. What remains is to consider some evidence about the activity of governments. Chapter 8 lays the groundwork for this. It reviews the economic case for government activity, discusses problems of measurement and interpretation, and outlines a number of explanations of government growth. Chapter 9 provides cross-country comparisons of government growth and offers suggestions about the role of different political institutions in these outcomes. Chapter 10 tests more formally a number of specific hypotheses and as a result raises serious doubts about the value of some claims in the politico-economic literature.

CHAPTER EIGHT

Theoretical Approaches to the Public Sector

This chapter returns to the central problem of political economics, the scope and level of state activity in the market economy. The fact that some state is active in an area is no guarantee that the activity is desirable. In principle, it is possible to justify state activity. For example, state production of public goods is defensible. But this implies neither that the state is producing an optimal quantity of public goods nor that the goods the state produces are in fact "public." The main difficulty of deciding whether intervention is justified lies in measuring the efficiency of state activity. *Efficiency* means that additional units are supplied up to the point where marginal cost just equals marginal benefit and to produce more would make marginal cost exceed marginal benefit. Given the role of market prices in the economic concept of efficiency, the difficulty lies in the absence of a market in which to establish a price for the state's output. Without a market for public output there is no way to establish that a particular quantity has been produced efficiently. There is also no way in principle to prove that it has been produced inefficiently.

Chapter 1 discussed the roles of the government set out by Adam Smith. He defined three areas of activity where he could see no alternative to centralized intervention: defense from external enemies, the maintenance of internal law and order, and the provision of certain public works that yielded social benefits but could not be privately profitable. Modern economists approach the public sector somewhat more analytically. A more contemporary classification of justifications of public sector activity includes provision of public goods, control of monopoly, and correcting for externalities. These establish a framework for understanding the recent controversy over the growth of government in Western industrial societies. We systematically outline major approaches to explaining the growth of the public sector. This topic has received enormous attention. Indeed, the literature on the growth of government has grown much faster than any government, and a recent paper even offered a review of review articles (Larkey, Stolp, and Winer, 1981).

ECONOMICS OF THE PUBLIC SECTOR

A presumption of the economics of public finance is that three sorts of roles can only be played by the state. These include the provision of public goods, intervention to correct imperfections in the market economy, and redistribution of income or wealth from rich to poor. Each of these requires the government to spend money. Any public expenditure requires taxation to generate revenue. Economics has given more theoretical attention to taxes than expenditures.[1] We will not discuss tax incidence and equity, important though these are. We are content for the most part to assume that an "appropriate" method of raising revenue is available, though we recognize the importance of studying both the administrative and incentive or aggregate production costs of any tax system.

PUBLIC GOODS

Public goods may be essential or desirable for a society to consume, but they cannot even in principle be provided by the invisible hand of market forces. It is widely believed that public goods should be sup-

1. For an introduction to analysis of taxes see Boadway (1979). A more advanced treatment, especially of "optimal taxation," is available in Atkinson and Stiglitz (1980). It is worth noting that the optimal tax literature, which on the whole treats the desirable level of revenue as a "given" and then asks about the optimal way to raise it with regard

plied by government and their cost financed by levying taxes. There is less agreement about which goods fall into this class.

The key characteristic of public goods is that, for any total amount of the good supplied, the benefit received by one individual does not affect the benefit available to another individual. With private goods, anyone's consumption of some amount directly precludes consumption of that amount by anyone else. Because a public good does not yield benefit only to an individual buyer, the decision about how much of a public good to produce cannot be left to the market bidding of individuals. Formally, optimal private good production is where marginal rates of substitution equal marginal rates of transformation.[2] Optimal public goods production requires the *sum* of individual marginal rates of substitution (across the whole economy) to equal the marginal rate of transformation. If one more unit of a private good is produced, the extra (marginal) benefit accrues only to the individual who consumes it. If one more unit of a public good is produced, the extra benefit is the sum of all the individual benefits accruing. Optimality requires producing all goods up to the point where the marginal benefit is just offset by the marginal cost, as long as the former is falling and the latter rising.

This dimension of public goods is joint consumption. Another is nonexcludability. Whether or not it can be jointly consumed, if a good once supplied cannot be restricted to the use of an individual purchaser, market allocation will again break down. If someone could not be excluded from consuming a good even though he had not paid for it, he would have the incentive to become a *free-rider*[3] and no incentive

---

to general welfare considerations, assumes a "productive" view of the state, while quite different "optimal" tax policies can be derived by assuming a responsive or protective state (Buchanan, 1967) or indeed an exploitative state (Brennan and Buchanan, 1981).

2. Consider an economy with all resources fully employed. To produce more of one good requires giving up some of another. The marginal rate of transformation is the ratio of the number of the other goods given up per extra unit of new good produced. This ratio may be different for each *composition* of output. Similarly, the marginal rate of substitution is the ratio of the extra subjective benefit (utility) of the new good produced as compared with the subjective benefit of the goods lost, holding total subjective well-being (utility) constant, that is, how much of one good would be required to compensate for the loss of a unit of another.

3. The free-rider problem arises wherever the benefit which can be appropriated by an individual is independent of his having to bear any of the costs involved in its production. Examples of this problem abound in the collective action literature, leading

at all to pay for the good. Public provision can make sense of this situation by providing the good free and financing it out of taxes, though there is a further problem to which we return below.

There are few clear examples of pure public goods. A classic case is national defense. Suppose a country has a missile system aimed outward around its borders. Suppose further that we live within this country. The fact that the system protects me in no way reduces the protection it gives you. Equally, it is not possible to exclude us from the benefit of that system short of ejecting us from the country. Of course, the benefits from constructing the defense system were private, though these may have been small in relation to the total benefit. In reality, most goods have private and public aspects. It is no easy matter to determine whether the good should be privately or publicly produced and/or provided free or through the market. The road system, for example, is often cited as a public good, though it is quite feasible to charge for road use, and congestion affects individual benefits.

Suppose we have identified a public good. How do the authorities decide how much of it to produce? In principle, the answer is easy: where the marginal rates of substitution and transformation are equal. In practice, the problem has no easy solution since there is no obvious mechanism for making individuals reveal their valuation or their benefits from a public good. If taxes were to be related to the benefit in any way, the free-rider problem means that there is an incentive to understate the benefit one received. Decisions about the provision of public goods are not typically made on narrow economic grounds but rather by elected politicians.[4] The optimality of state public good provisions rests on the assumption both of a benevolent state and of honest citizens or on the existence of (hitherto impractical) devices to get people to reveal their real preferences.

Downs (1957) to formulate a "paradox" of voting and Olson (1965) to hypothesize that interest groups should not form which cannot make the benefits they seek exclusive to their members. The problem has led some economists to stress the importance of ideology in motivating political activity (North, 1981), though there are other ways in which some of the apparent paradoxes can be resolved.

4. Johansen (1977) argues that the incentives of politicians offset the effects of public incentives to free-ride, reducing the magnitude of the problem.

In one special case a kind of market mechanism could lead to an optimal allocation of public goods (Tiebout, 1956). The provision of "local" public goods may yield benefits to a town or neighborhood but not outside. If a large number of localities offer different mixes of public goods and local taxes to pay for them, individuals can locate themselves in the area which gives their most desired combination of public goods. For this to be a means to an optimal result requires the restrictive and impractical assumption that there are no significant costs involved in relocating individuals. However, the model has inspired a considerable literature on the benefits of federal as opposed to unitary fiscal systems.

MARKET IMPERFECTIONS

Even in countries with a general commitment to a market economy, it is recognized that market allocations may fail. This could be cause for public intervention, though the benefits from it may be privately consumed (that is, not public goods). Market failure does not entail the *necessity* of public provision or even public intervention, though it has often been considered to do so. We deal with two major classes of market failure: the existence of monopolies and externalities.

Monopoly

The technology of some industries may create conditions such that competition does not survive. Economies of scale[5] at ranges of production sustained by the market size mean that a single large firm will be able to produce at lower cost than a number of small firms. This will drive out the small firms and leave production in the hands of at most a few large firms. For a few industries these economies of scale are so clear-cut for all ranges of output that these become known as *natural monopolies*. For example, it is pointless to have a telephone not connected to the same network as those of your friends and relatives. It is inefficient for two or more companies to supply electricity to one

---

5. *Economies of scale* mean that the average cost of producing an item declines with the number of such items produced by the firm.

house. The former is obvious. The latter is due to the fact that set-up costs are substantial relative to variable costs. Duplicated set-up costs would not result in lower market prices when only one set-up is necessary.

The objection to monopolies is that once they exist, even though they may have lower unit costs than smaller firms, they can exploit their position by restricting output and thus raising prices. Fewer goods will be supplied and at higher prices than is efficient. As a result, virtually every developed country has legislation aimed at controlling monopolies, though the type of intervention adopted varies from industry to industry and from country to country.

Three broad strategies are commonly adopted to offset the effects of monopolies. The first is to forbid formation of firms that have more than some specific share of a market. Normally such legislation incorporates escape clauses or "gateways" that enable "special cases" to survive. At the very least, however, this approach requires a public bureaucracy to monitor the position in each industry. The British Monopolies Commission is an example. Another approach is exemplified by the regulatory control of utilities in the United States. It is acknowledged that a monopoly must exist and the existing producers are effectively licensed. However, in exchange for the license, producers must submit to their pricing decisions being permanently monitored and controlled by a regulatory agency.

The third approach is to take the monopoly under public ownership or to nationalize it. Nationalization is often undertaken for social, ideological, or redistributive reasons. Some early European cases of nationalization in industries like tobacco were principally means of increasing state revenues. However, most industries commonly nationalized are exactly those which would be classified as natural monopolies: power supply, water supply, telephones, railways. One industry almost universally nationalized (even in the United States) is the postal service, though the critical economic factor determining this is far from clear.[6]

Monopoly has for a long time been used to justify state intervention

6. It is more likely that the ubiquitous state monopoly on postal services originated in the desire to monopolize revenues from stamps. Once the monopoly is created, competitive entry is inhibited. The success of private delivery services in the United States

in the form of regulation. Regulation in practice (and, of course, nationalization) has done at least as much to create and perpetuate monopolies as it has to alleviate their effects. Any licensing system necessarily institutionalizes the license holder and offers official protection against new entrants. Industries under public ownership have less incentive to increase efficiency because appropriability or property rights are attenuated in the public sector (McKean, 1974). In other words, those running nationalized industries cannot capture and retain the gains attributable to their actions. There is no reason in principle that they cannot act exactly like private sector entrepreneurs or even monopolists. However, they have no incentive to do so and indeed often have incentives to do otherwise.

Externalities

The second general reason for intervention in a market economy is that activities have effects on other than the immediate market participants. These external effects may be either positive or negative. Their existence reduces or eliminates the likelihood of markets producing an optimal allocation of resources. Identification of externalities depends on the assignment of property rights in the first place. The classic example of externalities is pollution where the operation of a factory may generate smoke or effluent to the detriment of the neighborhood. There are costs to people living nearby, but these costs are not reflected in the production decisions of the polluting firm. These costs may be internalized by taxing the producers and compensating the sufferers. However, it is more common to impose regulations requiring specific standards to be met.[7] Externalities typically cannot be cured by private entities because the benefits of curing them are impossible to appropriate.

State activity is not only intended to curb negative externalities. Government can participate actively in industry where the externality is positive or where there is a "consumer surplus" which exceeds any

---

and Britain suggest that markets exist for some services not provided by the state monopoly.

7. Setting up the compensation system so that penalties for causing negative externalities (for example, polluting) match the amount of the externality caused while not overly distorting production of goods is another serious problem of institutional design.

necessary subsidy. A simple example is a branch railroad which could profitably be run under "price discrimination" (where each consumer could be charged a different price according to his demand) but not under perfect competition where all can buy at the market price. Positive externalities imply underproduction of the good compared with the social optimum. Industries of strategic importance fall into this category as do communications to outlying regions or, indeed, public transport systems in general. For such industries the social benefits would exceed the size of subsidy necessary to keep the industry going. As a very minimum these loss-making enterprises must be subsidized if they are to survive, but very commonly they are taken over by public authorities.

REDISTRIBUTION

Curing market failures like externalities causes a redistribution of wealth. If a branch railroad is kept open by subsidy, the benefit to those who use it may well exceed the cost of the subsidy which is borne by all taxpayers. If the beneficiaries could be taxed exactly according to their benefit, no redistribution would take place, but the administrative cost of such a tax might well exceed the total benefit. In fact, almost every state action has such redistributive implications whether intended or not. Every action makes one person better off than another at least relatively. The range of areas where the redistributive element is more or less intended is large—education, health services, pensions, food stamps, unemployment benefits, and so on. The actual impact of a policy may be very different from what was intended (LeGrand, 1982). It turns out to be remarkably difficult to demonstrate that redistributive policies have had any significant effects on income distributions.

While state intervention causes redistribution, redistribution is often also claimed to justify state intervention. Whether this claim is valid or not cannot be settled by the efficiency arguments of neoclassical economics. It is not because forced redistribution reduces aggregate output since it need not do so. But the perfect competition model takes as given the endowments of wealth and abilities. It assumes economic actors make optimal decisions subject to those initial conditions. The resulting outcome may be described as efficient under some circumstances. There are certainly circumstances under which it would not be described as "fair." Moreover, given the nature of the Pareto-optimality criterion of efficiency in markets,[8] there are an infinite number of efficient outcomes, each corresponding to a different distribution of income among individuals. Distributional questions cannot be resolved by reference to efficiency arguments.

THE GROWTH OF GOVERNMENT

The previous section outlined why intervention in the market economy might be desirable. In some cases like the provision of public goods, the theoretical "optimum" level of provision can be defined. In practice it is impossible to obtain the information needed to solve the problem. Correction of externality is difficult since the effects are diffuse. What is the correct level of a subsidy? "Profit maximization" or "loss minimization" may not be socially optimal. There is little technical guidance available for decision-makers about "how big" public provision of goods and services, other interventions, and redistribution should be. These decisions are made by elected political representatives. A variety of economic, electoral, and ideological influences on their decisions may be important at any particular point.

A large literature tries to describe or explain government growth. As background we first discuss issues of measurement. We then review theories of the growth of government in its politicoeconomic context. For convenience we identify three aspects of these explanations: *policy* models, in which the growth of government appears largely as a by-product of other activities; *voting* models, in which the dynamics of growth are a characteristic of popular preferences; and *institutional* models, in which growth is explained by the structures, power, and incentives of different institutions.

8. Pareto efficiency exists if no transaction is available which would make at least one person be better off and no one else worse off.

STATISTICAL DESCRIPTION: WAGNER'S LAW

One of the earliest writers in a long tradition of studying the growth of government descriptively was Adolf Wagner, whose name is associated with "Wagner's law," sometimes called the "Law of Increasing State Activity." Wagner (1883) himself argued that some proportionality would be likely between income and expenditure.

There is thus a proportion between public expenditure and national income which may not be permanently overstepped. This only confirms the rule that there must be some sort of balance in the individual's outlays for the satisfaction of his various needs. For in the last resort, the state's fiscal requirements covered by taxation figure as expenditure in the household budget of the private citizen. (p. 8)

There must be a point where at the margin the individual no longer desires extra public provision. Wagner's law may say either that government expenditure will grow as a proportion of national income or that it will grow roughly in proportion with national income. A reasonable interpretation is that there is a more than proportionate increase of government expenditure during the transitional stage associated with industrialization, but after that the increase will be in proportion with the growth of national income (Chrystal and Alt, 1979).

Peacock and Wiseman (1961) studied the growth of public expenditures in Britain from the late nineteenth century to the mid-1950s. They conclude that during peacetime government expenditure grew roughly in line with GDP, but after each of the two biggest wars there had been a discrete upward jump in expenditure relative to GDP. They called this structural break the *displacement effect*. Similar effects can be found in other countries. Displacements take place after a major disruption like war or depression because demand increases for public provision as compensation for past sacrifices. This displacement effect is particularly clear in British data when expenditure is defined to include transfers and no allowance is made for military expenditure, which was only gradually reduced, especially after World War II.

Problems of Measuring Costs and Benefits

Government activity has grown in absolute size in most countries. It may not have grown more than in proportion to the whole economy. What is true even for one country over a single period depends on what measure of the size of government is used. A measure based on employment may differ considerably from a measure based on expenditures. Moreover, many aspects of government intervention are intrinsically difficult to measure and as a result usually go unmeasured.

Virtually any law which is passed will prohibit someone from doing something he might otherwise want to do, with implicit costs. A speed limit, for example, generates a variety of costs and benefits. The typical traveler will take longer to get to any destination which is costly in terms of time taken up. Some people may switch to airlines. Their journey will be more costly, but the airlines will benefit. Motel owners may benefit because drivers are longer on the roads or may lose because more people travel by air. Some people may live who would otherwise have died in road accidents. The demand for gasoline will fall, and so on. All these are effects of one piece of legislation. Some of the effects are a redistribution from one group to another. The net social benefit may be positive or negative. How do you value lives saved through reduced accident rates? *There are effects of some kind* which are not measured at all by any aggregate like government expenditure or tax revenue. If anything, the effects show up indirectly, in *private sector output*.

Cost-benefit analysis attempts to measure the net social cost or benefit of specific government interventions. It assesses the value of public sector investment projects where the benefits were not directly reflected in the internal profitability of the project. It was used to justify building an addition to the London Underground System, the Victoria Line, although the project would not be self-financing (Beesley, 1973). Diverse benefits included time saving and reduced congestion. These had to be evaluated in some way. The assumptions required for the analysis may be arbitrary and unwarranted. The alternative is to ignore entirely the existence of possibly considerable external benefits which would be otherwise unavailable.

A disadvantage of conventional cost-benefit analysis is that it deliberately nets out any redistributional effects. In some government interventions the redistributive impact is the most important. Regulation (or, indeed, deregulation) has net output effects, but its major impact is the imposition of a net cost on one group and a net benefit on another. From an economic point of view such interventions are the endowment of a capital resource (extension of property rights) upon one group and the removal of a capital resource (attenuation of property rights) from another.

Real policy effects which are hard to measure and not typically reflected in published statistics are not the only problem. Conversely, the statistics may appear to show change when in fact nothing "real" has happened. Some arbitrary features of government behavior could appear to have real effects if the statistics are taken at face value. For example, many benefits are implicitly paid through the tax system by allowing a deduction or credit against taxes. If the offsets were abolished and replaced by cash payments of equivalent value (to each person), nobody's financial position would change, but there would be an apparent increase in the size of the public sector as measured by tax revenue or gross expenditure. An example is the reform of Child Benefit in Britain. Child Benefit had been an allowance against income tax for each child. This tax deduction was received implicitly in (normally) a father's pay packet. The reform made it a cash payment to mothers. In principle, this could have been done so as to leave every family in exactly *the same* financial position. However, public expenditure and taxes would appear to *rise*. The Child Benefit reform was not neutral in reality because a flat rate benefit replaced an allowance whose value increased with the recipient's marginal tax rate, but this does not alter the point about measurement problems.

This "tax expenditure" problem is a special case of the general problem of measuring the size of the public sector by total public expenditure including transfer payments (all forms of grants and subsidies). This exaggerates the size of the public sector. Gross public expenditure including transfers is above 50 percent of GDP in several major countries. However, this statistic is misleading. Transfers do not consume resources in competition with the private sector. The maximum possible proportion of GDP "taken by" gross government expenditure is thus greater than 100 percent. If all output were produced by civil servants *and* civil servants' income were substantially redistributed to nonemployed persons through the tax system, the proportion of public expenditure to GDP could be close to 200 percent. But this is nonsense. Percentages are meaningless if they are not constrained to add up to 100 percent when the notion is implicitly one of sharing a cake.

The scale of public sector expenditures should be measured by considerations of resource cost. How much fewer resources are available for private sector use because of the existence of the public sector? An aggregate of "public sector expenditure on goods and services" (consumption) and "public sector gross fixed capital formation" (investment)[9] is better than a measure including transfers. Transfers should not be ignored. They can have significant effects. However, transfers consume resources only to the extent that they lead to higher tax rates than would otherwise have been necessary and to the extent that these tax rates are a disincentive to productive effort. Aggregate transfers cannot be included in "government" when the intention is to apportion shares of GDP.

THE TWO-SECTOR MODEL

The two-sector model (Baumol, 1967; Baumol and Oates, 1975) gives insight into the growth rather than the level of government expenditure. Suppose the economy is made up of an industrial sector and a government sector. The industrial sector produces some physical product with inputs of capital, labor, and raw material. The government sector produces nonmarketed public goods such as law and order. Labor productivity in the industrial sector can be measured as the number of units of output produced per unit of labor input. In the government sector there is a problem. The output of a policeman, a

9. Both adjusted for taxes. If the government hires an extra civil servant, it pays his gross salary as an expenditure but then receives back what he pays in taxes. He would also have paid taxes if otherwise employed, so the net calculation requires assuming what this would have been.

judge, or a fighter pilot cannot be measured, at least not in an obvious way.

While productivity can grow in the industrial sector, it cannot grow in the government sector since output cannot be measured. Normally public sector output is measured simply by the cost of the inputs. But measures of productivity relate outputs to inputs. With outputs measured by inputs, *measured* productivity in the government sector cannot increase *by definition*. Therefore, it will *always* appear that productivity growth as conventionally defined is poor in the government sector by comparison with the industrial sector.

The Baumol/Oates thesis starts by assuming that productivity in the government sector is lower. The government sector is more labor-intensive than the industrial sector. Suppose that wages are kept broadly in line between the two sectors. Keeping in mind the distinction between *actual* output and *measured* output in the public sector, what happens when there is balanced growth in the economy? Suppose that the actual output of both sectors grows in line. Clearly, for a constant real relative level of public services, relative public sector employment *is going to have to rise*. If wages are equal across sectors, there is a presumption that there will also be growing public expenditure relative to GDP.

REAL GROWTH AND PRICE DEFLATORS

The problem of establishing a price for government output has led to efforts to present comparisons between the growth of expenditure and national income in "real" or constant-price terms, with government consumption and aggregate GDP each deflated by *its own* price index. Government spending does buy a different bundle of goods from those which are used to make up the aggregate price index. If government expenditure reflects a higher proportion of wage costs than does private consumption, rising real wages will make the government price deflator rise relative to the GDP price deflator. Even though government is carrying out the same activities as before, when government expenditure is deflated by the GDP price index, the real activity of government will appear to have increased. Indeed, Beck (1976,

1979) shows that if a separate price index is used to deflate government expenditure, then government expenditure as a share of national income has not grown at all. Indeed, figures calculated from *National Accounts Statistics* show that the average annual rate of increase in the GDP price deflator in eight industrial countries from 1960–1977 was 5.8 percent, but the average annual increase in their government expenditure deflators is 8 percent.[10] Thus, the entire growth of government consumption in the West appears to be an illusory relative price effect of just over 2 percent per annum.

However, this interpretation can easily be misleading. If public employees' salaries are doubled, no effect will be observed in the share of the real public sector. The increase will simply be deflated out as a reflection of higher costs. But a discretionary increase in the relative scale of public compensation must be an expansion of the public sector. Deflating government consumption by the GDP price index is better, but not exactly right. The absence of a market "price" for government output means it is measured in terms of its input costs. Higher government costs may reflect relatively expensive goods (for example, labor) rather than extraction from the economy of more real goods. This is in the nature of government activities. Use of a separate government deflator to calculate real public expenditures will underestimate government growth whereas use of the GDP deflator or some other general price index can exaggerate public resource consumption by inflating the "price" of all nonmarket goods in the government sector. Believing that the almost right is better than the obviously wrong, any comparisons of real growth of government expenditures and GDP should deflate both by the same deflator.

How does the real output of the public sector actually behave? We do not know. Its measured output grows slower than that of private industry. The two-sector model makes it surprising that the public sector measured by current expenditure on goods and services has not grown faster relative to GDP than it actually has in most countries.

10. The GDP price deflator is a broad measure of the increase in prices of all goods and services in the domestic economy. The government expenditure deflator measures the price change of government inputs, mainly wages and salaries. The countries are those listed in Figure 9.2 in Chapter 9.

This may suggest that the real level of public sector services is in fact being reduced over time, though in the absence of direct evidence on the supply or quality of public services, no presumption in this regard is safe.

Finally, since the scale of public services is largely supply-determined, the nature of *demand* for them is ambiguous. It can reasonably be assumed that they are normal goods so that demand increases with income. The assumption of stable popular preferences leads to the expectation that government expenditure should maintain proportionality with national income. However, it is possible that, like other services, public services are luxury goods. Luxury goods have an income elasticity of demand greater than one. This means that consumers *would choose* to spend an increasing proportion of their income on these goods if they were free to do so and that government would grow disproportionately fast as income grows.

POLITICOECONOMIC EXPLANATIONS OF GOVERNMENT GROWTH

Many arguments in a variety of contexts provide a reason why "government" grows (relatively). The growth of government is a trend. Superficially, any other trend may appear to explain it. Models in such a case should explain many cases and do so parsimoniously. Unfortunately, all these proposed explanations of government growth are not mutually exclusive. Indeed, they are not independent models but can well be treated as different aspects of an overall view.

POLICY MODELS

Fiscal Drag

What are the origins of the apparent widespread tendency in recent years for government expenditure to grow as a proportion of national income? The simplest explanation is that ubiquitous progressive tax rates on incomes are not adjusted for inflation. This *fiscal drag* means that people whose real gross incomes remain constant pay a higher share of income in taxes as inflation drives their nominal incomes into higher tax brackets. Politicians exploit this to raise revenues without specific legislation and appropriate the gains from growth in nominal national income. However, explaining the recent introduction of indexing of taxes and some expenditures in several countries (see Organization for Economic Cooperation and Development, 1978) requires some other political motivation. For example, the 1981 Tax Act in the United States ties tax brackets to the Consumer Price Index after 1985. In Britain the Rooker-Wise Amendment has already done this. Old age pensions have been effectively indexed for some time. Fiscal drag in the past may not have been intended. The fiscal drag explanation of expenditure growth also requires that budget surpluses or the expectation of them *precede* expenditure rises. In fact, expenditure rises more commonly lead to deficits, which subsequently have to be financed.

Asymmetrical Stabilization Policy

One of the main recommendations of Keynesian economics was that governments should attempt to stabilize the economy. When there was a slump, they were to lower taxes and/or increase their expenditures. When there was "overheating," they were to do the reverse. This policy does not result in any trend since reductions in government expenditures in booms would exactly offset increases in slumps. However, it has been argued that there is, in fact, an asymmetry between booms and slumps (Buchanan and Wagner, 1977).

If the growth of government expenditures in slumps is not fully offset by reductions in booms, the result is trend growth in expenditures. This story is easy to rationalize in terms of the likely behavior of incumbent politicians. Instigating projects, increasing benefit rates, reducing taxes, and hiring public service workers are popular and pleasant things to do. Canceling projects, lowering benefits, and firing civil servants will be wasteful, time-consuming, unpopular, or, in some political contexts, impossible things to do (Rose and Peters, 1978). German local governments and trade unions are much more willing to accept increased federal support to offset recessions than to give it up in boom times (Knott, 1981). Raising taxes, however, while no more popular, may be easier if the costs of tax increases can be diffused across the board. The net result is that public expenditure rises through successive business cycles.

Another word of caution is due at this point. Government expenditures and taxes have been used for stabilization policy. Expenditures should rise at least in line with national income anyway. What this theory implies is that the actual growth is both unintended and excessive. Countries conducting active stabilization policy should show greater public sector growth than those not doing so. The United States and Britain are the two countries where Keynesian stabilization policy was most used (see Chapter 3). As we shall see in Chapter 9, the growth of government expenditure in these countries is not unusual: it is, if anything, relatively small.

Ideological Influences

If electorates had completely stable preferences, governments (or at least their policies) would never change. Since governments do change, either incumbent parties fail to deliver, the aspirations of individuals must change, or a desire must exist to "give the other side a chance." Consequently, it is possible to compare the behavior in office of political parties with different ideologies. Parties of the Left and Right can be compared either within a single country over time or across countries at the same point in time.

There are some common presumptions about how the behavior of parties of the Left and Right is likely to differ when in power (Chapters 2, 5, and 7). Right-wing parties are presumed to favor business interests and the better off. Their policies should, therefore, reduce the level of redistribution both by lowering taxes (especially high marginal tax rates on incomes and taxes on wealth) and reducing public expenditures. However, some expenditures benefit the rich more than the poor. These (for example, on the police which protect property) increase. In contrast, a left-wing government presumably reflects the interests of labor, the poor, and the underprivileged. Such governments should require taxes and expenditures for greater redistribution and better social services.

Many examples are consistent with this typology, but there are sufficient exceptions to warrant caution. The 1976–1979 Labor government in Britain slashed public investment programs by nearly half.

The Gaullist party in France and indeed the Conservative party in Britain have both been actively involved in expanding the public sector through the nationalization of industries (though, of course, not consistently). There will be differences between countries where Left participation in government has been sustained over a long period and those where it has been episodic.

VOTING BEHAVIOR MODELS

Redistributive Pressure

Most representative democracies base voting on the principle of one man-one vote. The distribution of votes is egalitarian whereas the distribution of income or wealth is highly skewed. Fifty-one percent of the population has a majority of the votes but a smaller fraction of the total income or wealth of the community. Democratic political systems should thus produce majorities in favor of redistribution from rich to poor. Meltzer and Richard (1981) offer a model of government growth along these lines. Oppenheimer and Frohlich (1980) extend it to the demand for transfer payments. Their argument is that as long as *the median voter* has an income less than the mean of all incomes, there will be a majority available to support a candidate promising further redistribution from rich to poor. Expansion of the franchise in countries like Britain and the United States was, in fact, accompanied by redistributive policies and the emergence of more popularly based governments. Whether the argument has contemporary relevance is another matter. Support for redistributive policy does not come only from the poor but also from among the better-off, who feel they can afford the cost (Alt, 1979). Political participation and power are skewed toward those with higher incomes. Why did Britain in 1979 and the United States in 1980 elect governments explicitly proposing to cut taxes and expenditures? Distributions of income and wealth have not been becoming consistently more egalitarian in recent years.

The Cost-Benefit Model and Fiscal Illusion

Suppose incumbent politicians maximize their own popularity. When they allocate expenditures, they will put them where they are most visible and, therefore, most likely to increase their popularity. Expenditures are more popular than taxes. There will be a strong temptation for governments to run deficits. Buchanan and Wagner (1977) claim that the principal consequence of the Keynesian revolution was to legitimatize government deficits. Politicians soon forgot that deficits were intended as a remedy for insufficient demand, not as a general course of action.

No general model that ascribes government growth to politicians' aversion to taxation and preference for spending can be sustained beyond the short term without a further assumption of some sort of popular "fiscal illusion." A *fiscal illusion* is a systematic tendency to misperceive the actual levels of cost and benefits in some tax-spending combination. Elected politicians' alleged preference for deficit finance requires people not to recognize that deficits have to be paid for as well. But deficits are widely perceived as harmful in the United States today. Moreover, although people may misperceive their tax burden, there is no evidence that they are more likely to underestimate it than to overestimate it. Fiscal illusion has also been used to justify arguments of insufficient public provision as well (Downs, 1965). Here, relative difficulty of perception leads people to underestimate the actual benefits (say, of defense expenditure) relative to tax costs. A lot thus depends on *visibility* of taxes and spending (Klein, 1976). A geographical variant of fiscal illusion is important in the class of models to which we turn next.

INSTITUTIONAL EXPLANATIONS

Bureaucracy and the Public Sector

The final class of explanations of public sector growth concerns public institutions. One version of potentially great importance in some countries attributes influence to the public employees themselves (Bush and Denzau, 1977). Public employees' salaries provide a direct interest in expanding public expenditure. Working conditions and employment prospects will depend on continued development of public services. This interest could be felt in electoral pressure. A large proportion of the electorate employed in the public sector is a significant vote for public sector expansion. However, evidence suggests that in fact the effect of such voting is small (Alt and Turner, 1982). Policy could also be affected by the preference of senior civil servants to expand their career base. "Spending" ministries can be constrained by the "control" ministry, that is, the Treasury or Ministry of Finance. Who wins depends on the sympathies of the elected government, the personalities involved, and the nature of incentives within the electoral system.

Niskanen (1971) argues that bureaucracy "supplies" government growth. His formal case is that "bureaucrats maximize the total budget of their bureau . . . subject to the constraint that the budget must be equal to the minimum total costs of supplying the output expected by the bureau's sponsor" (p. 42). In other words, the bureau has a sponsor in the legislature who demands the bureau's output with no means of either discovering the bureau's costs or reducing the price the bureau quotes for its output. In such a case, the bureau's level of activity will be greater than that of either a profit-seeking monopoly or a competitive industry (pp. 59ff.).

How do bureaus retain their price-fixing ability? There might be conflict with the private sector. Aranson and Ordeshook (1978) give conditions under which private sector suppliers of goods to the bureaucracy function as interest groups and facilitate oversupply. Romer and Rosenthal (1979) give circumstances under which all-or-nothing bids evade public control. On the other hand, Miller and Moe (1980) show that if the bureaucracy's legislative sponsors are modeled as monopsonists (single buyers of a good), the sponsor-bureaucracy problem becomes a bilateral monopoly with indeterminate results. This presumes that budget-maximizing bureaucrats are confronted by price-minimizing sponsors. Is there any reason to belive that, *ceteris paribus,* sponsors might not wish to minimize costs of public output?

Universalism and Reciprocity in Allocation

A series of papers (for example, Shepsle and Weingast, 1981; Fiorina and Noll, 1978) propose a model in which American congressmen have incentives to facilitate and maintain bureaucratic growth and to supply a level of expenditures higher than that which would result from simple majority rule. The model can be extended to other institutional contexts as well.

Legislators aid their reelection chances by being able to claim credit for doing things. Bureaucratic provision of services assists credit-claiming. Services provided automatically by automatic transfers and taxes are not easily identified with individual legislators. Legislators "solve" bureaucratic inefficiencies as a sort of casework for constituents. Legislators prefer a pattern of projects rather than uniform taxes or benefits. Given an "externality" like water pollution—rather than tax producers of pollution and transfer benefits to victims based on a uniform standard—the credit-claiming legislators prefer construction projects to clean water according to some standard. Such distributive projects appear as "gifts" to constituencies resulting from political efforts in Congress.

These incentives entail neither deficit finance nor government growth. The impact of two practices, universalism and reciprocity, on appropriation levels produce these. Universalism is roughly equal to "something for everyone," and reciprocity means not attacking another's appropriation or benefit in return for his not attacking yours. Under the usual rational choice assumptions, if legislators pursue their individual interests and if legislation requires some form of minimal winning coalition, the likeliest outcome of an appropriations debate is that nothing will be done. In general, a legislator will always vote against everyone else's appropriations on cost-benefit grounds while his own will, of course, also be defeated by everyone else. Omnibus bills with something in them for everyone (or nearly everyone) offer a way around this. They pass because people agree to let others' appropriations alone in return for theirs being let alone. The result is a higher level of expenditure than would result under normal majority rule procedures, which would produce either no bill or a cheapest winning coalition, protected somehow against individual deleterious amendments.

Universalism and reciprocity exist in other political systems, though by no means necessarily in the legislative branch. Heclo and Wildavsky (1974) quote cabinet ministers' reasons for never attacking the spending requests of other departments. They also describe the process of pairwise bargaining in the British system between the Treasury and other departments which leads to the final allocation of expenditures. Knott (1981) describes the same form of bargaining in ultimate decisions on spending in Germany. The implication of this is that it is the pairwise bargaining and agreement among component units that tends to push expenditure beyond the "natural" target of a constant proportion of national income.

Finally, what sets up the processes of universalism and reciprocity, and what keeps them going? The answers are uncertainty and fiscal illusion. Majority rule institutions could appropriate funds by "cheapest winning coalitions." Legislators who were uncertain about whether their proposals would be included but felt they would benefit in the long run from having projects adopted have an incentive to adopt universalist practice. Every legislator has the same incentives, so projects are oversupplied relative to majority rule. The practice is sustained by a particular fiscal illusion. Suppose revenues cover costs, costs are accurately perceived, and constituents accurately perceive their own benefits but mistakenly believe that other constituencies have not done as well. Constituents will then reward rather than penalize oversupply. The argument rests on the misperception of *others'* benefits, which people might indeed not be able to determine. Of course, the universalist strategy can be beaten by convincing electors that all districts share equally in the proceeds of omnibus legislation. But who has the incentive to do that?

SUMMARY

There are several well-established reasons for the presence of a public sector in a market economy. The most convincing are based on identification of areas of "market failure." Economic analysis provides a justification for intervention but no easily applicable method for determining the "correct" or "optimal" level of such activity. These decisions have to be made politically. The size of government has tended to grow—in all cases absolutely, in some relative to income, and in some cases in terms of spending relative to revenue (deficit). Many political and institutional theories about this growth have been proposed. Serious measurement difficulties hinder exact identification of the size of government. Some evidence about the merits of contending theories of the growth of government is presented in the next two chapters.

CHAPTER NINE

Comparative Government Expenditures

The previous chapter discussed the growth of government. This chapter and the next look specifically at government expenditures. Expenditures are not the only measure of government activity. If we were to analyze public employment, some results might be different. Moreover, our account of government expenditures would be enriched by considering the distribution of expenditures across subnational regions. Different functional categories of government services could also be considered. Nevertheless, it has been expenditures (and their financing through public revenues) that have attracted the most attention, and so it is at least worth considering these even if they do not tell the whole story.

Why is the growth of government expenditure so controversial? One argument goes back to Adam Smith. A growing *share* of national income or expenditure taken by the public sector "crowds out" private sector activities. There are two reasons why this might be held to be a bad thing. First, in the context of an exploitative state, growth might imply an increase in the exploitative potential of government. Moreover, as in Chapter 5, it might involve a transfer of utility from public to government rather than an increase in general social welfare. The other reason is the productive inefficiency of the state. This inefficiency could reflect low productivity in the public sector, though this could arise from measurement difficulties rather than be a demonstrated characteristic of state activity (see Chapter 8). If public officials choose projects on the basis of status and prestige rather than genuine social value (examples are the space program in the United States and the Anglo-French construction of the Concorde), relative inefficiency also arises. The alleged disincentive effects of taxes to finance state activities make the total impact on private sector output even greater.

Thus, increasing public sector expenditures and budget deficits in many Western industrial countries have recently received a great deal of attention, reflected in the publication of books with titles like *Democracy in Deficit* (Buchanan and Wagner, 1977) and *Can Government Go Bankrupt?* (Rose and Peters, 1978). Arguments about the political economy of public expenditures and revenues have proliferated while efforts to test them have lagged behind. A wide currency has been achieved by a number of theories like those reviewed in Chapter 8, for which there is, in fact, little supporting evidence. This chapter and the next will examine the evidence. We make four important points:

1. Trends in *national income* are important in determining *planned* public expenditures.

2. The institutions of expenditure *control* determine comparative rates of growth of public sector consumption expenditure.

3. Public expenditure has a small but significant role in economic *stabilization* policy.

4. *Electoral-cyclical* factors are relatively unimportant in determining public expenditure levels.

This chapter reports the experiences of a range of countries while the following chapter concentrates on Britain and the United States. Our view is that in peacetime, public expenditure grows for the most part because national income grows. If expenditure simply kept pace with national income, government growth would not be particularly controversial. But public consumption grows faster in some countries than in others. In most cases, though not all, it grows a little faster than national income. It grows roughly in proportion to national income because governments plan it to do so. This appears to be more or less true everywhere in the Western world. The demand for the kind of services governments provide could grow more than in proportion to income, as do demands for many services provided through the market. The extent to which growth in government exceeds growth in income depends on how these demands are politically articulated. International differences in the growth of public consumption can be fully understood only by looking at the evolution of budgets and the processes by which political conflicts over budgets are resolved. American and British government expenditures have not grown abnormally fast by international standards. What is exceptional about the experience of these two countries is not so much the growth of their government sectors but the lack of investment. Our account thus begins with a look at the shares of public expenditure and other components of national income.

TRENDS IN SHARES OF NATIONAL INCOME

The Keynesian view of the economy conventionally treats national income (Y) as identically equal to the sum of private consumption (C), gross fixed capital formation or investment (I), and government consumption of goods and services (G).[1] Chapter 3 discussed a Keynesian account of the relationships among these components. What actually happens to the shares taken by each of the three can be shown in terms of a triangular diagram of the sort shown in Figure 9.1a. The shares of national income taken by these three components for a particular country for a specific time period can be represented by a point in such a triangle. The closer the point is to a particular corner, the larger is that particular component in proportion or percentage terms. A country where C, I, and G take equal shares would be right in the middle whereas a country with, say, no investment would be on the side between C and G. One where private consumption took all income

1. $Y = C + I + G$ plus the difference between exports and imports. We shall ignore this last term in order to simplify exposition. While strictly speaking, we are talking about the composition of "national expenditure," we shall refer to "national income" as if it were equivalent.

would be right at the top corner, and one where consumption took the largest share but investment took more than government consumption would be above the middle and somewhat closer to the left-hand side. Most industrial countries look like this last case. Figure 9.1a provides a convenient and simple way to see the behavior of all three components at once. This can illustrate how government expenditure shares have grown and whether at the expense of investment or private consumption. We illustrate trends first with stylized stories and then present some data.

TWO STYLIZED STORIES OF
POSSIBLE TRENDS

Socialism in the 1930s

It often used to be argued in Britain (and sometimes still is) that its early industrialization had by the 1930s placed its basic industries in

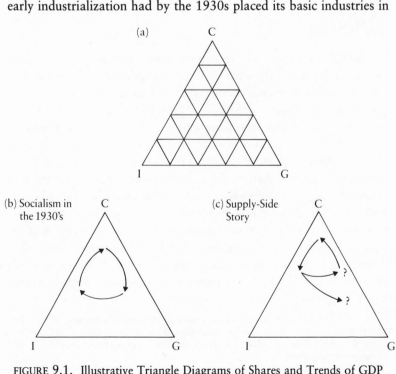

FIGURE 9.1. Illustrative Triangle Diagrams of Shares and Trends of GDP

a position of competitive disadvantage mainly because of outdated equipment. Members of the Labor party in the 1930s argued for nationalization of steel and other basic industries. They claimed that without state takeovers there could be no structural rationalization of the industry, harming employment prospects. The government could make up any deficiency of private capital in a rationalized steel industry directly. The hypothetical triangle diagram of Figure 9.1b describes the history of a country undergoing widespread nationalization as an initial shift toward G (toward the lower right corner from higher levels of C) followed by a shift toward I (across to the left) as investment increased, and finally a shift back up toward C as employment (and thus consumption) effects were felt. Although the final shares of G and I would probably be bigger than before, the path could eventually loop back right to where it began. The Labor party made it clear that they believed the country would now have higher aggregate income and that redistribution of consumption would take place from previous owners of industry to workers. Moreover, a complete description of government expenditure would distinguish public from private investment, here both contained in I.

A Supply-Side Story of Government Growth

Commonly given advice on how to make the economy grow stresses the initial stimulation of private disposable income, probably by a reduction in direct taxes. This may cause consumption to grow (a move away from G toward C in Figure 9.1c). If the reduction in taxes benefits most those most likely to invest, there will eventually be a movement toward I. As in the previous case, the long-run outcome could loop back to the beginning but at a higher level of income. Whereas the loop in the previous case moved clockwise, here it moves counterclockwise.

Suppose government now appropriates all the benefit from this growth either by overtly raising tax rates or covertly through inflation and fiscal drag? Two things can happen. If the extra revenue goes into programs (goods and services), there will be an increase in the share of G. This move toward the lower right corner will be at the expense of either C or I or both. If the extra revenue goes into transfers (entitlement-type cash benefits), the result will be that C rather than G will increase as long as the recipients do not convert benefits into investment. In either case, disincentive effects from larger government revenues are often claimed to cause investment to fall relative to both C and G.

BEHAVIOR OF INCOME COMPONENTS

Figure 9.2 plots the histories of investment and private and public consumption in eight countries from 1954 to 1980. Other countries could have been added but only at a major cost in readability. These eight industrial countries are located in a subspace bounded by government shares between 10 and 35 percent, investment between 15 and 40 percent, and private consumption between 50 and 75 percent. This area circumscribes the likely combinations of C, I, and G in industrial societies. Moving from, say, the corner labeled C of this smaller triangle to any point on the opposite side means that private consumption has decreased twenty-five percentage points. Whether G or I is consequently growing more depends on whether the path away from C is to the left or right of vertical. Move from upper right to lower left and investment is growing, and so on. Each of the countries is plotted with a dot marking the 1954 position and a series of arrows indicating the sequence of positions in 1959, 1964, 1970, 1977, and 1980.

Two general remarks are in order. First, nearly all the countries began the period with similar income shares. Except for Norway's high investment share, the countries could all have been enclosed by a much smaller triangle in 1954. This triangle would have been in about the same place on a left-right axis vis-à-vis the relative shares of investment and government. In every case it would have been at a higher level of private consumption. The early 1950s and indeed much of the immediate post-World War II era displayed the relative priority of private consumption. Second, subsequent developments have varied. The countries end up in very different positions. As in the case of differing unemployment-inflation responses in the 1970s (Figure 5.2 in Chapter 5), no single simple description is going to be adequate.

Nevertheless, Figure 9.2 contains a "typical" pattern. All countries moved noticeably toward I in the period 1954–1964, usually at the expense of C. To this extent the "supply-side" story of the 1950s as a peak period of investment appears correct. Only Norway's initially very high investment share does not increase during this decade. Among the rest, the smallest increase in the share of investment is in the United States, which also started with a comparatively low investment share. Later periods contain different trends, though most

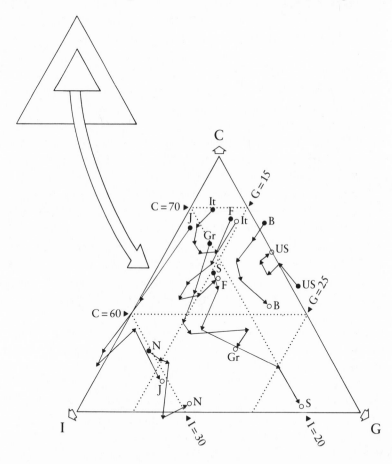

B	Britain	J	Japan	●1954　○1980
F	France	N	Norway	
Gr	Germany	S	Sweden	
It	Italy	US	United States	

SOURCE: International Monetary Fund, *International Financial Statistics*, May 1976 and May 1982.

FIGURE 9.2. Components of GDP, 1954–1980

involve some reduction in the share of investment. In some countries there is an evident growth of government consumption. This is particularly clear in Sweden but is also true of Britain, Germany, and Norway. Two cases, France and Italy, move back toward private, not public, consumption. Japan moves first toward private and then toward public consumption. The United States hardly moves at all. In fact, given that the scale of Figure 9.2 is reasonably fine, the best way to describe the United States in the last quarter-century is as a place where nothing changed as regards the distribution of national income between private and public consumption and investment.

Investment in Figure 9.2 is public as well as private. It can be argued that public investment is resource-consuming and therefore should be included in G. However, classical economists separated government capital goods (with long-lasting as opposed to short-lived benefits) from ordinary consumption, particularly in order to justify debt financing of capital goods. Moreover, capital is capital whether it is public or private. Even if rates of return on public investment are inferior (another hard-to-measure assertion), they are still likely to be positive especially if external benefits are included. Finally, there is no evidence that larger public shares of investment generally are connected with lower private investment. The country with the biggest investment share, Japan, also has the biggest public share in investment, about 25 percent. Most countries have about a 20 percent public stake in total investment.

Figure 9.2 has two important features. First, even if there is something in the supply-side story that government expropriated the gains from an earlier period of investment-led growth, *the story is nowhere less true than in the United States*. This account could explain developments in Germany, Sweden, and even Britain, though their individual histories are actually quite different. Other countries where government has grown have not given up investment, and in some cases government has not grown. Figure 9.2 also shows graphically that those three countries of the eight whose low growth by widespread agreement reflects troubled economies, the United States, Britain, and Italy, are in no way characterized by patterns of government growth. They are all characterized, however, by relatively low levels of investment. More important, they made the smallest movements in the 1950s toward higher levels of investment. All the other countries either were initially at much higher levels of investment, or moved toward them even if these higher levels proved transitory. Higher investment was sustained by many specifically aimed tax incentives in France (Norr and Kerlan, 1966), by more general tax incentives in Germany (Roskamp, 1974), and by active cooperation in credit rationing by government, central bank, and industry in Japan. By contrast, U.S. and British policy aimed to maintain high levels of private consumption in order to create a demand for investment indirectly. No account of the failure of the U.S. and British economies to sustain growth should be written without reference to this feature of their recent histories. It is ironic that those countries with the most sophisticated credit markets (the United States and Britain) are also those with low long-run investment shares. Institutional arrangements promoting market allocation of credit cannot guarantee that the credit will finance durable investment programs rather than short-run consumption.

COMPONENTS OF EXPENDITURES AND REVENUES

Government might not crowd out economic growth only by expanding its consumption of goods and services. There is also a plausible argument that poor economic performance stems from the expansion of entitlement programs, which redistribute consumption opportunities away from those likely to invest and provide a disincentive to productive enterprise. This subsumes two separate issues. One is the relationship between the growth of national product and the growth of transfers. The other is how the transfers have been financed.

Figures 9.3 and 9.4 present relevant data for those countries covered by the United Nations' *National Accounts Statistics*. Figure 9.3 presents the annual growth in real terms (constant units of the domestic currency) of gross domestic product (Y), transfer payments to persons (T), government consumption for defense (G_d), and for nondefense purposes (G_o). In each case, these growth rates are averaged for the 1960s and the period 1970–1980. Several conclusions are appar-

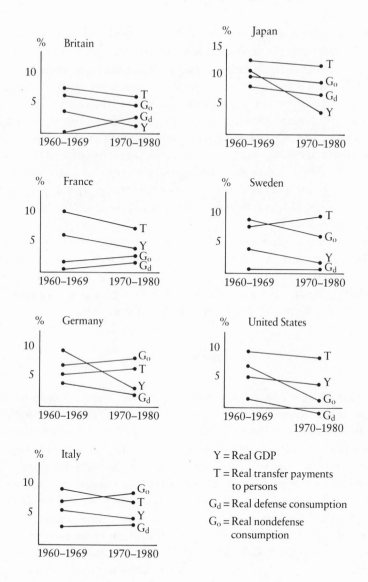

SOURCE: United Nations, *Yearbook of National Accounts Statistics,* 1978, updated from IMF, *Government Financial Statistics,* 1982.

FIGURE 9.3. Growth Rates of GDP and Selected Categories of General Government Expenditure, 1960–1980

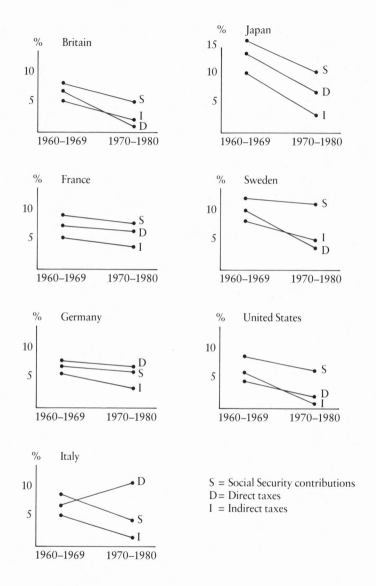

S = Social Security contributions
D = Direct taxes
I = Indirect taxes

SOURCE: United Nations, *Yearbook of National Accounts Statistics*, 1978,
updated from IMF, Government Financial Statistics, 1982; and OECD,
Revenue Statistics of Member Nations 1965–1980.

FIGURE 9.4. Real Annual Growth Rates of Selected General Government
Revenue Categories, 1960–1980

ent. First, obviously, growth rates of GDP declined everywhere in the 1970s from prevailing rates in the 1960s. Less obviously, in most cases the growth rate of government expenditures declined in much the same way as the growth rate of GDP. Nevertheless, transfer payments grew at a faster rate in the 1970s than the 1960s in Germany and Sweden. Even in this very rudimentary way, we observe a long-run constraining relationship between the growth of GDP and the growth of expenditure.

Second, in most cases the growth rates of transfers and nondefense consumption exceed the growth rate of GDP, and transfers are commonly the fastest-growing component of expenditures. Unemployment compensation is a major element in transfer payments. It is possible to ascribe the faster growth of transfers and their increased rate of growth relative to GDP in countries like Germany in the 1970s to the "automatic" effect of increased unemployment. However, other factors must be involved. We consider these in more detail below. There also appears to be no obvious connection between the rates of growth of transfer payments and the ability of countries to maintain relatively high shares of investment in GDP, as in Figure 9.2.

In nearly every case in Figure 9.3 the growth rate of defense expenditure is not only the lowest but is also below the growth rate of income. The last two decades have seen a tendency to substitute nondefense for defense consumption. This is by no means confined to the United States. This interesting trend is certainly consistent with accounts of the demand for public goods and the incentives for politicians to supply visible services. Finally, another point to which we return in detail below is that total (defense plus nondefense) consumption has grown just a little faster than GDP in many, though not all, cases.

What has happened on the revenue side of the account? Figure 9.4 is also complicated, but we can reasonably disentangle it in steps. First, real average annual growth rates of revenues declined in the 1970s, just like expenditures. That again simply indicates some long-run proportionality between the size of the public sector and GDP. Growth rates of revenue from indirect taxes (often a proportional tax on expenditure) are closest to being in line with the change in GDP. Second, the fastest revenue growth is nearly everywhere in Social Security contributions, just as the fastest growth in expenditures was in transfer payments. While transfer payments have increased, attempts have thus also been made to increase the direct financing of these payments.

A different question about finance is whether revenues have kept up with expenditures. Figure 9.5 shows that they have not. Deficits as a fraction of GDP have recently increased rapidly everywhere. Whether the fiscal deficit contributes directly to slower economic growth de-

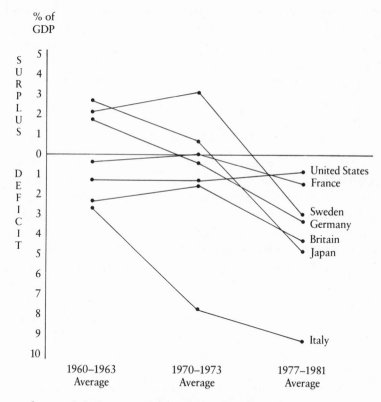

Sources: D. R. Cameron, "On the Limits of the Public Economy," presented to the annual meeting of the American Political Science Association, New York, September 1980, for earlier years; OECD, *Economic Outlook,* July 1981 and July 1982.

FIGURE 9.5. Budget Surplus/Deficit in Selected Countries, 1960–1981

pends at least on how much government borrowing is financed abroad. The effects, therefore, depend on whether many countries simultaneously run deficits. Figure 9.5 shows that running a sizable deficit was a widespread phenomenon in the late 1970s. This was the first extended period in recent decades when all countries did this simultaneously. In the United States an enormous amount of attention was lavished on the size of the federal fiscal deficit. The United States was not a leader in world terms in deficit financing. In fact, the U.S. budget deficit with state-level surpluses included was comparatively small as a fraction of GDP. However, it is dangerous to treat the deficits of the 1970s as the outcome of deliberate policy choices. A satisfactory explanation must include "automatic" effects of the depression after the oil crisis. Depressions increase deficits by reducing tax revenue while increasing such expenditures as unemployment benefits.

SOURCES OF VARIATION IN THE
GROWTH OF EXPENDITURES

Keynesian macroeconomics implies that government expenditure should be manipulated to control the economy. We argue that for the most part it grows in proportion to national income. It does so because politicians find it convenient to plan it that way. The plans once made are difficult to change. Expenditure is therefore not much used as a part of stabilization policy. Indeed, Knott (1981) makes it clear that the German government abandoned the effort to use expenditures this way after a brief experiment in 1974–1975 because the demands of policy timing and multilevel negotiation were incompatible. Moreover, administrations are large and represent many diverse interests, so it is difficult to amend expenditures for most purposes. That is the source of the unimportance of short-term factors, whether they reflect electoral ambitions or the requirements of stabilization policy. We demonstrate a link between public expenditures and national income in the next chapter with a simple model for Britain and the United States. However, for completeness we look first at the comparative experience of a number of countries.

Table 9.1 presents government consumption and GDP growth rates in nominal and real terms for the period 1951–1980. Growth rates of

TABLE 9.1   GROWTH OF GOVERNMENT CONSUMPTION
AND NATIONAL INCOME, SELECTED COUNTRIES,
1951–1980

Average Annual Growth Rate in Percent of

| Country | Nominal | | Real | | | |
	(a) Government Consumption	(b) GDP	(a) Government Consumption	(b) GDP	Difference (a) − (b)	Consumer Prices
Denmark	13.2	9.9	6.6	3.3	3.3	6.6
Finland	14.0	11.3	7.0	4.3	2.7	7.0
Sweden	12.3	9.8	6.3	3.8	2.5	6.0
Belgium	9.1	7.4	4.9	3.2	1.7	4.2
Ireland	12.9	11.2	4.9	3.1	1.7	8.0
Norway	11.2	9.8	5.2	3.8	1.4	6.0
Austria	10.7	9.3	6.2	4.8	1.4	4.5
Canada	10.9	9.6	6.4	5.1	1.3	4.5
Germany	10.4	9.3	7.2	6.1	1.1	3.1
Italy	13.1	12.2	5.8	4.9	0.9	7.3
Britain	10.8	9.9	3.3	2.4	0.9	7.5
Netherlands	11.1	10.3	6.3	5.5	0.8	4.8
United States	8.2	7.5	3.8	3.1	0.7	4.4
Japan	13.3	12.9	10.3	9.9	0.4	3.0
Switzerland	7.9	7.5	4.5	4.1	0.4	3.4
France	11.6	11.5	5.2	5.1	0.1	6.4

Note: Price figures for Japan 1951–1967 and Germany 1951–1960 are wholesale prices. GNP rather than GDP appears for Japan and Luxembourg. Data for Belgium are for 1953–1980. Government consumption is for all levels of government.
Source: International Monetary Fund, *International Financial Statistics,* May 1976 and May 1982.

income (GDP) and government consumption vary, with relatively low levels of real growth of both in the United States, Britain, and Switzerland, and high levels of growth of both in Japan.[2] Growth rates of

2. Naturally, some of the differences in expenditure growth rate will be attributable to the share of income taken by government consumption at the start of the period. It

nominal GDP cluster around 9 to 11 percent per annum and growth rates of nominal government consumption expenditure around 10 to 12 percent per annum. The difference between the real growth rates of government consumption and income does not vary much over many cases. Government consumption nearly everywhere appears to grow just a little (1 to 2 percent per annum) faster than national income.

Nevertheless, the data have two important features. First, small differences in growth rates accumulate over sufficiently long times into big differences. If nominal income grows by 10 percent per annum but public sector consumption grows by 12 percent per annum, after a quarter of a century the public sector will have grown by about 57 percent relative to income. The difference between government consumption growing 1.5 percent rather than 1 percent faster than income is substantial if sustained long enough. It is doubtful that people think about the long-run consequences of government spending growing by 11 percent per annum while income grows 10 percent. Many would probably think the government had done well to keep spending growth so nearly in line with the growth of national income.

The other feature is the evident differences between groups of countries in Table 9.1. No classification is perfect, but three groups emerge from the table:

1. The "Scandinavian" group, with relatively rapid increases in government consumption relative to income: the three countries where government consumption has grown more than 2 percent per annum faster than national income are Denmark, Finland, and Sweden. Norway has among the fastest growth rates of government consumption relative to

---

is clear that the biggest (the United States) grew slowest. Chrystal and Alt (1979) discuss extensively the absence of major differences with respect to the government consumption share of income. Particularly absent is any disproportionate growth in the share of income taken in public expenditure where income is larger. It is also possible that differences in administration between countries place some expenditures (say, health services) in consumption in some cases and in transfers in others (where an insurance system repays expenses rather than paying doctors directly). Nevertheless, data presented in Kohl (1980), using the EEC measure of "social expenditure" (which bridges the categories used here), confirms the broad outline of the rank ordering of Table 9.1, with Scandinavia high and France last. A complete account of cross-national differences in expenditure growth requires considering demographic differences and the role of different "price effects."

income of the remaining countries sampled, though it is considerably lower than the other Scandinavian countries.

2. A "low-growth" group, consisting of France, Switzerland, and Japan: it is evident in the data that there is a gap between the growth of government consumption in these countries and in all others. Indeed, in France it is worth pointing out that government consumption actually grew more slowly than national income between 1951 and 1974.

3. All other countries: in the rest, the norm is that government consumption grows on average about 1 percent per annum faster than gross domestic product. There are considerable differences between extreme cases. In the United States consumption has grown on average by 0.7 percent per annum faster than income. In Belgium or Ireland the gap between growth rates of consumption and income is 1.7 percent. Nevertheless, there is quite a diverse set of countries (Norway, Austria, Canada, Germany, Italy, Britain, the Netherlands) in a narrow range centered around government consumption growing at or just over 1 percent per annum faster than national income.

Why does expenditure nearly everywhere grow a little faster than income? The "low-growth" group have in common some institutions which are absent in other cases. However, among countries where expenditure grows somewhat faster than income, we can say more about the fastest-growing group than about differences among the countries in the middle.

First, there are some general points about similarities rather than differences. Government consumption growth has possibly outstripped national income growth because only very recently has it been suggested that a government which let nominal expenditures rise by 11 percent while income rose by 10 percent was not doing its fiscal duty. Moreover, some regimes attempting to use expenditure in a "Keynesian" way (expand during recessions, contract during booms) found it easier to persuade those involved (for example, local governments and public sector unions) to accept the increased expenditure during recessions than to accept the contractions during booms. Some conservative regimes (Britain in 1972 and the United States in 1981 are leading examples) have reduced taxation without making corresponding reductions in expenditures. Each of these arguments—no one noticed, local resistance to cuts, and easier to change taxes than expenditures—is plausibly the sort of thing that allows expenditures to grow. However, they do not say why expenditures should grow faster relative to income in some places.

The partisan complexion of governments is an obvious candidate to explain why expenditure growth is faster in some countries than in others. The underlying theory was discussed in Chapters 5 and 7. Evidence will be presented in the next chapter that partisan control in Britain has affected the rate at which transfer payments grew, even relative to income. Certainly, when one looks at the extreme groups in Table 9.1, it appears inviting to assign the presence, over extended periods, of socialist parties in governments in Scandinavia some influence over the higher rates of growth of expenditure there. The absence of socialist control in Japan, Switzerland, and for the most part in France could have something to do with low growth rates there. As Cameron (1978) points out, however, the correlation between socialist control and government growth is far from perfect. The United States and Canada, with no socialist governments, are there in the middle of the growth rate table with Belgium and the Netherlands, which have frequent socialist contributions to coalitions. The extent of electoral support for socialist parties does not differentiate Belgium and Norway from Finland and Denmark, but the latter two have the highest rates of public expansion.

The data in Table 9.1 are also loosely consistent with Cameron's (1978) argument that the expansion of the share of public revenues is increased by openness of the national economy (see Chapter 2). Cameron argues that the political effect of openness comes through the concentration of industry and industrial organizations. Concentrated labor organizations produce greater levels of socialist support, consistent with the argument above. Indeed, the upper half of Table 9.1 contains most of the open economies, and France, the United States, and Japan are the most closed economies. However, two of the most open economies, the Netherlands[3] and Switzerland, have among the

3. There could be a data error in Cameron's (1978) Figures 1 and 2. These purport to show that the Netherlands had the most rapid expansion of revenues in GDP between 1960 and 1975, over twenty percentage points. The Organization for Economic Cooperation and Development's (1980) Table 1 places the figure at about fifteen percentage points. This change weakens Cameron's reported correlation between public expansion and openness and strengthens the correlation between expansion and socialist support.

lowest rates of public consumption expansion. More important, openness does not require industrial concentration to affect public sector expansion. A high degree of openness also makes domestic outcomes (like unemployment) appear to be "externalities," the unplanned consequences of some other nation's economic activities. Extensive international trade presents many opportunities for governments to intervene on behalf of sectional interests in the domestic economy (see Chapter 4). Finally, *emulation* of other countries as well as ideology affects expenditure practice. National insurance was introduced in Britain because the working of the German model attracted Lloyd George. A concern to provide similar goods to one's neighbors accounts for some public sector growth in all the Scandinavian countries in spite of differences in the partisan complexion of their governments.

The fastest rates of expansion are concentrated in countries with open economies and sustained rather than episodic periods of socialist control of government. Openness and socialism do not explain trends in other countries. True, none of the countries with the slowest growing public sectors has significant periods of socialist control. There are, however, several countries with no socialist presence but more rapid rates of public expansion.

Different rates of public consumption growth in these countries reflect the conflict between institutions of central control over expenditures and the "universalism" and "reciprocity" practices discussed in Chapter 8. These practices describe a collusive resolution of decentralized bargaining, in which the result is a higher level of expenditure than simple majority rule would have provided. The incentives arise whenever politicians provide things to a constituency unlikely to have exact information about their share relative to other constituencies. Such situations are not restricted to electoral democracies. The functional division of ministries is also a basis for these practices if department heads negotiate to produce outcomes which benefit their sectors, and these expenditures are larger in aggregate than might have been "planned" or desired with stricter control.

Heclo and Wildavsky (1974) describe how Britain's departmental ministers evolve strategies of not attacking each other's spending requests in cabinet (see Chapter 8). Such agreements serve exactly the purpose that universalistic agreements over omnibus legislative bills serve in the American Congress. Collusion prevents individuals from the losses they might suffer if each spending request was submitted to a majority vote. Uncertainty about being on the winning side makes it rational for the individuals to prefer a universalistic solution. The result is settlement by bargaining at the highest levels of decision-making. Much the same thing happens in Germany, owing to the need for bargaining expenditure targets between federal and *Land* governments and major interest groups. The federal government begins the process by planning expenditures

to keep the public sector at a constant or slightly increasing proportion of GNP. . . . During discussions with spending ministries, labor unions, or other levels of government, the expected nominal growth in GNP is also the central figure around which discussions revolve. . . . The unions, the employers, and the states produce separate and different estimates of GNP growth. (Knott, 1981, p. 52)

The whole process of budgeting in Germany is characterized by this sort of decentralized bargaining, among ministries, among levels of government, and between government and interest groups.

There is evidence for the existence of institutions constraining such practices in the "low-growth" countries. These keep the size of government consumption more in proportion to income. Each of the three slowest-growing countries has such institutions. Switzerland subjects many expenditure decisions to popular referendum. This forces expenditures to come under the decision rule of ordinary majority voting. Not surprisingly, many spending referenda lose, forcing expenditures back to the status quo ante. Equally, pairwise bargaining and reciprocity are eliminated in France by virtue of the greater importance of the Ministry of Finance and its representatives in other ministries in allocating expenditures. Wildavsky (1975), Lord (1973), and Hayward (1973), among others, suggest very strongly that there is little scope in the French system for the sort of reciprocal agreements that push expenditure beyond original targets.

Spending ministers do not meet together to bargain out their differences. Each meets separately with the Minister of Finances, and if that is insufficient, possibly with the prime minister and the president. Only the Minister of

Finances, the prime minister, and the president need confront one another directly. (Wildavsky, 1975, p. 100)

There is certainly no role for the French parliament in the process, and little role for the representatives of individual ministries against the Ministry of Finance and what Wildavsky calls the "grand corps" of civil servants. The Japanese budgeting system achieves the same degree of central control through a complex set of rules. The Japanese practices of "fair shares" and contingent reserves again appear to concentrate control in the hands of the Ministry of Finance. The fair shares rules, balance, and other procedures of the Japanese system described by Wildavsky (1975) leave no room for the sort of reciprocal agreements that Shepsle and Weingast (1981) describe in the American Congress and that Heclo and Wildavsky (1974) find in Britain. This promotes the restriction of growth of Japanese public consumption to a fixed proportion of national income.

SUMMARY

Very different countries demonstrate remarkably consistent experiences. Government consumption expenditure grows everywhere roughly in proportion to income, though a fraction faster. Transfers have everywhere become the fastest-growing item of government expenditures, though Social Security payments are also the fastest growing sources of revenue. Socialist control in the context of economic openness explains the fastest cases of expenditure growth. Institutional differences between countries explain variations in other cases. Most important, however, the division of national income in the United States and Britain between government consumption, private consumption, and gross investment has not changed significantly in a quarter-century. This long-term stability is the context in which we turn to models of short-term variations in expenditures.

CHAPTER TEN

A Permanent Income Model
of Government Expenditure

Both economics and political science offer theories about the variability of government expenditures. Expenditures are supposed to be manipulated to control the economy, to help win elections, and to implement the preferences of the incumbent party. Much of what has been claimed is incorrect largely because the evidence has been ignored. We believe that the evidence favors a very different perspective. The fact to be explained is not the high variability of government expenditure but rather its *remarkable stability* with respect to the trend growth of national income. Other factors are important from time to time and place to place, but none is as all-pervasive.

THE PERMANENT INCOME APPROACH

The behavior of the institutions which determine public expenditure explains its stability. In at least two modern economies, the institutional procedures adopted for expenditure planning deliberately target expenditure growth on the expected growth of national income. For example, Price (1978) argues that in the case of Britain:

Public expenditure enjoyed an unchallenged pre-eminence in the original blueprints for postwar stabilisation policy, but in practice it surrendered this

220]

position to taxation and the manipulation of consumer demand. . . . By the end of the 1950s the avowed strategy had become to ensure that public spending was neutral vis-à-vis internal stability, with the public sector expanding at a rate consistent with the long-run growth of the economy, so that at least one sector would be free from cyclical disturbances. (p. 77)

Following the 1961 Plowden Report, expenditure planning in Britain was institutionalized in the Public Expenditure Survey Committee system known as PESC. The intention of this system was to plan public expenditure over a five-year horizon "in relation to prospective resources." Real public expenditure was projected as a stable share of the anticipated future level of real national income. Mistakes have been made in forecasting national income and in keeping expenditure to the planned share. This does not alter the underlying intention, which is the context in which expenditure decisions were made.

Knott (1981) offers a similar description of budgetary policy in West Germany. In drawing up their finance plan, the federal government is mainly concerned with the size of the public sector as a share of GNP. Their purpose is to keep the public sector "at a constant or slightly increasing proportion" of GNP. Negotiations with the *Länder* make explicit reference to the growth rate of nominal GNP. Indeed unions, employers, and the *Länder* all produce independent estimates of nominal GNP growth for use in budget negotiations. Knott quotes a budgetary official at the *Land* level as saying, when asked how they determined expenditure growth: "It is a rule of thumb and nothing exact. In general we try to orient the growth rate on the growth in GNP."

Against this institutional background, recalling the trends we observed in the previous chapter, we can specify this relationship between government expenditure and national income formally. Our basic hypothesis for the determination of aggregate public expenditures is simple, and it is familiar to economists in other contexts. Expenditure is planned to grow in proportion to expected or trend national income. In principle, this proportion could change from time to time (for example, with a new government). In practice, for Britain and the United States, there is no strong evidence that it has. Errors are made both in the implementation of expenditure plans and in the projections of actual national income, but these errors are assumed unrelated to each other. This relationship is the same as the Permanent Income Hypothesis, first formulated by Friedman (1957) for personal consumption expenditure.

This model implies that there is a good deal of inertia in government expenditures. They reflect commitments built up over time. Expenditure is planned in relation not to contemporaneous income alone but to levels of income over some time. Expenditure plans are too "sticky" to change in the light of short-term fluctuations in income. Only when those responsible for expenditure decisions are convinced that a change in income will be sustained is it incorporated in expenditures. This account applies to government consumption expenditure. Public investment is more variable, and transfers, as we have shown, have grown faster then income.

The baseline for any cogent explanation of public expenditure should be stability rather than volatility. Figure 10.1 shows the ratios to GDP of the annual values of three categories of public expenditure in Britain for the period 1955–1979. The expenditure series are all flat and smooth in comparison with variations in the revenue series. Government consumption, for example, starts and ends close to 20 percent of GDP, though there is evidence of slow growth in the period. Transfer payments to individuals grow faster but also smoothly. Public investment as a proportion of GDP does not grow at all, though early growth is cut back in the last few years. The key to explaining expenditure growth is an approach which accounts for this stability rather than one which regards these variables as highly flexible.

This commentary differs from the description of expenditures given in Klein (1976), who suggests that the proportion of gross national product taken by government expenditures rose from 36 percent in the late 1950s to 56 percent in 1974. In part, his picture of rapid growth stems from the choice of atypical start and end years. Any other choice of period would have made the contrast less extreme, as a look at Figure 10.1 confirms. Klein's percentages look so large because transfers are not actually *taken out* of GNP. In view of the dangers of measuring transfers as a proportion of GDP (see Chapter 8), we treat transfers separately. Moreover, the accelerations of expenditure as a fraction of GDP in Figure 10.1 could be caused by more spending or by declining GDP. All the same problems affect Nutter's (1978) comparative work. His study of the growth of government (measured by spending as a proportion of GNP) ends in the post-oil-crisis slump year of 1974–1975. A look through his appendices shows how much of the "growth" occurs during the economic contraction of that year. We analyze expenditure alone, rather than as a proportion of GDP, because of the danger of confounding trends in GDP with trends in expenditure.

We present below estimates of a "permanent income" model for Britain and the United States. Expenditures are disaggregated to three separate categories—consumption, transfers, and investment in Britain, and the first two in the United States. In the United States, we test the model at the federal level, where it should be confirmed, and at the level of aggregated state consumption, where it should not, since there is no single institution at the level of aggregate state expenditure which can perform the sort of planning we discuss. The separation of expenditures into these categories was based on three considerations.

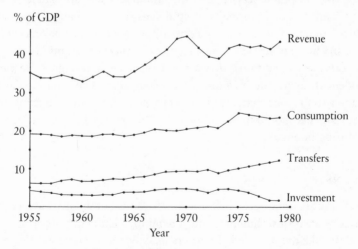

SOURCE: *Economic Trends Annual Supplements.*

FIGURE 10.1. Major Categories of Government Expenditure as Proportion of GDP, Britain, 1955–1979

First, Figure 10.1 suggested different time paths and therefore different estimated parameters for each. Second, the legislation involved is different in each case. Consumption involves programs and staff. Transfers involve entitlements and rates of benefit. Finally, the economic consequences imputed to these types of public expenditure are different. Public consumption and investment appear in arguments of crowding out (see Chrystal, 1979) and low productivity (Bacon and Eltis, 1976). Transfer payments are linked to financial burden and low incentives, but not crowding out, since transfers are redistributed within, not taken out of, private income. Quarterly data are employed to offer every opportunity of detecting short-term changes, which annual figures might obscure. Before presenting the estimates, we will say a word about each category of expenditure and what is to be expected in each case.

CONSUMPTION

Public consumption is composed of expenditures on current running costs of public services and the military: wages and salaries, fuel, rent, and so on. It should exemplify institutional inertia best since quick discretionary changes are difficult to make. Policymakers cannot hire and fire civil servants and instigate or cancel programs in response to transitory conditions, at least not on a large enough scale to be evident in aggregate government consumption. There may be some stabilization policy effects since Keynesian economics suggests that governments should increase spending during depressions and reduce it during booms.

TRANSFER PAYMENTS

These are not direct expenditures on goods but involve payments to persons. Pensions, student grants, unemployment benefit, food stamps, and the like are included. Transfers usually result from "entitlement" programs, in which legislation establishes a rate of benefit and a class of eligible recipients. The actual amount government spends depends on the number of persons qualifying for benefits. This can vary in the long term in response to demographic changes as, say, the proportion of old people changes. It varies in the short term in response to economic fluctuations as, say, the level of unemployment varies. Benefit *rates* are often indexed so that the outlay *per person qualifying* stays constant in real terms.

INVESTMENT

Government investment represents increases in the capital stock of the public sector, including equipment, buildings, roads, and the like. Investment is likely to be planned over a long horizon. Paradoxically, it is also the category which, at least in Britain, appears to be most affected by considerations of stabilization policy. This is because there is less political resistance to canceling capital projects if they have not begun or are "contracted out" to private firms. In contrast, running down programs involves firing public employees, and cutting benefit rates has immediate widespread effects. Consequently, many discretionary changes in public investment turn out to be cuts in plans rather than cuts in actual expenditures (Price, 1978).

ESTIMATES OF THE PERMANENT INCOME
MODEL

The emphasis on planning in the permanent income model means that expenditures should respond mainly to the trend or permanent level of national income rather than to its short-term variations. At an empirical level, one can represent this sort of sluggish adjustment process by setting expenditures to be a function of an infinitely long series of past values of income with declining weights. The Koyck transformation[1] provides a simpler operationalizing alternative. As a result of this transformation, current expenditure depends only on current national income and lagged expenditure. All influences on expenditure before the current period have already determined last

1. To achieve the Koyck transformation of an infinite sum with geometrically declining weights into a single lag formulation, reverse the steps of Chapter 7, n. 7.

period's spending, and their effects are captured in the lagged expenditure term. The only new piece of information is current income.

Equations 1–3 in Table 10.1 present a set of estimates of a permanent income formulation for British public expenditures for the period 1955–1979, in three separate categories: consumption, transfer payments to individuals, and public investment. The estimates reported in Table 10.1 are a good baseline for understanding the stability of public expenditures. In each case the fit is satisfactory, and there is little evidence of technical problems with the equations. A variety of subperiod estimates (not reported) suggest that the functions are stable and robust, except that the path of investment alters dramatically in the 1970s.

The interpretation of the coefficients is straightforward. Take, for example, the consumption function. An increase in GDP of £100 million would increase government consumption by £9.4 millions in the current quarter (based on the coefficient of GDP) and ultimately by £31 millions (9.4 divided by 1 − 0.718) *if sustained*. The other series require some seasonal adjustments, but the general interpretation is the same, with the long-term income shares lower than consumption in each case.[2]

To show that these results are not confined to Britain, the same functions were estimated for the United States. Equations 4–6 in Table 10.1 give the results. Equation 4 shows that federal nondefense consumption expenditures in the period 1950–1980 reflect the same pattern of response to sustained income growth that we discussed in the British case.[3] Equation 6 shows that the relationship between transfers and income is less well determined but still statistically significant. These equations may have other problems, but they lend credibility to the permanent income formulation as a guide to the time path of public

2. The "permanent" share of income taken by government consumption is lower when cyclical factors are included. See Table 10.4, below. The adjustment of investment downward in the second quarter could equally be represented as an adjustment upward in the first quarter. It probably reflects the practice of meeting annual targets by holding off some expenditure until the end of the fiscal year.

3. Defense expenditures were excluded to avoid having to estimate separately the period of the Vietnam War or finding some proxy for estimating the impact of the war on expenditures.

TABLE 10.1   PERMANENT INCOME MODEL

	Coefficient	T-Statistic	
Britain, 1955–1979			
(1) Government consumption =			
Govt. consump. (t − 1)	0.718	17.2	$R^2 = 0.99$
GDP	0.094	6.9	DW = 2.14
Constant	−3.35	6.0	
(2) Government transfers to individuals =			
Transfers (t − 1)	0.862	16.7	$R^2 = 0.99$
GDP	0.021	2.1	DW = 2.36
4th quarter 1972 on	1.172	7.0	
Constant	−0.86	1.5	
(3) Government capital investment =			
Investment (t − 1)	0.903	4.3	$R^2 = 0.90$
GDP	0.019	4.9	DW = 2.81
2nd quarter 1965–1970	−0.661	3.1	
2nd quarter 1971–1973	−1.873	6.2	
2nd quarter 1974 on	−2.960	13.0	
Constant	−1.23	4.3	
United States, 1949–1980			
(4) Federal government nondefense consumption =			
Govt. consump. (t − 1)	0.839	16.5	$R^2 = 0.97$
GDP	0.005	3.2	DW = 1.50
Constant	−0.01	1.9	
(5) State government total consumption =			
Govt. consump. (t − 1)	1.002	72.4	$R^2 = 0.99$
GDP	−0.00005	0.0	DW = 1.30
Constant	0.01	1.1	
(6) Federal transfer payments to persons =			
Transfers (t − 1)	0.969	42.6	$R^2 = 0.99$
GDP	0.006	2.0	DW = 2.03
Constant	−0.027	1.7	

Note: All estimates are by instrumental variables, based on quarterly data. GDP is an instrument created as the fitted variable of a regression on predetermined and exogenous variables including aggregate investment and exports. All expenditures and GDP are price-deflated, in Britain with the retail price index, and in the United States with the GDP deflator. Quarter variables are binary 0 − 1.

Sources: Data for Britain are from *Economic Trends,* various, from 1955.1 to 1979.4. Data for the United States are from Citibank, N.A. *Machine-Readable Data Bank,* from 1949.3 to 1980.2.

expenditures. A theory of public expenditure growth should at least start from the assumption that expenditures will take a stable share of national income in the long term.

The permanent income formulation should not work in some contexts. We have stressed the institutional procedures for bargaining and planning as the mechanism by which expectations of sustained income growth are translated into higher levels of expenditure. It would be strange to find the permanent income relationship where there was no institutional framework in which such planning could take place. There is no way for the states collectively to "plan" around their expected incomes. A test for aggregate government consumption at the state level in the United States is shown in equation 5. Here we find no income effect. Indeed, the expenditure series is purely "auto-regressive," that is, each successive value is a function of the previous observation, without any evident long-run income effects. Such long-run effects could show up *within* individual states. No institution corresponds to the aggregation of states, and there is no evidence of a permanent income effect. While there is still inertia in this case, there is no effect on this spending of short-term changes in GDP.

TESTS OF OTHER POLITICOECONOMIC HYPOTHESES

We turn now to a comparison of the permanent income formulation for the determination of public expenditures with other political-economic formulations. The most ambitious empirical politicoeconomic model in the literature is certainly the Frey-Schneider model (Frey and Schneider 1978a, 1978b, 1979).[4] Their model is an elaborate attempt to look at the manipulation of economic policy instruments in the reaction function context we discussed in Chapter 6. It attempts to introduce the electoral ambitions of politicians directly into a systematic model of expenditure determination in several countries. However, we will show that their model involves a relatively

4. A number of technical difficulties with their model are discussed in Chrystal and Alt (1981b) and need not be elaborated here.

small departure from our approach. While it appears to lead to very different results, we shall see that these results depend critically on one arbitrary restriction in their model, a restriction which is unjustified on statistical grounds.

The key variable in the Frey-Schneider approach is what they call the "popularity deficit" (DEF). At any time, the government is assumed to have some critical standing in the opinion polls such that if it leads the opposition by at least this amount, it is confident of winning the next election. This critical popularity level is defined arbitrarily as 8 percent behind the opposition immediately after an election, rising irregularly to eight percentage points ahead just before an election. The popularity deficit, DEF, is then equal to the difference between the actual lead in recent opinion polls and this critical standing.

The values of the expenditures which the government chooses to adopt depend critically upon whether DEF is positive or negative. If it is negative (the government's lead is less than its critical standing), the government engages in reelection effort by spending more and taxing less, the intensity of this effort depending on the size of DEF. If DEF is positive, "ideological" targets are pursued. In effect, this means that the party in power sets the expenditures by reference to DEF multiplied by GDP, with different target shares of GDP in expenditure assumed for Labor and Conservative incumbencies. Finally, there are, for all periods, variables reflecting "economic constraints," the balance of payments (BOP), and the real wage rate (W) in all cases and, additionally, unemployment in the case of transfers. Their model is thus of the following form, for any expenditure category E_t:

$$E_t = \text{constant} + a_1 D_1 \text{DEF} + a_{2i}(1 - D_1)D\ \text{DEF} \times \text{GDP}$$
$$+ a_3 D_1 E_{t-1} + a_4(1 - D_1)E_{t-1} + a_5 \text{BOP}_{t-1} + a_6 W_{t-1} \qquad (1)$$

where D_1 is one in periods of popularity deficit and zero otherwise, and the coefficient a_{2i} of GDP varies over parties of different ideologies.

Frey and Schneider provide estimates of their model for the United States, Britain, and Germany. Expenditures are affected by reelection strategies and ideology, as well as the economic constraint. In terms of our discussion, their model really raises three separate questions, and we shall deal with them one at a time. First, does the planning we have been describing stop in critical periods? That is, is there any evidence that the relationship we have been describing between expenditures and expected trend growth of GDP disappears at times because politicians adopt other strategies? Second, how much does party control matter? What differences in expenditures can be attributed to differing ideological commitments? Finally, what is the role in expenditure determination of the economic constraint, or, in our terms, how big is the role of stabilization policy?

DOES PLANNING STOP?

First, let us take the question of planning. According to Frey and Schneider, equation (1) does not contain GDP when popularity is in deficit (below the critical standard). In this case, its coefficient is *restricted* to zero. That is, when popularity is in deficit, $D_1 = 1$, so that $1 - D_1 = 0$, and the GDP term drops out of the equation. Thus (abbreviating the constraint terms), their model really has two different equations for periods of popularity deficit and surplus:

Deficit: $E_t = a_1 Def + a_3 E_{t-1} + \ldots$
Surplus: $E_t = a_{2i} Def \times GDP + a_4 E_{t-1} + \ldots .$

Their surplus period equation is much like our permanent income formulation, but with the extra complication that GDP is multiplied by DEF. In a period of popularity deficit, there is no target share of GDP in the equation, but it is replaced by the popularity deficit. Thus, their model assumes that governments in popularity deficit periods consider only their position in the polls and spend *without* consideration of national income.

The obvious way to test this restriction is to take their deficit period equation and add GDP to it. If the result of doing this is that a_1 is then found to be zero and that $a_3 = a_4$, then the apparent empirical success of their model rests on the erroneous omission of national income in periods of popularity deficit. We have done considerable statistical estimation which showed no differences even remotely approaching statistical significance between popularity deficit and nondeficit periods in the relationship between national income and expenditure. For example, the equation reported in Chrystal and Alt (1981b) for Britain from 1962 to 1974 provided estimates statistically consistent with $a_3 = a_4 = 0.54$, $a_1 = 0$, and $b_2 = 0.04$ regardless of which party was in power and whether or not popularity was in deficit or surplus. In no case have we been able to find a significant effect of popularity deficit on expenditure *if GDP was included in the equation as well.*[5]

The apparent impact of the popularity deficit on expenditures which Frey and Schneider report rests on the unwarranted exclusion of GDP from their model in periods of popularity deficit. If GDP really predicts expenditures in deficit periods, then its omission will cause whatever replaces it to pick up the GDP effect. There is a strong presumption that this is what happens in the Frey-Schneider model since (according to all the studies reviewed in Chapter 7) it is probable that the popularity deficit is itself partly a function of GDP through the effect of income on popularity.

ELECTORAL CYCLES AND PARTISAN SHIFTS

In the estimates discussed above, there were several cases in which party control of government appeared to affect expenditure, but these could not be estimated at satisfactory levels of statistical significance. In Chapter 5, we saw that in Britain, at least, the targets of policy, unemployment, and inflation probably did not display electoral-cyclical movements. If governments change their behavior before elections, the changes should appear in the figures for revenues and expenditures even if they are reversed before affecting unemployment or output. It is therefore important to see whether such behavior shows up in our model. (It is possible that some changes are just announcements for effect, and these are beyond the scope of this approach.)

Chrystal and Alt (1981a) provide an extended discussion of a search for short-term cycles reflecting electoral ambitions in the series for consumption and transfers. We pursued the strategy of entering

5. In their reply to Chrystal and Alt (1981b) Frey and Schneider claim further to defend their model through its superior forecasting ability. What they actually demonstrate is that their model *including* the economic constraint outperforms a version of ours from which the constraint has been *excluded*. Their reply thus demonstrates nothing about the importance of reelection strategy in determining expenditure. All the points we have just made apply equally well to forecasting tests.

into the permanent income equations reported in Table 10.1 each of a set of terms designed to capture some characteristic fluctuation in expenditure: the popularity deficit as defined by Frey and Schneider, dummy variables representing both the two and four quarters before general elections, a dummy variable designed to pick up an acceleration in the four quarters before an election (rather than a constant shift), and, finally, a dummy variable separating Labor and Conservative incumbencies, to pick up the sort of partisan or ideological differences suggested by Frey and Schneider, among others.

Only in one case, transfer payments to individuals, did any of these "political" formulations achieve statistical significance as a determinant of expenditures. This result is presented in Table 10.2. Transfer payments have generally been higher under Labor administrations. The precision of this estimate is not great, and we shall see below that there is good reason to believe that the effect is really confined to the Labor administration of 1964–1970. Nevertheless, it appears that transfers are higher under Labor, and the magnitude of the difference, when the coefficient is rescaled by the magnitude of expenditures in the equation, is about £15 millions, or about 3 percent of transfer payments in 1964.[6]

Tufte's (1978) argument (reviewed in Chapter 5) rests on the assertion that real income increases unusually fast in election years. This atypical increase is somehow fueled by governmental tampering with the amount of money expended in transfer (particularly Social Security and veterans' benefits) payments. Tufte emphasizes the timing of Social Security benefit increases before the 1972 election and the creation of a "window" in benefit-cost relationships owing to the deferment of increased contributions until after the election, while benefits are increased before it. A recent critique by Winters et al. (1981) agrees that "windows" of the sort Tufte describes are evident in 1972 and 1976.

---

6. It is worth remembering that a long-standing literature on expenditures in subnational units has tried and failed to provide any evidence that party competition stimulates (especially welfare) expenditures. Some of the literature is theoretically misconceived, but the general proposition is that in competitive systems elected politicians will bid up expenditures to gain votes whereas in one-party systems there will be no incentive to do so, producing *ceteris paribus* higher levels of expenditure in competitive systems. This has never found empirical confirmation. The latest paper to make this point is Jennings (1979).

TABLE 10.2   ELECTORAL CYCLES AND SHIFTS IN BRITISH
TRANSFER PAYMENTS

	Coefficient	T-Statistic	
Transfer payments =			
Transfers (t − 1)	0.848	16.6	$R^2 = 0.99$
GDP	0.021	2.1	DW = 2.39
4th quarter 1972 on	1.210	7.3	
Labor incumbency	0.200	2.0	
Constant	−0.779		

Note: See Table 10.1. Labor incumbency is defined as one between 1964.4 and 1970.2 and between 1974.2 and 1979.2, and zero otherwise.
Sources: See Table 10.1.

However, such windows are, in fact, common, and not confined to election periods. Most (and the largest) windows occur well away from preelection quarters.

To look at the possible role of electoral manipulation in transfer payments, Figure 10.2 plots the residuals which are the differences between observed values and those predicted by the transfers function

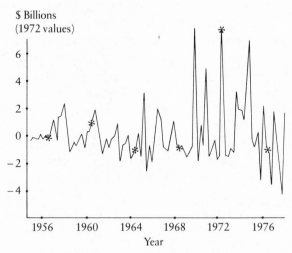

*Presidential election quarter

FIGURE 10.2. Residuals from the Permanent Income Federal
Transfers Equation

reported in Table 10.1, equation 6. A high positive residual reflects aggregate transfers higher than the overall function would predict for that quarter. Three things are immediately clear in the figure. First, the residual for the election (fourth) quarter of 1972 was extraordinarily large and positive, confirming that transfers that quarter were unusually high. Second, there is no regular occurrence of high positive residuals in election quarters. Finally, as Winters and his colleagues suggest, most of the outlying positive residuals (big quarterly increases) lie well away from election quarters. Thus, the figure reveals the exceptional quality of the election of 1972, so prominent in Tufte's account.

STABILIZATION POLICY CONSIDERATIONS

The third consideration is stabilization policy and the economic constraint. Does public expenditure display the characteristics of government reactions to the state of the economy? It is conventional to distinguish between responses to economic change which are *automatic* (require no formal intervention, such as the rise in unemployment benefits paid when unemployment rises) and those which are *discretionary* or require some formal intervention such as a cut in planned public investment. Either sort of response may be modeled as a reaction function for an economic instrument in terms of economic targets and its own lagged values.[7] Unemployment rates, inflation rates, and the balance of payments are generally agreed to be the targets of economic policy in Britain (though note that Frey and Schneider's choice is different). We accordingly incorporate them in the basic model.

Table 10.3 gives estimation results for consumption and transfer payments.[8] The balance of payments never enters significantly into the government consumption function. Equation 1 in Table 10.3 provides

7. A properly specified reaction function would include some measure of the difference between actual and "desired" values of the targets. Only discretionary changes would relate to these differences whereas automatic changes would relate to actual levels only.

8. The picture with respect to stabilization policy and investment is clouded by the need to make a variable seasonal adjustment, as in Table 10.1. This requires too lengthy a discussion of estimates for the present context, but the likeliest interpretation is that there was some consistent reaction to the balance of payments only and that this was confined to the period before 1972.

TABLE 10.3   STABILIZATION POLICY AND EXPENDITURES
IN BRITAIN

	Coefficient	T-Statistic	
(1) Government consumption 1955–1979 =			
Govt. consump. (t − 1)	0.627	8.9	R^2 = 0.99
GDP	0.101	5.7	DW = 1.99
Unemployment (t − 1)	0.167	2.0	
Inflation (t − 1)	0.067	3.9	
Constant	−3.29	6.3	
(2) Government consumption 1955–1972 =			
Govt. consump. (t − 1)	0.619	9.0	R^2 = 0.99
GDP	0.102	6.0	DW = 1.84
Unemployment (t − 1)	0.185	2.1	
Inflation (t − 1)	0.012	0.6	
Constant	−2.80	5.6	
(3) Government consumption 1955–1979, excluding 1973.2–1976.2 =			
Govt. consump. (t − 1)	0.626	11.1	R^2 = 0.99
GDP	0.100	7.1	DW = 1.89
Unemployment (t − 1)	0.266	3.3	
Inflation (t − 1)	−0.004	0.2	
Constant	−2.77	5.6	
(4) Transfer payments 1955–1979 =			
Transfers (t − 1)	0.619	7.9	R^2 = 0.99
GDP	0.046	4.0	DW = 2.24
4th quarter 1972 on	1.002	6.0	
Unemployment (t − 1)	0.344	4.1	
Labor incumbency			
1964–1970	0.386	3.5	
Constant	−2.190	3.4	

Note: See Tables 10.1 and 10.2. Inflation is defined as the annual change in the retail price index. The unemployment rate is in percentages.
Sources: See Tables 10.1 and 10.2.

a set of estimates which include the permanent income formulation discussed above, but with apparently significant effects attributable to unemployment and inflation as targets. Since the coefficient attaching to unemployment is positive, government consumption is higher when unemployment is higher. This is a discretionary response by the authorities in line with orthodox stabilization policy. (Higher unemployment would not increase consumption automatically.)

The sign of the inflation coefficient is the opposite of that indicated by stabilization policy. Expenditure should be cut, not increased, when inflation is high. Subperiod comparisons reveal that the effect of inflation is a transitory phenomenon. The same function estimated for the period through 1972 (equation 2 in Table 10.3) indicates no inflation effect, with other estimates largely unchanged. The inflation effect is confined to the period from mid-1973 to mid-1976. The third equation shows that if these twelve quarterly observations are omitted, the estimates are unchanged from the early period. There is no evidence that the experience of the last three years is different in any way from the period before mid-1973. Why the effects of inflation on government consumption should have been so severe in the mid-1970s is hard to say. A variety of explanations present themselves, including differential cost increases in the public sector and overzealous application of inflation supplementation, a practice ended in early 1976. Net of these short-term influences, the long-run share of income taken by government consumption is $0.10/(1 - 0.626)$, or about 26 percent, roughly in line with the present share shown in Figure 10.1.

Neither inflation nor the balance of payments appears in the transfers function, but there is a large and significant coefficient attaching to the unemployment rate. The effect of unemployment is larger than in the consumption equations (the coefficient is larger and aggregate transfer payments are less than consumption). At least part of this effect is the automatic response to changes in unemployment of unemployment benefit, a major component of transfers. The inclusion of unemployment also eliminates any upward shift due to Labor partisanship after 1974. This "ideological" difference between parties with respect to transfers appears only in the 1964–1970 Labor government. The higher levels of transfers between 1974 and 1979 are entirely due to the higher levels of unemployment prevailing in that incumbency rather than to the ideological preferences of parties.

SUMMARY

Public expenditure—and particularly public consumption—grows roughly in proportion with national income. It maintains this proportion initially because politicians and administrators plan it that way. In part the growth of national income is a handy reference standard for negotiations about individual expenditure allocations, but expenditure plans are also too rigid to change in line with short-term fluctuations in income. In such a context, when growth rates fell sharply after the 1973 oil crisis, government expenditure continued to grow until it became clear that the income losses would be sustained. We believe that it was this transitory episode of apparently rapid government growth as a share of GDP that sparked the enormous surge in the literature on the growth of government. In fact, the growth in the government share of GDP in that period was principally the consequence of a contraction in GDP. British government consumption was cut between 1976 and 1978 in line with the apparent permanence of the national income contraction following 1973. Investment was cut more drastically. Government consumption expenditures as a share of GDP in the United States did not grow at all in the late 1970s.

Public expenditure is only one aspect of the central question of the appropriate role of government in a market economy. We hope to have at least heightened the awareness of readers to the misconceptions and distortions which abound even in apparently technical studies of the subject. There are effects of stabilization policy and even of partisan differences, though those, in the case of transfer payments in Britain, were episodic rather than sustained. Individual expenditure decisions are certainly political, and cases can be found which are consistent with any of the models in Chapter 8. In terms of the aggregates which appear in macroeconomic models, the principal characteristic of expenditure is a close relationship to trend national income.

Conclusion

The subject of political economics is the economic role of governments. The economic policies of elected governments can be fully understood only in the light of a variety of influences. Economic theories provide both the ideas about the appropriate economic role of government and the framework for analysis of what governments have actually done. Political influences affect the way policies are formed by incumbent politicians in the context of the political institutions. Politicians consider many aspects other than the pure economics of a problem. Chosen policies must be feasible both in the historical and institutional context of the domestic economy and in that provided by international institutions and the world economy. In this chapter, we expand upon these themes as they have arisen in this book.

POLITICAL ECONOMICS IN RETROSPECT

To ask sensible questions about the economic role of government requires having clear ideas about the working of a market economy as a system. This is addressed by economics, especially within the general equilibrium tradition. Chapter 1 provides a history of economic thought in this area as a foundation for subsequent arguments. Formal analysis of the market economy provides clear definitions of areas in which "market failure" is likely. Such "failures" present opportunities for some form of "government" action to make the outcome "better."

Exactly what kind of action should the government take and how does the decision get made? Economic theory is very useful in setting up the problem. It is less helpful in providing realistic solutions. Even where analytical solutions are available in the abstract, they rely upon concepts, such as "social welfare," which are no visible guide to the policymaker. Indeed, when questions of distribution arise, and the problem is to choose between Pareto-efficient points, economists frequently throw up their hands and state that the problem is "political." Economists, by implication, have done their job. The rest is for someone else.

Economics can be taken both further and less far than this. It can be taken further because the methods of economic analysis can be successfully applied to explicitly political problems. The economic analyses of policymaking in Chapter 6 and of voting in Chapter 7 are good examples. It can be taken less far because even the standard economics is much more political than economists usually admit. An example is the way policy outcomes are affected by institutional constraints. Understanding macroeconomic policies requires understanding the division of responsibility between the finance ministry and the central bank (Chapter 2). Possible uses of fiscal policy are limited if, as in the United States, the president cannot rely on getting his proposed budget passed by Congress (Chapter 5). Indeed, the need for a Keynesian type of fiscal policy arises in economies only where the polity cannot accommodate more effective control mechanisms (Chapter 3).

Better understanding of political factors will improve economists' conception of "government" or the state. When economists do include government as an actor in their models, it is sometimes as a disembodied and disinterested puppeteer pulling strings from on high, with nothing more in mind than to improve the lot of the puppets. If it is not this, then it is an evil witch entering an idyllic scene where everybody is as happy as could be already. Neither of these is a sensible conception of government when trying to make constructive comment about the role of government in any *real* economy. Government is an institution within the system made up of the actors of the system. It is a useful procedure to think of economic policy in terms of the control of abstract models. But the story should not end there. Sensible policy recommendations also must be thought through in their full institutional context.

The general idea of optimization is important as a means of understanding behavior. Optimization, however, is "context-bound." The economy and polity are adjusted to an institutional framework. Any change in economic and political institutional structures will cause actors to adapt to the new arrangements. The costs of such adaptation can be substantial. They must be offset by the benefits of the institutional change. Because of the adjustment costs, what would be the optimal policy in the absence of existing arrangements may not be the optimal policy net of the extra adjustment costs. Indeed, it need not even offer guidance as to the general direction in which the optimal policy net of adjustment costs might be found. The effects of changing a tax system exceed the straightforward changes in the prices of goods that result. But the idea applies in broader contexts as well. To argue that the United States can learn how to make economic policy from the Japanese requires a demonstration that the institutional changes which would be required would not cause even greater adjustment costs as well.

Part II specifies the institutional arrangements on which policy outcomes and adjustment costs depend. Chapter 2 outlines the political institutional framework. Chapter 3 describes the development of thought about how the macroeconomy works and the role of "government" within it. Chapter 4 points out that none of these issues can be viewed in purely "domestic" terms. The domestic economy is not isolated from what is going on in the rest of the world economy— there are spillovers at all levels of activity. People in most countries have been aware of this for some time. It was brought home to the United States by the OPEC oil price rise of 1973. Political constraints are also imposed by membership of the international community through treaty obligations and membership in international organizations.

A substantial literature attempts to demonstrate the influence of political factors upon economic policy. Much of this literature is superficial and tendentious. The most popular story tells of an incumbent party which manufactures boom conditions in order to win re-election. Chapter 5 and Chapter 10 argue that this part of the literature is neither theoretically convincing nor supported by the evidence. It displays bad economics, poor empirical support, and, most of all, scant attention to the workings of the political institutions themselves. We have tried to make clear what the contribution of such an account would be and suggested areas where progress is being made.

Chapter 6 outlines analysis of policymaking viewed as maximization of some objective function subject to constraints. Indeed, it is hard to see how else it can be viewed especially if aggregate empirical studies are required. Setting up the problem this way requires careful attention to how an objective function may be formulated and what happens if no unified objective function exists. There is also a need for a thorough understanding of how an economy works and the institutional constraints within which policies operate. The advantage of the framework is that it lays out the assumptions necessary for applied policy analysis. It also clarifies the difficulties of interpretation which arise in any empirical analyses of the behavior and motives of policymakers.

Actors in the economic system express their preferences for most goods (subject to the constraints of incomes and prices) by their spending in the marketplace. They express their preferences for those things which are provided by the polity by political activity and thus *in part* by their voting behavior. Nothing is lost and much is gained by viewing voters' choices as a special case of economic choice problems. Voters vote for the party which offers the greatest expected utility of outcome. Upon what specific factors does this utility depend, and what does this add to our understanding of voting behavior? Chapter 7 calls attention to the importance of understanding the difficulties underlying even apparently simple calculations of economic advantage, as well as the important role in these models for media influence, the impact of exogenous shocks, and the formation of standards of evaluation. This is one more aspect of the general problem of how to decide upon the appropriate level of state activity. Voters' choices reflect their information, which depends on the prevailing intellectual climate which supplies analyses of what government should or should not be doing.

What should the public sector do? Chapter 8 reviewed the welfare economics analysis based on identification of market failure such as monopoly, externalities, or providing public goods, and redistribution. The fact that the public sector exists causes less contention than the fact that it has grown, and, by implication, excessively. The problems of measuring "government" cannot be stressed too often. Arguments have been put forward that this growth is the unintended by-product of other policies, the intended political result of ideological programs, or a consequence of incentives and power in institutional structures. There is no reason to believe that government growth has only one cause. Many of the arguments may have been valid in some places and at some times.

Deciding between competing explanations is a question of evidence, which Chapters 9 and 10 confront. The evidence does not support the view of government as manipulative and destabilizing in the short term. Government consumption expenditures in both the United States and Britain as a proportion of national income are remarkably stable. Partisan control and stabilization policy have limited effects. Different institutional structures in which expenditure decisions are made are an important determinant of international variation. In general, it is best to start the study of government expenditure from a presumption of institutional inertia.

POLITICAL ECONOMICS IN PRACTICE

THE CONTEMPORARY SCENE

The elections in 1979 and 1980 of Margaret Thatcher in Britain and of Ronald Reagan in the United States, following on the Social Democrats' defeat in Sweden in 1976 after nearly half a century in power, appeared to many to herald the triumph of a new conservative economic doctrine. As *Newsweek* put it after the first Reagan budget:

The age of conservative economics has arrived, and its implications for all Americans are immense. Not only did last week's tax bill reverse decades of social engineering to provide important new incentives for the rich, it also permanently reduced the government's role in economic life. By voting to index future tax rates to protect citizens against the encroachment of inflation, Congress junked the great engine that has financed the growth of Big Government in the postwar period—and greatly reduced its own power in the process. "We have the largest tax cut in the history of the world," exulted Treasury Secretary Donald T. Regan, "and when you add indexation to that, it changes the whole concept of how fiscal matters will be handled in Washington in the decades ahead." (August 10, 1981, p. 21)

Was there a worldwide movement to the right? The defeat of the Swedish Social Democrats involved energy policy and foreign affairs as much as taxation. The defeat of the Labor government in Britain in 1979 owes a great deal to their commitment to an economic policy that led to the deferral of full employment targets and a squeeze on the incomes and benefits of much of their working-class constituency. Thus, if there was a movement to the right, it was in the economic policies of the Labor government at least as much as in the ideology of the electorate. Moreover, France in the same period moved in the opposite direction and elected a socialist president for the first time since the foundation of the Fifth Republic whereas Sweden returned the Social Democrats to office in 1982. These elections all reflect growing public concern about the economic difficulties of the 1970s. They reflect a widespread public reaction to economic problems that takes the form of blaming incumbents for economic failure and trying the remedies proposed by those out of power. They reveal little evidence of growing public conviction that the best answers lie with the Right.

There is a "new conservative economics." It is a doctrine unified principally by opposition to government intervention. It owes much to Monetarism, for "sound money" (low inflation) is an important aspect of its policy. The new conservative economics derives from New Classical economics the belief in "rational" actors, natural rates of output and employment, and efficient markets. It has leaned heavily on supply-side economics, seeking policies to encourage productivity in the private sector. High marginal tax rates are seen to be a disincentive to work and wealth creation. Contracting the scope of government activity will provide a stimulus to economic growth.

Prime Minister Thatcher and President Reagan believe in this "new conservative economics," though Thatcher has more commonly been called "monetarist" in the British media. The economic policies of both these leaders represent considerable changes from those of their predecessors. Whether what they have actually done is consistent with the tenets of the new conservative economics is another matter. While many domestic programs have been cut, defense spending has been increased. One year after the passage of the 1981 Tax Act, Congress passed "the largest tax increase in American history." The Thatcher administration's commitment to reduce the size of the public sector did not materially affect the relationship we have analyzed between government consumption and national income, at least in her first year in office. The difficulty of cutting expenditure was heightened by increased numbers receiving unemployment benefits. Expenditures combined with recession-reduced revenues to produce government deficits. The need to finance these deficits interfered considerably with the government's proposed monetary strategy.

It is difficult to dissociate policy from the ideas which influence policy. No politician does something without *some* reason and without some expectation of what the outcome will be. Whether a policy is judged to be good or bad depends largely on the ideas of the time, though these will almost certainly change over time. Nothing illustrates this better than the changing attitude to budget deficits.

Before the 1930s it was widely accepted that governments should balance their budgets except in times of severest crisis like external wars. Keynesian economic policy regarded it as a positive virtue for governments to run deficits from time to time. In the 1970s and early 1980s, the emergence of massive budget deficits in several major countries was accompanied by a growing belief that deficits are almost entirely "bad things." In the United States there is even the possibility of a constitutional amendment requiring a balanced budget. The objection to deficits is an aspect of the drift to more conservative policy attitudes but is worthy of some elaboration.

Deficits were thought to be good for one reason, and one reason alone. A deficit arises when government spending exceeds tax revenue. This represents a net injection of spending into the economy (in Keynesian terms) which will stimulate production and thereby increase growth until "full employment" is reached. Economic objections to deficits are largely along the lines of "crowding out." There are many popular misconceptions in this area. A common argument is that since a deficit has to be funded by borrowing, the extent of such borrowing will be associated with a one-to-one reduction in borrowable funds available for the private sector. There would thus be a corresponding reduction in private sector investment. This argument is almost entirely fallacious. The deficit may, for example, be entirely funded by borrowing from abroad. Even in a closed economy the deficit has complex effects. For example, the supply of saving and the demand for investment will change so that the overall impact on domestic investment is uncertain, even as to direction let alone magnitude. This is not to say that government debt sales strategies cannot put upward pressure on nominal interest rates at times and that this pressure is a disincentive to investment. These effects, however, need not always dominate. It is possible to have economic growth and very high real interest rates, though most of the cases where this has happened have also been countries whose size and institutional structure permitted policies of directing finance to specific growth-oriented industries.

Another economic objection to deficits is that ultimately they cause inflation. This reflects either increased pressure on real resources or unwillingness and inability of governments to control the money supply. This would be true if printing money (or, more commonly, borrowing from the central bank) were an easier and more popular method of funding than raising taxes or borrowing elsewhere. From a political point of view the attitude toward deficits depends upon whether they were accidental or deliberate. Where they are accidental, the incumbent party can incur the wrath of the electorate for apparent incompetence. Where they are deliberate, the implications depend very much upon the attitudes of the time—or at least the balance of pros and cons reflected in the dominant intentions of the legislative assemblies.

SOME RECURRENT THEMES

Political economics is a coherent area of inquiry which draws ideas from a number of sources—notably politics and economics—and applies them to an analysis of economic policy in a real world setting. Political economics is about the study of economic policy in its political context. Economic policy is not made in the classroom, in the factory, or in the bank. In this sense at least politics and economics are inseparable. The intentions of policy are strongly influenced by contemporary economic theories. The realities of policy are constrained by political feasibility. To reinforce this perspective it is convenient to draw out recurrent themes or implications developed in the analysis.

International Differences

Blindly transferring analytical perspectives from one country to another without a careful regard for the institutional differences between them is dangerous. Those who proffer economic advice freely to governments of many countries on the basis of what they think they know about their own economy make this mistake. Less well understood by political scientists are the implications for economic policy (both external and internal) of the position of the sectors of the domestic economy (of the country concerned) with regard to the structure of the international economy. For example, a country which is small in financial markets and has a fixed exchange rate cannot usefully be described as having an independent monetary policy. If it is small in the markets for its imports and exports, commercial policy will not influence its terms of trade.

Politics and Economic Policy

The greater part of economic theorizing about policy has been concerned with the objective of maximizing income for the economy as a whole. This is a useful way to proceed for some purposes, but problems arise as soon as there are both gainers and losers from any policy. However, it seems pertinent to observe that the *politics* of economic policymaking is dominantly concerned with distributive aspects of the impact of various policies on the public. But all economic policies have distributive aspects, and, consequently, all have a "politics" as well as "economics." This is true *whether or not the major intended impact of the policy is redistributive.*

Virtually any policy you can think of will affect some groups more than others. Changing income tax rates affects the rich more than the poor. Changing a tariff affects the import competing industry directly as well as potential consumers of the import. Subsidizing a branch railroad benefits those who use it at a cost to those who wouldn't, even at the subsidized price. Deregulation of air fares in the United States affected the airlines and travelers. Cutting expenditures on some social program affects the workers hired on this program as well as the recipients of benefits, at some gain perhaps to the taxpayer. Political leverage of potential gainers and losers affects policy outcomes, as does information about benefits and costs.

Discretion and Constraint

We have repeatedly drawn attention to the importance of making a distinction between areas in which policymakers have discretion and areas in which they are constrained. In practice, everything is difficult or costly to change. Not all policies are "up for grabs" at any point in time. Only a fraction of tax rates or expenditure is even considered for change in any particular policy stage. Policies are made at the margin. The status quo survives unless there is an active will to change it. The status quo is the cumulative weight of the entire history of policy as well as the evolution of social and economic institutions. Thus, history has generated a kind of capital stock which must be treated as given in deciding what are feasible policy outcomes. This point is important in understanding international differences. Policy toward labor markets in Britain cannot ignore the union structure which largely evolved in the nineteenth century. Analyses of fiscal policy in the United States requires understanding the division of responsibility between federal and state authorities whose roots are even older.

More things constrain policy than simply inertia or the laws of nature. Ideas about how the economy works may be equally binding constraints on policy. Many constraints will in practice be "chosen" by policymakers. If a monetary growth rule is adopted, this will constrain other areas of policy. From the point of view of policy analysis, it will be sensible to look at the choice of other instruments as if the growth rule were a constraint, though a full account would presumably need an explanation of why the growth rule was adopted.

The most important example of this kind of shifting constraint is given by the abandonment of fixed exchange rates by major countries in the 1971–1973 period. Fixed exchange rates represented a severe and binding constraint upon macroeconomic policy, especially in countries like Britain, which tended recurrently to drift into balance of payments deficits. The switch to floating exchange rates gave policymakers more freedom. However, it soon became clear that their resultant actions were doing little good and in many cases were inflicting much harm. The *idea* which resulted from this experience was that governments should *choose* to severely limit their activities. This led to the recurrence of talk about balanced budgets, the widespread adoption of monetary targets, and cooperative exchange-rate-fixing policies like the European Monetary System.

Platforms and Policies

Political candidates can promise to solve all sorts of problems if elected. Once in office, both the realities of power in political institutions and the workings of the economy interfere. Economic structures can dominate ideological commitments. A well-known example was the abandonment of the British Labor government's expansionary policies in the face of exchange rate and balance of payments constraints in the late 1960s. Ideas are thus easier to change than structures. Political expedience demands that the strongest commitments crowd out the weakest parts of economic theory. The Reagan administration abandoned the part of the supply-side argument that cuts in tax rates would be self-financing through economic growth. The commitment to build defense appeared to be stronger than the economic arguments about harmful effects of deficits. The result was an economic policy compromise which balances: (1) increased defense spending, (2) the need to raise taxes to pay for it without creating deficits which cause disorder in financial markets, and (3) the alleged disincentive effects of the increased taxes.

What all this means is that preelection commitments and rhetoric give way ultimately under the pressure of economic and political constraints. In an extended period of economic problems, this produces the appearance of repeated economic policy failures by incumbents. Opposition candidates adopt increasingly adventurous policy promises as a result. Nevertheless, even though sweeping changes are intended, after the event only small changes appear to have been achieved. Reversals of direction in midterm are nothing more than an admission of institutional reality. Given the nature of some recent electoral platforms, in our view it is something of a blessing that politicians cannot achieve more.

References

A comprehensive bibliography of the subject would run to thousands of citations, even of works from the last few years. We have referred at a number of places in the text to good review articles from which interested students can derive further reading. To facilitate organization of readings, we have added to each reference (in brackets) the chapter or chapters of this book where the reference occurs.

Abrams, R., R. Froyen, and R. Waud. "Monetary Policy Reaction Functions, Consistent Expectations, and the Burns Era." *Journal of Money, Credit, and Banking* 12 (1980):30–42. [Chapter 6]

Akerlof, G. "The Market for 'Lemons': Quality, Uncertainty, and the Market Mechanism." *Quarterly Journal of Economics* 90 (1970):599–617. [Introduction]

Allison, G. T. *The Essence of Decision: Explaining the Cuban Missile Crisis.* Boston: Little, Brown, 1971. [Chapter 6]

Alt, J. E. *The Politics of Economic Decline.* Cambridge: Cambridge University Press, 1979. [Chapter 5]

———. "The Evolution of Tax Structures." Presented at the Carnegie-Mellon Conference on Political Economy, April 30–May 1, 1982, at Carnegie-Mellon University, Pittsburgh, Penna. [Chapter 2]

————. "The Dynamics of Partisanship in Britain." In *Electoral Change in Advanced Industrial Societies,* edited by P. Beck, R. Dalton, and S. Flanagan. Princeton: Princeton University Press, 1983. [Chapter 7]

Alt, J. E., and J. Turner. "The Case of the Silk-Stocking Socialists and the Calculating Children of the Middle Class." *British Journal of Political Science* 12 (1982):239–48. [Chapter 8]

Anderson, L. C., and J. L. Jordan. "Monetary and Fiscal Actions: A Test of Their Relative Importance in Economic Stabilization." Federal Reserve Bank of St. Louis *Monthly Review,* November 1968. [Chapter 3]

————. "The Political Bases of Public Sector Growth in a Representative Democracy." Mimeographed. 1978. [Chapter 8]

Arrow, K. J., S. Karlin, and H. Scarf. *Studies in the Mathematical Theory of Inventory and Production.* Stanford: Stanford University Press, 1958. [Chapter 6]

Atkinson, A. B., and J. E. Stiglitz. *Lectures in Public Economics.* New York: McGraw-Hill, 1980. [Chapter 8]

Bach, G. L. *Making Monetary and Fiscal Policy.* Washington, D.C.: Brookings Institution, 1971. [Chapter 2]

Bacon, R., and W. Eltis. *Britain's Economic Problem: Too Few Producers.* London: Macmillan, 1976. [Chapters 3, 10]

Bain, G. W., and R. Price. *Profiles of Union Growth: A Comparative Statistical Portrait of Eight Countries.* Oxford: Basil Blackwell, 1980. [Chapter 2]

Baran, P. A., and P. M. Sweezy. *Monopoly Capital: An Essay on the American Economic and Social Order.* New York: Monthly Review Press, 1966. [Chapter 1]

Bates, R. H. *Markets and States in Tropical Africa: The Basis of Agricultural Policies.* California Series on Social Choice and Political Economy. Berkeley and Los Angeles: University of California Press, 1981. [Introduction]

Baumol, W. J. "Macro-Economics of Unbalanced Growth." *American Economic Review* 57 (1967):415–26. [Chapter 8]

Baumol, W. J., and W. E. Oates. *The Theory of Environmental Policy.* Englewood Cliffs, N.J.: Prentice-Hall, 1975. [Chapter 8]

Beck, M. "The Expanding Public Sector: Some Contrary Evidence." *National Tax Journal* 29 (1976):15–21. [Chapter 8]

————. "Public Sector Growth: A Real Perspective." *Public Finance* 34 (1979):313–56. [Chapter 8]

Beck, N. "Parties, Administrations, and American Macroeconomic Outcomes." *American Political Science Review* 76 (1982):83–93. [Chapter 5]

Beesley, M. E. *Urban Transport: Studies in Economic Policy.* London: Butterworths, 1973. [Chapter 8]

Behrman, J. R. *Development, the International Economic Order, and Commodity Agreements.* Reading, Mass.: Addison-Wesley, 1978. [Chapter 4]

Bergsten, C. F. *The Dilemmas of the Dollar*. New York: New York University Press, 1975. [Chapter 4]

Black, S. "The Use of Monetary Policy for Internal and External Balance in Ten Industrial Countries." Presented to the American Political Science Association Annual Meeting, New York, September 1981. [Chapter 6]

Blinder, A., and S. Goldfeld. "New Measures of Fiscal and Monetary Policy, 1958–73." *American Economic Review* 66 (1976):780–96. [Chapter 6]

Boadway, R. W. *Public Sector Economics*. Cambridge, Mass.: Winthrop, 1979. [Chapter 8]

Brennan, H. G., and J. M. Buchanan. *The Power to Tax: Analytical Foundations of a Fiscal Constitution*. Cambridge: Cambridge University Press, 1981. [Chapters 1, 8]

Brown, T., and A. Stein. "The Political Economy of National Elections." *Comparative Politics* 14 (1982):479–97. [Chapter 5]

Brunner, K., and A. H. Meltzer. "Government, the Private Sector and 'Crowding Out.'" *The Banker,* July 1976, pp. 765–69. [Chapter 3]

Bryant, R. C. *Money and Monetary Policy in Interdependent Nations*. Washington, D.C.: Brookings Institution, 1980. [Chapter 6]

Buchanan, J. M. *Public Finance in Democratic Process: Fiscal Institutions and Individual Choice*. Chapel Hill: University of North Carolina Press, 1967. [Chapter 8]

Buchanan, J. M., and R. Wagner. *Democracy in Deficit*. New York: Academic Press, 1977. [Chapters 8, 9]

Budge, I., and D. Farlie. *Voting and Party Competition*. London: Wiley, 1977. [Chapter 7]

Bush, W. C., and A. T. Denzau. "The Voting Behavior of Bureaucrats and Public Sector Growth." In *Budgets and Bureaucrats: The Sources of Government Growth,* edited by T. Borcherding. Durham, N.C.: Duke University Press, 1977. [Chapter 8]

Cameron, D. R. "The Expansion of the Public Economy: A Comparative Analysis." *American Political Science Review* 72 (1978):1243–61. [Chapters 2, 9]

———. "On the Limits of the Public Economy." Presented to the Annual Meeting of the American Political Science Association, New York, September 1980. [Chapter 9]

Caves, R. E., and R. W. Jones. *World Trade and Payments: An Introduction*. Boston: Little, Brown, 1973. [Chapter 4]

Chrystal, K. A. "International Money and the Future of the SDRs." *Princeton Essays in International Finance* No. 128. Princeton: Princeton University Press, 1978. [Chapter 4]

———. *Controversies in British Macroeconomics*. London: Philip Allan, 1979. [Chapter 10]

Chrystal, K. A., and J. E. Alt. "Endogenous Government Behavior: Wagner's

Law or Götterdämmerung?" In *Current Issues in Fiscal Policy,* edited by S. T. Cook and P. M. Jackson. London: Martin Robertson, 1979. [Chapters 8, 9]

————. "Public Sector Behavior: The Status of the Political Business Cycle." In *Macroeconomic Analysis,* edited by D. Currie, R. Nobay, and D. Peel. London: Croom Helm, 1981. [Chapter 10]

————. "Some Problems in Formulating and Testing a Politico-Economic Model of the U.K." *Economic Journal* 91 (1981):730–36. [Chapter 10]

Clower, R. "The Keynesian Counter-Revolution: A Theoretical Appraisal." In *The Theory of Interest Rates,* edited by F. H. Hahn and F. P. R. Brechling. London: Macmillan, 1965. [Chapter 3]

Coolidge, C., and G. Tullock. "Firm Size and Political Power." In *The Economics of Firm Size, Market Structure, and Social Performance,* edited by J. J. Siegfried. Federal Trade Commission, 1980. [Chapter 2]

Cowart, A. "The Economic Policies of European Governments." *British Journal of Political Science* 8 (1978):285–311, 425–39. [Chapter 6]

Crotty, J. "Post-Keynesian Economics: An Overview and Evaluation." *American Economic Review Papers and Proceedings* 70 (1980):20–25. [Chapter 3]

Downs, A. *An Economic Theory of Democracy.* New York: Harper & Row, 1957. [Chapters 7, 8]

————. "Why the Government Budget Is Too Small in a Democracy." In *Private Wants and Public Needs,* edited by E. Phelps. New York: Norton, 1965. [Chapters 2, 8]

Dunleavy, P. "The Political Implications of Sectoral Cleavages and the Growth of State Employment." *Political Studies* 28 (1980):364–83, 527–49. [Chapter 2]

Emmanuel, A. *Unequal Exchange: A Study of the Imperialism of Trade.* New York: Monthly Review Press, 1972. [Chapter 4]

Fair, R. "The Effect of Economic Events on Votes for President." *Review of Economics and Statistics* 60 (1978):159–73. [Chapter 7]

Feige, E., and D. Pearce. "Economically Rational Expectations." *Journal of Political Economy* 84 (1976):499–522. [Introduction]

Figlewski, S., and P. Wachtel. "The Formation of Inflationary Expectations." *Review of Economics and Statistics* 63 (1981):1–10. [Chapter 7]

Finer, S. *The Changing British Party System.* Washington, D.C.: American Enterprise Institute, 1980. [Chapter 7]

Fiorina, M. P. *Retrospective Voting in American National Elections.* New Haven: Yale University Press, 1981. [Chapter 7]

Fiorina, M. P., and R. C. Noll. "Voters, Bureaucrats and Legislators: A Rational Choice Perspective on the Growth of Bureaucracy." *Journal of Public Economics* 9 (1978):239–54. [Chapter 8]

Frey, B. *Modern Political Economy*. London: Martin Robertson, 1978. [Chapter 5]

Frey, B. S., and F. Schneider. "An Empirical Study of Politico-Economic Interaction in the United States." *Review of Economics and Statistics* 60 (1978):174–83. [Chapters 6, 10]

———. "A Politico-Economic Model of the United Kingdom." *Economic Journal* 88 (1978):243–53. [Chapters 6, 10]

———. "An Econometric Model with an Endogenous Government Sector." *Public Choice* 34 (1979):29–43. [Chapters 6, 10]

Friedman, M. *Theory of the Consumption Function*. Princeton: National Bureau of Economic Research, 1957. [Chapter 10]

———. *Capitalism and Freedom*. Chicago: University of Chicago Press, 1962. [Chapter 1]

———. "The Role of Monetary Policy." *American Economic Review* 58 (1968):1–17. [Chapter 3]

Friedman, M., and R. Friedman. *Free to Choose*. New York: Harcourt Brace Jovanovitch, 1980. [Chapter 1]

Galbraith, J. K. *The Affluent Society*. 3rd ed. 1958. Reprint. Boston: Houghton Mifflin, 1976. [Chapter 2]

Golden, D., and J. Poterba. "The Price of Popularity: The Political Business Cycle Reexamined." *American Journal of Political Science* 24 (1980):696–714. [Chapter 5]

Gourevitch, P. "International Trade, Domestic Coalitions, and Liberty: Comparative Responses to the Crisis of 1873–1896." *Journal of Interdisciplinary History* 8 (1977):281–313. [Chapter 2]

Hadjimatheou, G., and A. Skouras. "Britain's Economic Problem: The Growth of the Non-Market Sector?" *Economic Journal* 89 (1979):392–415. [Chapter 3]

Hahn, F. H. *Money and Inflation*. Oxford: Basil Blackwell, 1982. [Chapter 3]

Hayek, F. A. "Socialist Calculation: The Competitive Solution."*Economica* n.s., 7 (1940): 125–49. [Chapter 1]

———. *The Road to Serfdom*. Chicago: University of Chicago Press, 1944. [Chapter 1]

Hayek, F. A., ed. *Collective Economic Planning*. London: Routledge & Kegan Paul, 1935. [Chapter 1]

Hayward, J. *The One and Indivisible French Republic*. New York: Norton, 1973. [Chapter 9]

Heclo, H., and A. Wildavsky. *The Private Government of Public Money*. London: Macmillan, 1974. [Chapters 8, 9]

Heidenheimer, A., H. Heclo, and C. Adams. *Comparative Public Policy*. 2nd ed. New York: St. Martin's Press, 1983. [Chapter 2]

Hibbs, D. "Political Parties and Macroeconomic Policy." *American Political Science Review* 71 (1977):1467–87. [Chapter 5]

———. Letter. *American Political Science Review.* 73 (1979):185–90. [Chapter 5]

———. "The Dynamics of Political Support for American Presidents Among Occupational and Partisan Groups." *American Journal of Political Science* 26 (1982):312–32. [Chapters 5, 7]

———. "Economic Outcomes and Political Support for British Governments Among Occupational Classes: A Dynamic Analysis." *American Political Science Review* 76 (1982):259–79. [Chapters 5, 7]

Hibbs, D., and H. Madsen. "Public Reactions to the Growth of Taxation and Government Expenditure." *World Politics* 33 (1981):413–35. [Chapter 7]

Hibbs, D., and N. Vasilatos. "Macroeconomic Performance and Mass Political Support in the United States and Great Britain." In *Contemporary Political Economy,* edited by D. Hibbs and H. Fassbender. Amsterdam: North-Holland, 1981. [Chapter 7]

Hinrichs, H. H. *A General Theory of Tax Structure Change During Economic Development.* Harvard Law School International Tax Program. Cambridge, Mass.: Law School of Harvard University, 1966. [Chapter 2]

Hodgman, D., and R. Resek. "Determinants of Monetary Policy in France, the Federal Republic of Germany, Italy, and the United Kingdom: Some Preliminary Findings." Mimeographed. Champaign: University of Illinois, 1981. [Chapter 2]

International Monetary Fund. *Documents of the IMF.* Washington, D.C.: IMF, 1969. [Chapter 4]

Jackson, J. E. "Issues, Party Choices, and Presidential Votes." *American Journal of Political Science* 19 (1975):161–86. [Chapter 7]

Jacobs, R., and R. Jones. "Price Expectations in the United States 1947–75." *American Economic Review* 70 (1980):269–77. [Chapter 7]

Jacobson, G. C., and S. Kernell. *Strategy and Choice in Congressional Elections.* New Haven: Yale University Press, 1981. [Chapter 7]

Jennings, E. "Competition, Constituencies, and Welfare Policies in American States." *American Political Science Review* 73 (1979):414–29. [Chapter 10]

Johansen, L. "The Theory of Public Goods: Misplaced Emphasis?" *Journal of Public Economics* 7 (1977):147–52. [Chapter 8]

Katzenstein, P. *Between Power and Plenty.* Madison: University of Wisconsin Press, 1978. [Chapter 4]

Keeley, M., and P. Robins. "Work Incentives and the Negative Income Tax." *Challenge,* March–April 1979, pp. 52–55. [Chapter 3]

Keohane, R. "Economics, Inflation, and the Role of the State." *World Politics* 31 (1978):108–28. [Introduction]

Keynes, J. M. *The General Theory of Employment, Interest, and Money.* 1936. Reprint. London: Macmillan, 1973. [Chapter 3]

Kinder, D., and R. Kiewiet. "Sociotropic Politics—The American Case." *British Journal of Political Science* 11 (1981):129–61. [Chapter 7]

Klein, R. "The Politics of Public Expenditure: American Theory and British Practice." *British Journal of Political Science* 6 (1976):401–32. [Chapters 8, 10]

Knott, J. H. *Managing the German Economy: Budgetary Politics in a Federal State.* Lexington, Mass.: Lexington Books, 1981. [Chapters 2, 8, 9, 10]

Kohl, J. "Trends and Problems in Post-War Public Expenditure Development in Western Europe and North America." In *The Development of Welfare States in Europe and America,* edited by A. J. Heidenheimer and P. Flora. New Brunswick, N.J.: Transaction Books, 1980. [Chapter 9]

Kohler, H. *Welfare and Planning.* London: Allen & Unwin, 1968. [Chapter 1]

Korpi, W. "Social Policy Strategies and Distributional Conflict in Capitalist Democracies." *West European Politics* 3 (1980):296–316. [Chapter 2]

Kramer, G. "Short Run Fluctuations in U.S. Voting Behavior, 1896–1964." *American Political Science Review* 65 (1971):131–43. [Chapter 7]

———. "A Dynamical Model of Political Equilibrium." *Journal of Economic Theory* 16 (1977):310–34. [Chapter 7]

Krasner, S. *Defending the National Interest: Raw Materials Investments and U.S. Foreign Policy.* Princeton: Princeton University Press, 1978. [Chapter 2]

Kuklinski, J. H., and D. M. West. "Economic Expectations and Voting Behavior in United States House and Senate Elections." *American Political Science Review* 75 (1981):436–47. [Chapter 7]

Lange, O., and F. M. Taylor. *On the Economics of Socialism.* 1938. Reprint. New York: McGraw-Hill, 1964. [Chapter 1]

Larkey, P., C. Stolp, and M. Winer. "Theorizing About the Growth of Government: A Research Assessment." *Journal of Public Policy* 1 (1981): 157–220. [Chapter 8]

LeGrand, J. *The Strategy of Equality: Redistribution and the Social Services.* Winchester, Mass.: Allen & Unwin, 1982. [Chapter 8]

Lindberg, L., and C. Maier, eds. *The Political Economy of Global Inflation and Recession.* Washington, D.C.: Brookings Institution, 1983. [Introduction, Chapter 2]

Lindblom, C. E. *Politics and Markets: The World's Political-Economic Systems.* New York: Basic Books, 1977. [Introduction, Chapter 2]

Lord, G. *The French Budgetary Process.* Berkeley and Los Angeles: University of California Press, 1973. [Chapter 9]

Lucas, R. "Econometric Policy Evaluation: A Critique." *Journal of Monetary Economics* 1, suppl. series (1976):19–46. [Chapter 6]

Lucas, R., and T. Sargent. "After Keynesian Macroeconomics." In *After the Phillips Curve: The Persistence of High Inflation and High Unemployment.* Federal Reserve Bank of Boston, Conference Series No. 19, 1978. [Chapter 3]

MacKuen, M. "Social Communication and the Mass Policy Agenda." In *More Than News* by M. MacKuen and S. Coombs. Beverly Hills: Sage, 1980. [Chapter 7]

———. "Political Drama, Economic Conditions, and the Dynamics of Presidential Popularity." *American Journal of Political Science* 27 (1983). [Chapter 7]

MacRae, D., Jr. *Parliament, Parties, and Society in France, 1946–1958.* New York: St. Martin's Press, 1962. [Chapter 6]

MacRae, G. D. "A Political Model of the Business Cycle." *Journal of Political Economy* 85 (1977):239–63. [Chapters 5, 6]

Makin, J. H. "Constraints on Formulation of Models for Measuring Revealed Preferences of Policy Makers." *Kyklos* 29 (1976):709–32. [Chapter 6]

Markus, G., and P. Converse. "A Dynamic Simultaneous Equation Model of Electoral Choice." *American Political Science Review* 73 (1979):1055–70. [Chapter 7]

Martin, A. "Political Constraints on Economic Strategies in Advanced Industrial Societies." *Comparative Political Studies* 10 (1977):323–54. [Chapters 1, 2]

Marx, K. "Estranged Labor." In *Economic and Philosophical Manuscripts of 1844,* edited by D. Struik. London: Lawrence & Wishart, 1970. [Chapter 1]

McClam, W. "Targets and Techniques of Monetary Policy in Western Europe." Banca Nazionale del Lavoro *Review* (1978):3–27. [Chapter 6]

McCracken, P., et al. *Towards Full Employment and Price Stability.* Paris: Organization for Economic Cooperation and Development, 1977. [Introduction]

McKean, R. "Property Rights Within Government, and Devices to Increase Governmental Efficiency." In *The Economics of Property Rights,* edited by E. Furobota and S. Pejovich. Cambridge, Mass.: Ballantine, 1974. [Chapter 8]

McKelvey, R. "General Conditions for Global Intransitivities in Formal Voting Models." *Econometrica* 47 (1979):1085–1112. [Chapter 7]

McKinnon, R. I. *Money in International Exchange: The Convertible Currency System.* New York: Oxford University Press, 1979. [Chapter 4]

Meltzer, A. H., and S. F. Richard. "A Rational Theory of the Size of Government." *Journal of Political Economy* 89 (1981):914–27. [Chapter 8]

Miller, G., and T. Moe. "Bureaucrats, Legislators, and the Size of Government," Mimeographed. 1980. [Chapter 8]

Mishan, E. *Introduction to Political Economy*. London: Hutchinson, 1982. [Chapter 1]

Monroe, K. "Econometric Analyses of Electoral Behavior: A Critical Review." *Political Behavior* 1 (1979):137–73. [Chapter 7]

——. "Presidential Popularity: An Almon Distributed Lag Model." *Political Methodology* 6 (1980):43–69. [Chapter 7]

Mosley, P. "Towards a Satisficing Theory of Economic Policy." *Economic Journal* 86 (1976):59–72. [Chapters 5, 6]

——. "Images of the Floating Voter, or the 'Political Business Cycle,' Revisited." *Political Studies* 26 (1978):375–94. [Chapter 7]

Mueller, J. "Presidential Popularity from Truman to Johnson." *American Political Science Review* 64 (1970):18–34. [Chapter 7]

Mullineaux, D. "Inflation Expectations and Money Growth in the United States." *American Economic Review* 70 (1980):149–61. [Chapter 7]

Musgrave, R. A. *Fiscal Systems*. New Haven: Yale University Press, 1969. [Chapter 2]

Niskanen, W. *Bureaucracy and Representative Government*. Chicago: Aldine, 1971. [Chapter 8]

Noll, R. *Reforming Regulation*. Washington, D.C.: Brookings Institution, 1971. [Chapter 1]

Nordhaus, W. "The Political Business Cycle." *Review of Economic Studies* 42 (1975):169–90. [Chapters 5, 6]

Norr, M., and P. Kerlan. *Taxation in France*. Harvard Law School International Tax Program. Chicago: Commerce Clearing House, 1966. [Chapter 9]

North, D. *Structure and Change in Economic History*. New York: Norton, 1981. [Chapters 1, 8]

Nutter, G. *Growth of Government in the West*. Washington, D.C.: American Enterprise Institute, 1978. [Chapter 10]

O'Connor, J. R. *The Fiscal Crisis of the State*. New York: St. Martin's Press, 1973. [Chapter 1]

Odell, J. *U.S. International Monetary Policy: Markets, Power, and Ideas as Sources of Change*. Princeton: Princeton University Press, 1982. [Chapter 4]

Okun, A. *Political Economy of Prosperity*. Washington, D.C.: Brookings Institution, 1970. [Chapter 6]

Olson, M. *The Logic of Collective Action*. Cambridge, Mass.: Harvard University Press, 1965. [Chapters 2, 8]

————. *The Rise and Decline of Nations*. New Haven: Yale University Press, 1982. [Chapter 2]

Oppenheimer, J., and N. Frohlich. "Post-Election Distributive Strategies of Representatives." Presented to the American Political Association Annual Meetings, Washington, D.C., September 1980. [Chapter 8]

Organization for Economic Cooperation and Development. *The Adjustment of Personal Income Tax Systems for Inflation*. Paris: OECD, 1978. [Chapter 8]

————. *Long-Term Trends in Revenues of OECD Member Countries, 1955–1980*. Paris: OECD, 1980. [Chapter 9]

Page, B. I., and C. C. Jones. "Reciprocal Effects of Policy Preferences, Party Loyalties, and the Vote." *American Political Science Review* 73 (1979):1071–89. [Chapter 7]

Paldam, M. "A Preliminary Survey of the European Theories and Findings on Vote and Popularity Functions." *Journal of Political Research* 9 (1981):181–200. [Chapter 7]

Parkin, M., and R. Bade. "Central Bank Laws and Monetary Policies: A Preliminary Investigation." Mimeographed. London, Ont.: University of Western Ontario, 1978. [Chapter 2]

Peacock, A., and J. Wiseman. *The Growth of Public Expenditure in the United Kingdom*. Princeton: Princeton University Press, 1961. [Chapter 8]

Pechman, J. A. *Federal Tax Policy*. 3rd ed. Studies of Government Finance. Washington, D.C.: Brookings Institution, 1977. [Chapter 6]

Phillips, A. W. H. "The Relation Between Unemployment and the Rate of Change of Money Wage Rates in the U.K., 1861–1957." *Economica*, November 1958, pp. 283–99. [Chapter 3]

Pissarides, C. "A Model of British Macroeconomic Policy, 1955–69." *Manchester School of Economic and Social Studies* 40 (1972):245–59. [Chapter 6]

————. "British Government Popularity and Economic Performance." *Economic Journal* 90 (1980):569–81. [Chapter 7]

Pittman, R. "Market Structure and Campaign Contributions." *Public Choice* 31 (1977):37–52. [Chapter 2]

Popkin, S., J. W. Gorman, C. Phillips, and J. A. Smith. "Comment: What Have You Done for Me Lately? Toward an Investment Theory of Voting." *American Political Science Review* 70 (1976):779–805. [Chapter 7]

Price, R. W. R. "Public Expenditure." Chapter 3 of *British Economic Policy 1960–1974*, edited by F. Blackaby. Cambridge: Cambridge University Press, 1978. [Chapter 10]

Rawls, J. *A Theory of Justice*. Cambridge, Mass.: Harvard University Press, 1971. [Chapter 1]

Romer, T., and H. Rosenthal. "Bureaucrats Versus Voters: On the Political

Economy of Resource Allocation by Direct Democracy." *Quarterly Journal of Economics* 93 (1979):563–87. [Chapter 8]

Rose, R., and G. Peters. *Can Government Go Bankrupt?* New York: Basic Books, 1978. [Chapters 8, 9]

Roskamp, K. W. "Twenty-Five Years of Fiscal Policy Advice in West Germany." *Public Finance* 29 (1974):214–20. [Chapter 8]

Royama, S. "Monetary Control in the Japanese Financial System." Mimeographed. 1980. [Chapter 6]

Salamon, L. M., and J. S. Siegfried. "Economic Power and Political Influence: The Impact of Industry Structure on Public Policy." *American Political Science Review* 71 (1977):1026–43. [Chapter 2]

Salert, B. *Public Support for Presidents.* Modules in Undergraduate Mathematics and Its Applications. Boston: Educational Development Corp., 1978. [Chapter 7]

Schneider, F. "Different (Income) Classes and Presidential Popularity: An Empirical Analysis." *Munich Social Science Review* 2 (1978):53–69. [Chapter 7]

Schumpeter, J. A. *Capitalism, Socialism, and Democracy.* London: Allen & Unwin, 1966. [Chapter 1]

Shepsle, K. "The Strategy of Ambiguity: Uncertainty and Electoral Competition." *American Political Science Review* 66 (1972):555–68. [Chapter 7]

Shepsle, K., and B. Weingast. "Political Preferences for the Pork Barrel: A Generalization." *American Journal of Political Science* 25 (1981): 96–111. [Chapters 8, 9]

———. "Institutionalizing Majority Rule: A Social Choice Theory with Policy Implications." *American Economic Review* 72 (1982):367–71. [Chapter 7]

Shonfield, A. *Modern Capitalism: The Changing Balance of Public and Private Power.* London: Oxford University Press, 1969. [Chapter 2]

Skocpol, T. "Political Response to Capitalist Crisis: Neo-Marxist Theories of the State and the Case of the New Deal." *Politics and Society* 10 (1980):155–201. [Chapter 2]

Smith, A. *An Inquiry into the Nature and Causes of the Wealth of Nations.* 1776. Reprint. Oxford: Clarendon Press, 1976. [Chapter 1]

Sodersten, B. *International Economics.* 2nd ed. London: Macmillan, 1980. [Chapter 4]

Stokey, E., and R. Zeckhauser. *A Primer for Policy Analysis.* New York and London: Norton, 1978. [Chapter 6]

Theil, H. *Optimal Decision Rules for Government and Industry.* Amsterdam: North-Holland, 1968. [Chapter 6]

Tiebout, C. "A Pure Theory of Local Expenditures." *Journal of Political Economy* 64 (1956):416–24. [Chapter 8]

Tinbergen, J. *On the Theory of Economic Policy.* Amsterdam: North-Holland, 1952. [Chapter 6]

Triffin, R. *Gold and the Dollar Crisis: The Future of Convertibility.* New Haven: Yale University Press, 1960. [Chapter 4]

Tufte, E. *The Political Control of the Economy.* Princeton: Princeton University Press, 1978. [Chapters 5, 10]

Vogel, D. "Why Businessmen Distrust Their State: The Political Consciousness of American Corporate Executives." *British Journal of Political Science* 8 (1978):45–77. [Chapter 2]

Volcker, P. A. "A Broader Role for Monetary Targets." Federal Reserve Bank of New York *Quarterly Review* 2 (1977):23–28. [Chapter 6]

von Mises, L. "Economic Calculation in a Socialist Commonwealth." 1920. In *Collective Economic Planning,* edited by F. A. Hayek. London: Routledge & Kegan Paul, 1935. [Chapter 1]

Wagner, A. *Finanzwissenschaft.* 1883. Translated and reprinted as "Three Extracts on Public Finance." In *Classics on the Theory of Public Finance,* edited by R. A. Musgrave and A. T. Peacock. London: Macmillan, 1962. [Chapter 8]

Weber, M. "Power." In *From Max Weber: Essays in Sociology,* edited by H. Gerth and C. Mills. New York: Oxford University Press, 1958. [Chapter 1]

Wildavsky, A. *Budgeting: A Comparative Theory of Budgetary Processes.* Boston: Little, Brown, 1975. [Chapter 9]

Williamson, J. *The Failure of World Monetary Reform, 1971–74.* London: Nelson, 1977. [Chapter 4]

Williamson, O. *Markets and Hierarchies.* New York: Free Press, 1975. [Introduction]

Winch, D. *Economics and Policy.* London: Hodder & Stoughton, 1969. [Chapter 3]

Winters, R., C. Johnson, P. Nowosadko, and J. Rendini. "Political Behavior and American Public Policy: The Case of the Political Business Cycle." In *Handbook of Political Behavior,* vol. 5, edited by S. Long. New York: Plenum Publishing, 1981. [Chapter 10]

Wood, G. E. "The Monetary Policy Decision Process in the United Kingdom." Mimeographed. Champaign: University of Illinois, 1981. [Chapter 2]

Woolley, J. T. "Monetary Policy Instrumentation and the Relationship of Central Banks and Governments." *Annals of the American Academy of Political and Social Science* 434 (1977):151–73. [Chapter 2]

———. "Monetarists and the Politics of Monetary Policy." *Annals of the American Academy of Political and Social Science* 459 (1982):148–60. [Chapter 3]

Wright, G. "The Political Economy of New Deal Spending: An Econometric Analysis." *Review of Economics and Statistics* 56 (1974):30–38. [Chapter 2]

Recommended Reading

There are many places to look for more information on political economics, apart from the writings reviewed in the course of our discussion. The semiannual *Economic Outlook* published by the Organization for Economic Cooperation and Development is an excellent source of data and discussions of contemporary economic developments in many countries. The same organization publishes an annual *Economic Survey* of each of its member countries. The International Monetary Fund and Bank for International Settlements both publish an *Annual Report*. Other OECD and IMF publications have been referred to in the figures and tables. Central bank reports are good sources of discussions of policy issues. These include the Federal Reserve *Bulletin,* the Bank of England *Quarterly Bulletin,* and the Deutsche Bundesbank *Monthly Bulletin* (in English). The Brookings Institution publishes many monographs on relevant topics. Of special note are two of their series, *Setting National Priorities,* an analysis of issues underlying each year's budget, and their *Papers in Economic Activity.*

On general issues in the history of economic thought, see D. O'Brien, *Classical Economists* (New York: Oxford University Press,

1979); or M. Dobb, *Theories of Value and Distribution Since Adam Smith* (Cambridge: Cambridge University Press, 1973). For an introduction to welfare economics, there is Mishan (1982). Many important papers in this tradition of analysis are reprinted in K. Arrow and T. Scitovsky, *Readings in Welfare Economics* (Homewood, Il.: Irwin, 1969). For an overview of choice theory, see J. Mueller, *Public Choice* (Cambridge: Cambridge University Press, 1979). J. K. Galbraith, *Economics and the Public Purpose* (Boston: Houghton Mifflin, 1973), offers both a contemporary defense of the planned economy and opposition to the views of the new marketeers discussed in Chapter 1. For a balanced discussion of the conflict between wealth creation and distribution, see A. Okun, *Equality and Efficiency: The Big Trade-off* (Washington, D.C.: Brookings Institution, 1975).

For a historical survey of economic development from a political point of view, see North (1981). Important histories of economic policy include Winch (1969); M. Friedman and A. Schwartz, *A Monetary History of the United States* (Princeton: Princeton University Press, 1963); M. Friedman and A. Schwartz, *Monetary Trends in the United States and the United Kingdom* (Chicago: University of Chicago Press, 1982); and J. Garraty, *Unemployment in History* (New York: Harper, 1978). For more on policy and institutions, see Katzenstein (1978) and Lindberg and Maier (1983). For details and examples of corporatist modes of organization, see G. Lehmbruch and P. Schmitter, *Varieties of Corporatism* (Beverly Hills: Sage, 1982). The January 1980 issue of *West European Politics* was devoted to comparative studies of union activity. In addition to the works discussed in Chapters 2 and 9, aspects of fiscal policy and budgeting with further sources for individual countries are covered in Wildavsky (1975). Recent studies of American budgeting include L. LeLoup, *Budgetary Politics,* 2nd ed. (Brunswick, Ohio: King's Court, 1980); and J. Havemann, *Congress and the Budget* (Bloomington: Indiana University Press, 1978). A. Schick, *Congress and Money* (Washington, D.C.: Urban Institute, 1980), contains a wealth of detail. The Report of the Treasury and Civil Service Committee on *Monetary Policy* (London: H.M.S.O., 1981) is a thorough discussion of British monetary policy. For the United States, see S. Maisel, *Managing the Dollar* (New York: Norton,

1973); and J. Woolley, *The Federal Reserve and the Politics of Monetary Policy* (New York: Cambridge University Press, 1983). Various OECD publications discuss monetary and fiscal policy in other countries.

To go further into contemporary economics, A. Okun, *Prices and Quantities* (Washington, D.C.: Brookings Institution, 1982), offers a discussion of problems of aggregate supply. John Flemming's *Inflation* (London: Oxford University Press, 1976) discusses different theories of inflation. Important data and details can be found in L. Krause and W. Salant, *Worldwide Inflation* (Washington, D.C.: Brookings Institution, 1977). Good places to read more about the international monetary system and the effects of exchange rate regimes on domestic economic strategies are J. Williamson (1977); S. Black, *Floating Exchange Rates and Domestic Economic Policies* (New Haven: Yale University Press, 1976); and V. Argy, *The Postwar International Monetary Crisis: An Analysis* (London: Allen & Unwin, 1981). There are also two important Brookings Institution studies: Bryant (1980) and C. F. Bergsten, T. Horst, and T. H. Moran, *American Multinationals and American Interests* (1978). A. MacBean and P. Snowden, *International Institutions in Trade and Finance* (London: Allen & Unwin, 1981), is a description of major international institutions. A readable survey of the problem of inequality in the world economy can be found in the Brandt report, *North-South: A Program for Survival* (Cambridge, Mass.: MIT Press, 1980). The theoretical development of North-South models is surveyed in E. Bacha, "An Interpretation of Unequal Exchange from Prebisch-Singer to Emmanuel," *Journal of Development Economics,* December 1978.

Index

Designer: Lisa Mirski
Compositor: Interactive Composition Corporation
Printer: Vail-Ballou Press
Binder: Vail-Ballou Press
Text: 10/13 Sabon
Display: Sabon